The Working Class in European History

The Logic of Solidarity

THE LOGIC OF SOLIDARITY

Artisans and Industrial Workers
in Three French Towns
1871–1914

Michael P. Hanagan

University of Illinois Press

Urbana   Chicago   London

LIBRARY OF CONGRESS CATALOGING IN PUBLICATION DATA

Hanagan, Michael P.   1947–
   The logic of solidarity.

(The Working class in European history)
Bibliography: p.
Includes index.
1. Strikes and lockouts—France—Saint-Étienne region
(Loire)—History.   2. Strikes and lockouts—France—
Rive-de-Gier—History.   3. Strikes and lockouts—France—
Saint-Chamond—History.   4. Strikes and lockouts—France—
Chambon-Feugerolles—History.   5. Labor and laboring
classes—France—Saint-Étienne region (Loire)—History.
6. Saint-Étienne region, France (Loire)—Social condi-
tions.   I. Title.   II. Series.
HD5376.S3H36   331.89′2944′581   79-13181
ISBN 0-252-00758-1

For Miriam

Contents

Preface		*xiii*
One	Artisans and Industrial Workers	*3*
Two	The Formation of the Stéphanois Working Class	*33*
Three	Economic Structure and Strike Activity	*56*
Four	Artisans and Industrial Workers in Rive-de-Gier, 1871-1914	*87*
Five	Artisans and Industrial Workers in Saint-Chamond, 1871-1914	*126*
Six	Artisans and Industrial Workers in Le Chambon-Feugerolles, 1871-1914	*165*
Seven	Conclusion	*209*
Appendix		*218*
Bibliography		*222*
Index		*253*

Table

1. Textileworkers in France, England, and the United States, 1900–1901 *8*
2. Labor Force and Union Membership in the Arrondissement of Saint-Etienne, 1896 *49*
3. Wage Structure, 1896 *70*
4. Wage Structure in the Arrondissement of Saint-Etienne, 1896 *71*
5. Daily Wages, 1896 *71*
6. Cost of Living Index, 1890–1908 *76*
7. Wage Index in Paris and Saint-Etienne *79*
8. Real Wages for a Forger in Saint-Etienne, 1853–1911 *80*
9. Number of Strikers(Glassworkers and Metalworkers) in Rive-de-Gier, 1885–1914 *88*
10. Duration of Strikes (in Days) in Rive-de-Gier, 1885–1914 *88*
11. Worker-Days Lost in Strikes in Rive-de-Gier, 1885–1914 *88*
12. Strike Contributions from Metalworkers and Glassworkers in Rive-de-Gier *91*
13. Strike Contributions by Geographic Distribution, Rive-de-Gier *91*
14. Residential Patterns in Rive-de-Gier, 1891: Individual Sample of Glassworkers and Nonglassworkers *100*
15. Workers in the Richarme Glassworks by Department of Birth, 1894 *108*
16. Residential Patterns in Rive-de-Gier, 1891: Individual Sample of Metalworkers and Nonmetalworkers *118*
17. Number of Strikers (Metalworking, Textiles, and Construction) in Saint-Chamond, 1880–1914 *128*
18. Duration of Strikes (in Days) in Saint-Chamond, 1880–1914 *128*
19. Worker-Days Lost in Strikes in Saint-Chamond, 1880–1914 *128*
20. Age Distribution of Semiskilled Metalworkers at the Compagnie des aciéries de la marine, 1901 *134*
21. Residential Patterns of Turners and Adjusters in Saint-Chamond, 1891 *136*
22. Residential Patterns in Saint-Chamond, 1891: Family Sample of Metalworkers *137*
23. Residential Patterns in Saint-Chamond, 1891: Family Sample of Textileworker Heads of Household *146*
24. Residential Patterns in Saint-Chamond, 1891: Family Sample of Textileworker Members of Household *146*
25. Geographic Distribution of Textile Plants in Saint-Chamond, 1894 *147*

26. Residential Patterns of Masons and Plasterers in Saint-Chamond, 1891 *148*
27. Number of Strikers (Metal Trades) in Le Chambon-Feugerolles, 1885–1914 *166*
28. Duration of Strikes (in Days) in Le Chambon-Feugerolles, 1885–1914 *166*
29. Worker-Days Lost in Strikes in Le Chambon-Feugerolles, 1885–1914 *166*
30. Sex and Age Distribution of Metal Trades in Le Chambon-Feugerolles, 1906 *197*
31. Worker Residential Patterns in Le Chambon-Feugerolles, 1901: A File Factory and a Metal Plant *199*
32. Principal Occupations of Workers, 1891 *220*

FIGURES

Figure
1. Department of the Loire *36*
2. The skill hierarchy in glassmaking, 1862 *97*
3. Nineteenth-century housing for glassworkers, 1974 *99*
4. The city of Rive-de-Gier, 1887 *101*
5. Location of industry *102*
6. Nineteenth-century glassworkers' *quartier* in the southeast section of Rive-de-Gier *103*
7. The *bourse du travail* in the rue de la Barrière *104*
8. Floor plan of a medium-sized metal factory, 1892 *116*
9. A large metal plant: Marrel Frères, c. 1910 *117*
10. General view of the Compagnie des aciéries de la marine, c. 1910 *130*
11. A large-face plate lathe at the Compagnie des aciéries de la marine, c. 1910 *134*
12. Workshop for apprentices at the Compagnie des aciéries de la marine, c. 1910 *135*
13. The city of Saint-Chamond, 1887 *139*
14. A strike kitchen *(soupe communiste)* in 1910 *179*
15. The city of Le Chambon-Feugerolles, 1887 *182*
16. Whole families goto the strike kitchen *191*

GRAPHS

Graph
1. Strikes in Saint-Chamond, 1870–1914 *58*
2. Strikes in Le Chambon-Feugerolles, 1870–1914 *58*

 3. Strikes in Rive-de-Gier, 1870–1914 *58*
 4. Strikes in Saint-Chamond *60*
 5. Strikes in Le Chambon-Feugerolles *60*
 6. Strikes in Rive-de-Gier *60*
 7. Stéphanois Price Index, 1870–1908 *75*
 8. Total Trade Union Membership in Rive-de-Gier, 1890–1913 *120*
 9. Total Trade Union Membership in Saint-Chamond, 1890–1913 *154*
10. Fileworkers' Union Membership, 1889–1900 *176*
11. Metalworkers' Union Membership, 1901–13 *176*

Preface

The evolution of French strike conflicts in the late nineteenth century reveals aspects of French working-class life previously ignored by scholars. For too long the actions of the national leaders of the trade union movement have obscured the actions of hundreds of thousands of French workers. But the reasons for this one-sided emphasis on leaders are understandable. The student of working-class history finds many aspects of syndicalist theory and most of its leaders appealing; the syndicalist theoreticians who stressed the need for the self-development and independent activity of the working classes seem especially attractive in an era when the major European trade unions, Communist and socialist alike, appear dominated by unresponsive bureaucracies. Contemporary European labor leaders bear little resemblance to syndicalists like Jean Allemane, Fernand Pelloutier, or Victor Griffuelhes, who were authentic working-class heroes and who dedicated the greater part of their lives to a high conception of working-class democracy.

Yet the concentration of scholars on the leaders of French trade unionism and their ideologies has led historians to ignore many equally important characteristics of French strike protests. Many militant strikes occurred before the rise of revolutionary ideologies within the French trade union movement, and syndicalism itself was successful because it expressed concerns which arose from the daily experience of ordinary workers. Throughout the entire period, industrial and technological change had significant effect in shaping workers' goals and their participation in strike conflicts.

Over the last decade French historians have begun to broaden their conception of the prewar French labor movement. Studies like those of Michelle Perrot, Joan Scott, Edward Shorter and Charles Tilly, Rolande Trempé, and Claude Willard have used new methodologies to ask new questions about the French working-class movement. Instead of a universe bounded by the "five major socialist parties" and yearly trade union and social-ist congresses, the universe of French working-class history has expanded to include demography, quantitative methods, and an-thropological, economic, and sociological theory. The result has been the production of a fuller and more complete picture of French working-class life. In some ways syndicalist leaders would have been pleased by this recent work, which is close to the kind of detailed economic and social history of working-class life for which Pelloutier, Merrheim, and Monatte pleaded. Recent historical research fulfills some old syndicalist objectives. While it may detract from the personalities of syndicalist leaders, it reveals in considerable detail the struggles of actual working-class people and their goals.

In my own attempt to examine mass strike actions I found it necessary to examine many different aspects of French strike activity, and I often turned to other scholars for advice and assistance. First of all, I would like to thank my wife, Miriam Cohen, who has taken time from her own historical research to read and criticize many drafts of this book and of the dissertation on which it was based. Time and again her advice proved helpful in tightening the analytic framework, and many of her suggestions, both large and small, have been incorporated into the final draft. From its inception my advisor, Charles Tilly, helped me to clarify my research proposal and provided encouragement and valuable advice throughout. His work has continually inspired my own thinking about the history of strike conflict; his seemingly tireless attention to his students' work and his wide-ranging knowledge make him a model mentor, and made my graduate education at the University of Michigan a very special experience. Joan Scott, a pioneer in the field of Third Republican labor history, has also served as a guide; for her insight and patience I am most grateful. Many teachers, colleagues, and friends have offered advice and support. I particularly wish to thank John Bowditch, Raymond Grew, Edward Malefakis, John Merriman, and William Rosen-berg. Through comments upon earlier drafts of this manuscript and related articles, the following people have suggested how I might improve this study: Ron Aminzade, Robert Bezucha, Joseph

Butwin, Frank Couvares, Bruce Fireman, Christopher Johnson, Lynn Lees, Jim Lehning, Harold Livesay, Leslie Moch, Otto Pflanze, Elizabeth Pleck, Harvey Smith, Charles Tamason, and Louise Tilly.

French scholars were also helpful to a young researcher inexperienced in the delicate art of working in regional archives. I spent the year of 1973–74 in France, where François Furet, Michelle Perrot, and Jean Maitron were all helpful in the initial stages of my research, and suggeted avenues of investigation which proved useful. Yves Lequin graciously welcomed me to Lyon and encouraged me to use the facilities of the Centre d'histoire économique et sociale at the Université de Lyon. His own work, which appeared after this manuscript was completed, provides a macro-view of the working classes in the region around Lyon. Jean Lorçin and Claude Cherrier acquainted me with the strengths and weaknesses of the departmental archives, and I also benefited from Jean Merley's perceptive discussion of the Stéphanois workers' movement. I thank Jean-Paul Martin for lending me his mémoire, "Le syndicalisme révolutionnaire chez les métallurgistes de l'Ondaine." The personnel at the archives in Saint-Etienne were consistently helpful and provided valuable assistance. I wish to thank particularly Mlle. Elaine Viallard, the director of the Archives départementales de la Loire, and her staff, and M. Menard, the archivist, now retired, of the Archives municipales de Saint-Etienne.

Also, I would like to thank Pem Larsen, who took several of the photographs, and Mrs. Mildred Tubby, who did a superb job of typing the manuscript.

Finally, I only wish that my father, Francis Patrick Hanagan, who first encouraged me to become a historian, had lived to see the manuscript's completion. His love and support, as well as that of my mother, Berenice Henke Hanagan, made everything easier.

The Logic of Solidarity

CHAPTER ONE

Artisans and Industrial Workers

The more I study the facts, the more I become convinced that alongside of those fleeting convictions which the workers find in books or in
their clubs, there are others, more permanent, more deeply held,
and reflected on, which inspire them. . . . It is in the regime of
manufacturing that these convictions have been born and grow, in
spite of the rules, the fines, the forced silence and many indignities, or
rather because of these fines and rules. . . .[1]

Louis Reybaud, 1859

The May Day strike of 1906 in Le Chambon-Feugerolles and in the
whole Stéphanois region was one battle in an industrial war in
France between 1890 and 1914. In shops and factories throughout
the country a tremendous struggle raged over the control of the
production process. Everywhere employers strove to seize control
on the shop floor and acquire a monopoly of expertise over the
manufacturing process; everywhere skilled workers resisted these
attempts. The growing power of the machine gave the employers an inestimable advantage in the conflict, but they faced a
determined and resolute opponent.

The battle for the command of the work process in late
nineteenth-century France was fought between employers and
skilled workers. In this context, "workers' control" meant skilled
workers' control, and it could not have been otherwise. In late
nineteenth-century France "workers' control" was not a cry of the
offense, as in the twentieth century, but a defense of the status quo
against employer attack. Moreover, skilled workers were the only
ones who could effectively contest such a key issue; the monopoly
of skills enjoyed by artisanal workers enabled them to stoutly resist
employers' attempts to regiment them.

Because these conflicts were confined to skilled workers, labor
historians have tended to ignore the nineteenth-century struggles to
defend the workers' autonomy in the workplace and concentrated

instead on the struggles of industrial workers. But recently these battles of skilled workers have attracted new attention. As demands for "workers' control" began once more to emerge from factories, historians looked to the past for precedents, and discovered that the "workers' control" so frequently dismissed as utopian was only lately a reality. Moreover, because of the enormous industrial conflicts it generated, the war over the regulation of the workplace is of crucial importance in understanding the French workers' movement of the late nineteenth century. When artisanal workers set their faces against employers' encroachment on their skills, they were setting themselves squarely against one of the major lines of contemporary capitalist development. And on this question neither employer nor artisan had much leeway to compromise. Furthermore, as these struggles over workers' control grew more bitter, skilled workers joined together with industrial workers to oppose their bosses. In so doing artisans exerted a formative influence on the shape of the French industrial workers' movement.[2]

To understand French strike conflict in the years between 1870 and 1914, worker militancy must first be placed in its industrial context. The French artisanal economy will be set against the background of the economies of other, more advanced countries by showing the exceptionally wide variety of artisanal workers in France touched by technological change. We will also discuss the different strategies used by artisanal workers in resisting employers' attempts to control the workplace, as well as how technologically threatened artisans were led to form coalitions with industrial workers, coalitions which often produced mass strikes. Finally, these general discussions will be followed by a brief introduction to the three towns chosen as case studies for our examination of work group, technological change, and social protest.

The French Economy: An Artisanal Economy under Stress

Perhaps the most important feature of late nineteenth-century French industrial structure was the continued predominance of artisanal industry. Since the seventeenth century manufacturing had been more concentrated in artisanal industry in France than in England. Once established, this pattern of French artisanal production and British industrial production tended to be self-reinforcing; it widened in subsequent centuries.

The origins of this international division of labor in Western Europe can be traced to the early seventeenth century and were rooted in the state-making process. Long ago John U. Nef pointed out that strong French monarchs were more able to impose their own designs on industry than were their weaker English counterparts. Monarchical plans for industry emphasized luxury, artisanal industries whose products could be easily exported to other European nations and would yield the gold so essential to the raising of armies and the building of fleets. The royal plan also involved government-enforced standards of quality which, although often benefiting artisanal industries, sometimes served as a pretext for government exactions from nonartisanal industries.[3]

French predominance in artisanal industry increased during the seventeenth and eighteenth centuries while English industry was preparing for the Industrial Revolution. English historians such as G. N. Clark and K. Berrill have argued that the high costs of production of French luxury goods made French industrialists loathe to risk their capital in overseas trade or the mass internal markets, which were increasingly attracting British industrialists. The French economic historian François Crouzet disputes this interpretation and maintains that both French and English producers were well suited to the different conditions prevailing in their respective internal markets. According to Crouzet, French industry produced high-quality, artisanal goods for its extravagant aristocracy and low-quality goods in domestic artisanal industry for its impoverished masses. In contrast, English industry increasingly oriented itself toward production of medium-range goods of uniform quality for an expanding middle-class market. He adds that standardized production for this middle-class market particularly encouraged technological change and the growth of factory industry.[4]

Whether the diverging path of Franco-Britannic industrial development is attributed to production costs or the nature of demand makes no difference for our argument. For our purposes it is sufficient that an international division of labor already existed on the eve of the English industrial revolution and helps explain the different rates of technological change in the two countries during the nineteenth century. While English industrial production underwent a whole series of dramatic technological changes between 1780 and 1820, the more artisan-oriented French industrial production resisted mechanization for almost a century longer. Between 1800 and 1850 the growing gap between the British and French economies became a yawning chasm. The French economist Tihomir Markovitch has described the first two-thirds of the nineteenth century as a period of substantial growth but little fundamental transformation, observing that, "contrary to a widespread belief, industrial structure at the time of the Second Empire had not yet undergone fundamental changes in contrast to what it was at the end of the eighteenth century."[5]

France's reputation as a producer of quality goods continued throughout the nineteenth century. Although an evaluation of these products using census material is almost impossible, contemporaries were agreed that they represented a significant section of the French economy. In 1870 Armand Audiganne, discussing Parisian industry, remarked:

> [there are a whole series of] . . . products so varied that it is necessary to designate them as Parisian products *par essence*. These are the art, fashion, and luxury industries. They form a group so well known, and so renowned and without rival in the world in many cases [that they are called] *articles de Paris*: artificial flowers, umbrellas, toys, knick-knacks, morocco leather products . . . pearl buttons . . . etc. This includes fine metalworking and a whole procession of its artistic applications: fine jewelry, imitation jewelry . . . all kinds of gold and silver work, engraving, metal sculpting, setting and twenty other delicate operations. [It comprises] furniture-making with all its more or less splendid branches which include cabinetmaking and furniture joining, upholstering, bronzeworking, wallpaper making etc. This summary enumeration of groups finishes with carriagemaking, a luxury industry if there ever was one, and all its applications, including those more modest specialties which are its natural accessories. . . .[6]

Using data from the 1860 Parisian census, Audiganne estimated that approximately 110,000 Parisian artisanal workers were employed in these industries, and this list did not include an estimated 34,000 workers in optics and precision instruments, 78,000 carpenters, or any of the tens of thousands of skilled artisans involved in the Parisian textile or garment trades. French luxury goods production was not by any means confined to Paris and it figured significantly in the national economy, particularly in the export sector. Markovitch estimates that the export of French quality goods in the first half of the nineteenth century played a pivotal role in financing the importation of machine technology.[7]

One direct consequence of the importance of French artisanal industry was the large size of the French artisanal workforce during this period. High-grade French products were the creation of very skilled workers. The carriagemakers referred to by Audiganne provide an example of this upper aristocracy of French labor. In 1900 there were 102,000 workers employed in carriage- and wagonmaking in France compared with 87,000 in England and 67,000 in the United States. In 1884 a skilled carriagemaker noted that more than forty separate crafts were involved in making a luxury coach.[8] In the most highly skilled stages of carriage manufacture, work was subcontracted to an individual artisan who bargained for the job and hired several assistants to help him complete it. The factory furnished the worker with the materials and, later, the machine tools, but the worker himself drew up the precise blueprint and selected the exact method of carrying out the job.

When the automobile appeared at the turn of the century, it initially developed as a branch of carriagemaking, which accounts for the early prominence of France in automotive engineering. Eric Hobsbawm has described the irony of the French official in the early 1900s who boasted that while America could compete with France in mass-produced articles, it could never compete in an industry where ingenuity and craft skill were decisive: the manufacture of automobiles.[9]

The expansion of French quality production to fill a growing worldwide demand did not generate substantial external economies or large-scale capital concentration, and so did not encourage industrial transformation in other sectors of the economy. Where necessary, French industrialists copied English methods; but in their own areas of strength little industrial progress was made in the first half of the nineteenth century.

Even outside the quality sector, artisanal methods of production remained largely intact. While the majority of French workers were not labor aristocrats like the carriagemakers, neither were they industrial workers. In textiles, which was everywhere the entering wedge of the Industrial Revolution, the majority of French workers were involved in artisanal domestic production even in the late nineteenth century (see Table 1). Thirteen percent of the total French industrial workforce was concentrated in textiles, compared with 12 percent in England and 6 percent in the United States.[10] In contrast to the American and English labor force, which was concentrated in industries which were rapidly mechanized between 1815 and 1860, the French labor force was concentrated in industries which were slowly transformed between 1860 and 1914. English and American textiles were dominated by the highly mechanized cotton industry. Forty-seven percent of all English textileworkers were employed in this industry, as were 45 percent

Table 1

Textileworkers in France, England, and the United States, 1900–1901 (labor force as number of workers engaged in an occupation and as percentage of total industrial workforce)

	France		England		United States	
	Number of Workers	Percent of Workforce	Number of Workers	Percent of Workforce	Number of Workers	Percent of Workforce
Linen	117,000	14	146,000	13	22,000	3
Cotton	167,000	20	530,000	47	308,000	43
Wool	166,000	20	210,000	19	164,000	24
Silk	172,000	20	35,000	3	68,000	10
Dyeing	50,000	6	60,000	5	31,000	5
Lace	114,000	14	36,000	3	9,000	1
Hosiery	55,000	6	35,000	3	86,000	13
Unclassi- fied	0	0	76,000	7	0	0
Total	841,000	100	1,128,000	100	688,000	99

Sources: Censuses of France (1901), England and Wales (1901), United States (1900); Paul Bairoch *et al.*, *The Working Population and Its Structure* (Brussels: Editions de l'institut de sociologie de l'Université Libre de Bruxelles, 1968).

of all American textileworkers. Indeed, the incompletely mechanized wool industry and the artisanal silk industry equaled the cotton industry in size, while old homeworking industries like lace enjoyed a prosperity which was denied them in England and the United States. An equally ancient home industry, linen, was strongly represented in both England and France but only barely existed in the United States.

Even in the late nineteenth century, when French industry did begin to mechanize, the very presence of large numbers of skilled artisanal workers encouraged French employers to rely more on skilled labor than did employers in England or the United States, where the scarcity of skilled labor further stimulated mechanization. At the beginning of the eighteenth century France had been one of the most industrialized European nations. Even before the Industrial Revolution a large skilled workforce operating out of small workshops existed within the French economy. Throughout much of the nineteenth century these decentralized and highly skilled work groups showed remarkable flexibility in meeting the challenge of mechanization. In 1898 Peter Kropotkin, the Russian anarchist and a keen observer of European society, noted:

> When a crisis breaks out in some branch of the petty trades there is no lack of writers to predict that the trade is going to disappear. During the crisis which I witnessed in 1877 amidst the Swiss watchmakers, the impossibility of a recovery in the trade in the face of the machine made watches was a current topic in the press. The same was said in 1882 with regard to the silk trade of Lyons, and, in fact, whenever a crisis has broken out in the petty trades. And yet, notwithstanding the gloomy predictions, and the still gloomier prospects of the workers, that form of production does not disappear. . . . It undergoes various modifications, it adapts itself to new conditions, and it struggles without losing hope of better times to come.[11]

While French sociologists, economists, and politicans vied with one another to describe and analyze the rise of an industrial economy in France, they all but ignored the intact artisanal economy which everywhere surrounded them. Kropotkin concluded that he had never "guessed from the little attention to [small-scale industry] by orthodox economists, what a wide, complex, important, and interesting organization would appear at the end of a close enquiry."[12] The government survey of French industry prepared by the Ducarre committee in 1877 charged that social commentators had been too concerned with the new heavy-industry phenomenon and had exaggerated its importance in the French economy. The committee affirmed the continued signif-icance of small industry in "adapting the [products of heavy industry] to the consumers' needs and tastes."[13]

Many small-scale, artisanal industries which survived into the late nineteenth century were revived by the expansion of electrifi-cation and the growth of demand for consumers' goods which occurred between 1880 and 1900. Where steam had concentrated industry, electricity allowed it to disperse. Sewing machines and machine tools could now be powered at home. The growing home market also created a need for consumer goods, to which small industry catered. Electrification and the growing consumers' mar-ket explain the *decrease* in industrial scale in the French manu-facturing sector which was recorded between 1896 and 1901 and again between 1901 and 1906.[14] One enthusiastic commentator, Camille Sabatier, writing in the *Revue d'économie politique*, be-lieved he saw in this trend the repeal of the Industrial Revolution.[15]

But artisanal industry was not limited to tiny shops; it often existed concealed under the plant roof. Markovitch has noted the tendency of French manufacturing surveys to include as industrial establishments many plants only barely touched by mechaniza-tion.[16] According to the French economist, in the small "industrial" establishments of the 1860s, more increases in productivity came from centralization and coordination (the division of labor) than actual mechanization. Economist C. K. Harley has similarly found evidence that in many British industries, such as engineering, employers used their abundant supply of skilled labor to compete successfully with processes accomplished by machines in Amer-ica.[17] The small size of the French metal-manufacturing industry suggests that a similar kind of substitution was taking place in France, and probably to an even greater extent. In 1900 most French metalwork was done in shops which, on average, employed between five and fifty workers; few French metal plants in any branch of the industry employed over 500 workers.[18]

In France the inclusion of highly skilled artisanal workers in the factory did not automatically do away with artisanal autonomy. Nowhere was artisanal survival inside the factory more clear than in metalworking. Although shut behind factory walls, metalworking artisans continued to behave as if they were in their own small shops: they consulted their friends whenever they felt it necessary, they took their own workbreaks, and they expected their supervisors to treat them as equals. In 1904 an English skilled metalworker, who had worked in shops in both England and France, commented:

> In the workshop [in France] there is much more freedom than, I believe, exists in English factories. Discipline is by no means of a cast iron character. If Maurice or Jules have a sudden idea which they wish to communicate to Henri at the other end of the shop, they go at once, without looking around to see where the foreman is, or pretending to go on business. A good quarter of an hour is lost each morning in shaking hands and passing salutations with comrades in all parts of the factory. To omit the handshake or the "salut comarades" is a serious breach of manners. In most workshops in France smoking is allowed . . . in a few of the larger and more modern plants only, smoking is forbidden . . . provided there is no deliberate wasting of time or shirking of work, the workman has the utmost freedom in the workshop, and any attempt to limit this freedom is resented as deeply as an attack on the economic position of wages and hours. The French workman attaches an importance, altogether unrecognized in England to such matters as personal freedom and treatment, courtesy of foremen and masters and so on.[19]

More than anything else, even the superior American machinery, a delegation of French bronzeworkers visiting American factories in 1890 remarked on the contrast between the behavior of American and French workers on the shop floor: "Work in the American shops is altogether different from what it is in France. Nobody talks, nobody sings, the most rigorous discipline reigns. The men come and go by the clock, a half-hour is given for the noon-day meal; the week's work is fifty-eight hours in summer and fifty-nine in winter. To get off for a while one has to go through the greatest amount of red tape."[20] An American unionist visiting French factories in 1896 was also struck by the difference:

> The Frenchman does not work very hard. He takes life rather

leisurely. There are multitudes of industries in which hand labor still prevails. While there are many large factories, machinery has not so generally supplanted hand production as in the United States. Even when operating a machine the workman does not rush. He will stop the machine while he chats with his fellow workman. Occasionally he takes ten minutes off for a cigarette or a glass of wine. If a workman were deprived of this privilege the whole factory would strike. They particularly object to any importation of American high-pressure rates of industry. They ask me why our people do not make a stand against the hurry and rush of our factory system.[21]

Still, even as observers were remarking on the independence of French workers on the shop floor, profound changes were occurring which were eventually to destroy this independence. Although an increase in the scale of industry did not automatically signify the disappearance of the artisanal workers, the increase in scale did, for the first time, make it financially worthwhile for the industrialist to attack the artisans' relatively independent status by mechanizing key artisanal skills, developing his supervisory staff so as to give it an authority which had formerly belonged to the workers, and establishing his own training programs without regard to those maintained by workers. The high wages and shop-floor autonomy of the skilled workers were obstacles to the industrialist's control of the factory and the pursuit of profits; mechanization allowed the industrialist to attack the position of the skilled worker and install a new discipline. In 1901 Charles Limousin noted:

> As a result of the new situation [mechanization] . . . the industrialists hire the first workers who present themselves. . . . They [the industrialists] look for certain qualities of the laborers during the first days of their employ. If [these workers] do not possess them, they are fired and replaced by others. These workers must have the virtues of sobriety, manageability, and dependability. . . . They must arrive on time, must not quarrel with their workmates, must not lose time gossiping. . . .[22]

Toward the turn of the century a new industrial working class of semiskilled workers began to make its appearance in France. These workers emerged in industries like metalworking and machine production which had heretofore been dominated by artisanal work organization. The "second industrial revolution" of the late nineteenth century represented a new kind of challenge to artisanal workers. Previously the transformation of the work process had led to the replacement of skilled artisans by unskilled women and children whose wages were dramatically lower than those of the skilled worker. The new transformation was far more insidious: skilled artisans were gradually replaced by less skilled, employer-trained, male operatives whose wages were lower than those of artisans but much higher than those of the unskilled female and child proletariat. By 1900 this new industrial working class could be found in large numbers in French heavy industry.[23]

Artisanal Resistance to Technological Change

Although French artisanal industry was marked by adaptability and survivability, artisanal workers were under constant pressure from mechanized industry and the increased division of labor. In the years between 1871 and 1914, the relationship between employers and workers was changing; mechanization was only the most typical of a whole series of changes, such as speed-ups, new management techniques, and elaborate systems of payment, which fundamentally altered work relations. Each innovation strengthened the employer's hand and gave him greater leverage to attack the skilled workers' position. The presence of a sizable artisanal sector in late nineteenth-century France is a surprise partly because the drama's outcome is known. Despite the hopes of an anarchist like Peter Kropotkin or a petty-bourgeois economist like Camille Sabatier, the future did not lie with small-scale industry. The survival of French artisanal industry into the late nineteenth century only meant that its agony was extended longer than in other, more industrialized countries. Because of the marked slowness of the French economy to industrialize, the history of the French labor movement is *par excellence* the history of the strategies used by artisanal workers struggling with employers armed with machines and new methods of work organization.

In order to understand how late nineteenth-century French workers confronted the threat of mechanization and industrial reorganization, an examination of the kind of technological changes taking place and the tools of protest available to French workers is first necessary. French artisans had successfully withstood the threat of dequalification during the greater part of the nineteenth century for two chief reasons. First, as already mentioned, in many cases decentralized artisanal methods of production proved competitive with machines for a much longer time than is generally realized. Second, artisans were a cohesive and highly paid group which was easily organized. Frequently artisanal workers could force employers to maintain artisanal production methods even though they were no longer the most efficient technology, or to pay artisanal wages for semiskilled industrial tasks, thus incorporating the machine into the artisanal wage structure. While changes in the structure of work had serious consequences for artisanal life, artisans also had some influence on work structure.

Although they labored for an employer, large sectors of the French working class still asserted claims to control key elements of the productive process. Their refusal to relinquish these claims was rooted in their daily work experience; artisans were highly skilled, possessed a wide range of skills, and exercised some control over the admission of workers into their trades. Each of these three defining elements of artisanal work needs to be looked at separately. "Skill" is defined as a scarce ability which takes time and effort to acquire. The definition of skill is a broad one and includes the manual dexterity of the wood joiner and the shoe laster as well as the extraordinary physical capacity of the forger. In any case, an evaluation of the relative share of dexterity and capacity in determining skill is frequently impossible. Should the source of the puddler's skill be located primarily in his metallurgical knowledge or in his facility in performing demanding physical labor in a difficult environment? The preceding definition says that if any reasonably strong man could perform the job it should be considered unskilled, while if it requires really unusual muscular development it may be considered skilled.[24]

A second important characteristic of artisanal industry was that workers learned a variety of valuable skills. In artisanal industry the employers specialized their product while, in contrast, the workers generalized their skills. Apprenticeship programs prepared the workers for the needs of the whole industry by specifying that they had to be proficient in many aspects of the trade. This requirement provided the employer with a workman who could be assigned almost anywhere in an emergency situation, but, by increasing the potential market for the worker's skill, it also strengthened his bargaining power vis-à-vis his employer. A final characteristic of artisanal industry was the presence of a worker-controlled apprenticeship program. This usually took the form of training in domestic industry or in the regulation of apprenticeship by informally agreed-upon worker custom or formal trade union rules. The ability to control admission to a trade was an important weapon in the skilled workers' arsenal.

The characteristics of artisanal work explain artisans' determination to assert their independence on the shop floor. As highly skilled workers, they believed that they knew more about how the job should be done than their supervisors or employers. As workers who possessed a variety of skills, they felt superior to the employer who specialized in some narrow branch of the trade. Finally, as members of a group that decided who should be admitted to apprenticeship positions, they felt a collective responsibility for production not inferior to that of their employers.

Changes in the work structure had the most serious repercussions for artisanal workers because its influence extended well beyond the shop-floor routine established by the pace of work and method of discipline. Different work structures defined alternative types of working-class lifestyles. Artisanal work involved the subordination of one worker to another within a worker-controlled job hierarchy; the existence of this chain of command, combined with the artisanal tradition of technical decision-making and diverse skills, encouraged informal artisanal worker contact. This familiarity was reinforced by the tendency of small-scale establishments in the same industry to huddle together in their own quarter of the city so as to rapidly respond to market conditions. The geographic proximity of small-scale industrial establishments was also imitated by its workers, who customarily lived near their workplace and gathered together in bars to exchange job information. In contrast, industrial work scattered workers across the factory and the city. Industrial workers had little contact with one another on the job, and they were separated even after they had left work. Similarly, large factories did not group together but sought their own private expanse of cheap land on the edge of a town or in the suburbs.[25]

Artisanal and industrial forms of production thus had different consequences for working-class mobilization. Because the kind of labor workers performed determined skill requirements and the level of informal shop contacts, it also powerfully influenced the workers' ability to form a trade union, build a strike fund, or sustain a long strike. Artisanal work structure helps explain why artisans played a much more important role in nineteenth-century protest than did industrial workers. Because of their skills, artisanal workers earned relatively high wages and could afford to finance, first, mutual aid societies and, then, trade unions. The structure of artisanal work, which encouraged worker contacts both on and off the job, created group cohesion among artisanal workers. This informal solidarity made it relatively easy for artisans to evolve formal organizations from their strong informal group. Industrial workers, on the other hand, who had lower wages and less group cohesion, found it much more difficult to build strong trade union organizations.

Nineteenth-century French observers clearly perceived these differences between artisanal and industrial workers. A late nineteenth-century social reformer, Charles Limousin, explained that one powerful reason behind the employers' decision to mechanize was

> . . . the desire of putting an end to strikes. . . . For, the industrialists have understood that professional specialization, which makes certain work the monopoly of certain workers, by putting these workers together and promoting their coming to a mutual understanding, facilitates strikes which result in serious losses; while the employment of "laborers" who are not specialized and not unionized, who are always abundant on the labor market, would render these strikes difficult if not impossible.[26]

Victor Griffuelhes, the revolutionary syndicalist leader of the Confédération générale du travail (CGT), concluded after viewing the work situation of mechanized weavers in the Nord: "[T]he misery, the demoralizing work of the factory, the near certainty of the weaver of his powerlessness, allied to his habitual submission, and his lack of experience in rebelling . . . the atmosphere in which he passes his life . . . determines in our proletariat a particular mentality. He is the victim quietly sighing about his lot, convinced of the uselessness of any effort although he has never actually tried."[27]

Griffuelhes's comments suggest that mechanized textile workers in France were not as militant as sometimes alleged. Impressions of textile militancy arise because textile and cloth production comprised a large percentage of the French workforce; as a result, the absolute number of French textileworkers on strike was substantial. Shorter and Tilly show that in the years between 1890 and 1914 the number of strikes per 100,000 textileworkers was among the lower occupational strike rates. Scholars have used the large numbers of textile strikes as examples of unrest among unskilled workers; but, as already noted, French textiles were particularly concentrated in slowly mechanizing branches of textiles, and many textile strikes were led by skilled artisans, such as the ribbonweavers, dyers, and cloth printers.[28] This point is reinforced by the low strike participation rates of female workers, a group disproportionately concentrated in unskilled textile jobs. Between 1896 and 1906 over 70 percent of the workforce in textile and cloth products were women; in the same period less than half of the strikers in textiles and cloth were female.[29]

Artisanal skills facilitated organization which, in turn, made it possible for artisans to defend themselves against employers' attempts to undercut their position. Artisanal workers had good reason to defend their trades because their skills not only gave them more autonomy on the job but provided them and their families with a relatively high standard of living. By the late nineteenth century no group of French skilled workers was unaware of the potential dangers of mechanization. In 1863 Anthime Corbon, a Parisian skilled worker, remarked wryly that "the worker who follows with a lively interest the happy transformations which occur in other trades cannot be persuaded . . . that a happy transformation is able to occur in his own trade."[30]

It is easy to sympathize with these workers' suspicions—they were in fact threatened by a whole complex of unfamiliar changes which was eliminating the need for their skills. Technological change could overtake the skilled workers in a variety of ways.

That particular type of technological change which suddenly transformed an entire trade, as the power loom revolutionized weaving in the early nineteenth century, remained exceptional. Somewhat more typical of late nineteenth-century technological change was the kind of slow transformation occuring in metalworking, where the gradual rise of the semiskilled worker possessing a few specialized skills took place at the expense of both artisan and unskilled industrial worker.

While technological change made itself felt almost everywhere, its impact was greater in some industries than others. In glassmaking and pottery the spread of the Siemens oven augmented productivity without altering workers' skills. Even though skills were left untouched, productivity increases usually created unemployment, which brought wage levels down. Some kinds of changes were permanent but only affected a small part of the total array of skills possessed by the artisans; the extensive introduction of machine tools into carriagemaking did not seriously affect the status of the carriageworker because the most crucial skills remained in his control. Other kinds of change were gradual but cumulatively transformed a trade, as the sewing machine, stitcher, and lasting machine transformed shoemaking in the course of two decades. For many workers, such as shoeworkers, technological change was not a brief searing experience, as it is often described, but a continual menace. The threat of technological change played an important role in shaping the attitudes and actions of skilled workers in the late nineteenth century.[31]

Artisanal workers in France developed a number of strategies for dealing with technological change. In general, they accepted the inevitability of mechanization but did not concede that mechanization involved any attenuation of their control of the work process or any reduction of the skilled worker's position. Artisanal workers responded to technological change in two ways. First, they acted to strengthen their own formal trade union organization and to increase their union's monopoly over the skills which remained to them. Second, they acted to incorporate machine work into the existing work structure by demanding that artisanal wages be paid for machine work. Where small-scale industry dominated, powerful artisanal unions could apply great pressure on individual employers, and artisanal chances of success were improved. Conditions were also favorable for artisanal success when an industry catered to a local market which made strong national organization unnecessary and freed workers from the dangers of national or international price competition. The French economy, dominated by family firms and protected by high tariff walls, was an ideal theater of operations for artisanal unions.[32]

French artisanal workers could hope to set the terms by which machinery would be introduced into the factories because the process of mechanization was seldom rapid enough to enable employers to dispense completely with the artisans' services. In cases where rapid change did occur, completely transforming the trade, skilled workers could do little. In these cases the artisans' bitterness sometimes turned against the industrial workers who replaced them. But in most cases when employers tried to make artisans pay the cost of mechanization and to take complete control of the work process, workers still possessed sufficient skills and resources to carry out a prolonged struggle. In many instances artisanal strategies brought skilled workers into alliances with industrial workers. If skilled workers could substantially raise the price of machine work, the result would be to slow down the pace of mechanization no matter who actually worked the machines. Under these circumstances artisans and industrial workers could work together under the banner of wage increases.

Middle-class observers generally ridiculed and dismissed the attempts of nineteenth-century artisanal workers to preserve their position. For these observers, any attempt by artisanal workers to defend themselves was "to attack the machine," and "to attack the machine is to attack civilization."[33] Yet the artisans' attempts were neither so foolhardy nor so unsuccessful as middle-class commentators were inclined to claim. In some industries, such as the construction trade and printing, artisanal workers successfully maintained their position against the threat of unemployment or attempts to undermine their skills. And in many other industries artisans succeeded in slowing down potentially catastrophic changes to manageable proportions. If workers succeeded in retarding the destruction of their trade by even a few years, they gave older workers time to leave the trade and younger workers time to enter other occupations.

Industrial and Political Change: The Formation of a Working-Class Coalition

Thus far attention has been focused primarily on the industrial composition of the French labor force and the effects of changes in industrial structure on the behavior of artisanal workers. It has been argued that artisanal workers played a large role in the nineteenth-century French economy, that artisanal workers were particularly able to carry out organized protests, and that the reaction of artisanal workers to employers' attempts to undermine their position significantly influenced the goals of workers' protest during this period. From the industrial world, which shaped workers' demands and their ability to protest, it is time to turn to the political world to which every mass strike belonged. The argument in this section is that industrial change and political liberalization joined together to powerfully shape the French working-class movement. It did so chiefly by promoting the development of organizational and political coalitions of industrial workers with artisanal workers threatened by technological change. These coalitions produced the mass strikes which swept France in the years between 1890 and 1914.

The republican majority which took control of the Third Republic in 1877 inherited the "social question" as well as a variety of social "solutions" from the preceding regimes. Where Napoleon III and Marshal MacMahon had failed, the liberal republicans hoped to succeed, but first they had to deal with the legacy of brutality bequeathed by earlier administrations. Between 1851 and 1876 French trade unions and working-class political organizations had been harassed and persecuted continuously. In the fifties Napoleon III had used police spies and imprisonment to crush the independent working-class movement, while the union organizations, grown up in the last years of the Second Empire, were smashed by the massacres and deportations stemming from the suppression of the Paris Commune. As a result of decades of repression, in 1876 all sections of the French working class remained outside the political system, unorganized and unrepresented.[34] Almost every republican agreed that the political estrangement of the working class, its increasing disillusionment with the republic, was a serious danger to the regime's existence.

French republican legislators faced with this problem studied the example of their English neighbors. Where in 1840, French middle-class politicans had feared the legalization of trade unions because they might encourage peaceful French workers to imitate their seditious English comrades, by 1880 these politicians hoped that the legalization of trade unions would encourage embittered French workers to imitate their conservative English brothers. It was not coincidental that the law of March 21, 1844, which legalized French trade unions, almost exactly copied the act of 1824 which legalized English unions. Basically, French middle-class politicians like Leon Gambetta and Pierre Waldeck-Rousseau hoped that the legalization of trade unions would create a conservative, wage-oriented, craft unionism capable of being drawn into the existing political system as had their counterparts in England and America. The legalization of trade unions was only one in a series of stratagems designed to tie the workers' movement to the republican camp; others included the dispatch of republican-financed workers' delegations to international expositions and the establishment of municipally subsidized labor exchanges, the *bourse du travail*. The attempts of these middle-class republicans to mold the French working class along Anglo-American lines miscarried for several reasons, all of which grew out of the peculiar industrial development of late nineteenth-century France.[35]

First, the appearance of a new group of well-paid, semiskilled industrial workers alongside the great mass of French artisanal workers encouraged French artisans to form industrial unions instead of craft unions. This new semiskilled working class had little in common with the industrial proletariat created by the first industrial revolution. In the early and mid-nineteenth century most industrial workers were in the textile industries, which mainly employed poorly paid women and children. In the second half of the nineteenth century a new proletariat engaged in heavy metalwork and machine construction was in process of formation;

these metal workers were adult, semiskilled men who received relatively high pay. The craft exclusiveness which gradually took over in English and American trade union organizations was powerfully shaped by the low potential for collective action of industrial workers during the early and mid-nineteenth century when Anglo-American unions emerged; the very different potential for collective action possessed by the late nineteenth-century industrial working class pulled the French trade union movement in a very different direction.

The Anglo-American trade union movement was created and developed during the fifty-year period between 1830 and 1880, when the French trade union movement was, for the most part, outlawed and repressed. In both England and the United States craft unions evolved from the collapse of mass industrial unions, the British Grand National Consolidated Craft Unions of the thirties and the American Knights of Labor of the eighties. These unions, though industrial in form, had been composed mainly of artisanal workers; both failed because of the pace of mechanization, which transformed their constituency, and the resulting rapid growth of an unskilled proletariat of women, children, and penniless immigrants, incapable of supporting mass trade union organization. Out of the ruin of these organizations developed narrow craft unions led by conservative leaders who scorned the mass of unskilled workers and maintained an authoritarian control over their own membership. Only much later, and against the strong opposition of their leaders, did some of these craft unions evolve into industrial unions composed mostly of industrial workers.[36]

From its revival in the nineties, the French labor movement showed the same tendency toward "artisanal" industrial unionism as its Anglo-American precursors. But while, under the pressure of mechanization, the embryonic Anglo-American industrial organizations proved weak and unstable, in France industrial unionism showed considerably more resilience and flexibility. The industrial unionism of the early CGT stemmed from the clear predominance of artisanal workers in industry; when there were several different groups of skilled craftsmen working in an industry, all of whom possessed the same amount of bargaining power, it made sense for them to unite together and enjoy the benefits of their collective strength. But while the French trade union movement of the late nineteenth century would never have assumed an industrial form had it not been for the large size of the French artisanal work-force, the superior strength of French industrial unionism can be explained by its ability to incorporate industrial workers into its organization.[37]

Second, the Third Republic gave French workers the right to organize politically at a time when the threat of technological change politicized many French artisanal workers and drove them into electoral alliances with industrial workers. Once granted the right to form their own political organizations, French artisanal workers began again, as in 1848, to engage in mass politics. The sudden increase in working-class political strength was more than the existing electoral coalitions, based on the gradual doling out of meager benefits by conservative republicans, could bear, and independent working-class parties began to emerge. The increasing politicization of threatened artisanal workers led them to try to rally industrial workers to their side because, together, artisans and industrial workers could dominate local elections.[38]

In contrast with England, the formative period of trade unionism in France occurred after French male industrial workers had acquired the electoral franchise and were thus valuable allies. In America all native-born and naturalized white males were admitted to the franchise by the early nineteenth century, but precisely because of their long political history it was difficult to involve American trade unionists in a specifically "trade union" movement. Local unions were so deeply involved in coalitions with one or another of the existing parties that it was not easy to unite them around expressly trade union issues.[39]

The battle over control of the work process raging in late nineteenth-century French factories ensured that trade union questions emerged as the central issue of French working-class political life. Initially, technological change almost always strengthened trade union organization among threatened artisans, and, once organized, artisans inevitably became involved in the politics of the trade union movement. Union solidarity played an important role in bringing artisanal and industrial workers together. Artisans felt that only their union stood between them and the destruction of their trade. In this atmosphere the open anti-unionism of large industrialists angered artisanal workers who saw "union busting" anywhere in their community as a prelude to an assault on their own organization. Industrial workers could only benefit from these new allies.

Union solidarity was not the only reason French artisans were driven to form coalitions with industrial workers. Artisanal workers turned to independent politics as a result of their own experience in defending their job interests. Strikes and industrial unrest brought artisans into conflict with the political authorities, judges, and police officials, who frequently had direct connections with the major industrialists. In addition, artisans began to develop their own political demands. Artisans hoped that legal measures such as the eight-hour day, prohibitions on private employment bureaus, and the regulation of child labor would enable them to maintain and tighten their control over the trade. Typical of dozens of resolutions passed by workers' congresses during the Third Republic are the resolutions of the 1901 shoeworkers' congress:

> [T]he Congress adopted the resolutions on the following questions on the agenda; complete suppresion of work in prisons, in work related to the shoe industry; suppression of master bootmakers in the army for they give unfair competition to licensed shoemakers; suppression of employment bureaus, placement should be reserved to the trade unions through the creation of *Bourses du travail* by municipalities . . . the incessant progress of mechanization allows only one solution, the socialization of the means of production; suppression of female labor, or, as frequently occurs where women work for vile wages to the detriment of men's salaries, for similar work, a salary equal to that of a man; suppression of child labor under 16 years; on the question of the hours of work . . . the eight hour day.[40]

A final reason for the difference between the French and Anglo-American trade union movements is that there existed in France a nucleus of politicized artisanal workers who had grown increasingly disenchanted with the republic and embraced socialist ideas. Almost everywhere in the nineteenth-century industrial world, artisanal workers spread socialist doctrines. On the basis of very impressionistic evidence, mostly drawn from the secondary literature, it seems that there were more politicized worker-militants in France than in either England or the United States. If so, this would be explained partly by the strength of the revolutionary tradition and partly by the larger size of the French artisanal working class.[41]

In any case, the spread of socialist ideas in France acted to promote the growth of solidarity among workers and to discredit the already precarious influence of republicans on the working class. As Bernard Moss has shown, politicized French artisanal workers, who for a long time had placed their faith in the creation of worker-controlled cooperatives, were disillusioned by the failure of liberal republicans to aid them once the republic was established. In desperation these artisanal workers turned to a revolutionary strategy based on a decentralized "trade socialism." While this trade socialism was based on the craft interests of skilled workers, it appealed to all French workers and encouraged cooperation between artisans and industrial workers.[42]

The formation of trade union and political coalitions of artisanal and industrial workers promoted strike coalitions between these two groups. Membership in the same union gave artisanal and industrial workers a shared interest in the common defense of their trade union organization; a defeat for industrial members of the union was an attack on the prestige of the whole organization as well as a crippling blow to its treasury. Moreover, the growing political awareness of threatened artisans increased their desire to support the spread of militant unionism among industrial workers. Artisanal workers knew from their own experience that strike militancy increased political consciousness. Finally, the spread of socialist ideas helped to persuade both artisanal and industrial workers that they had a common interest in uniting together to oppose the employers.

The Design of This Study

An examination of a few specific mass strike actions provides the best opportunity of finding out more about artisanal-industrial worker coalitions and what impact different forms of work organization had on social protest. A case study can explore such complex changes with precision. Since sources at the national level—industrial censuses, production estimates, and government reports—are intractable in yielding information about skill levels and shop organization, local studies are of invaluable assistance. It has been suggested that the concentration of strikes into "strike wave" years and the rapidly growing participation of industrial workers during these years were associated with an increase in the number of threatened artisans. One way of testing this proposition is to choose an area of France with these characteristics and see if artisanal-industrial coalitions were formed. To determine whether different goals and methods of worker protest could be distinguished, three different towns were chosen which all had a record of high strike activity but different industrial composition. Of the three towns selected one was predominantly artisanal, one predominantly industrial, and one mixed artisanal-industrial.

Setting down formal, *a priori* procedures to dictate the choice of an area seemed preferable to making an arbitrary selection or, worse yet, making a selection with the fore-knowledge that the area chosen would support the argument. Accordingly, criteria were established for finding strike wave areas, and then these criteria determined the choice of the area. A detailed description of this procedure can be found in the Appendix, "The Selection of a Region."

As a result of this selection process, three cities were picked within a twenty-mile radius of the city of Saint-Etienne, in the area of France called the "Stéphanois." Each town had a rich history of strike activity, and in 1891 the industrial composition of the towns differed considerably. Le Chambon-Feugerolles, whose inhabitants were known as "Chambonnaires," was a predominantly artisanal town; Saint-Chamond, the home of the "Saint-Chamonnais," was a predominantly industrial town; and Rive-de-Gier, with its "Ripagériens," was a mixed artisanal-industrial town.

Subsequent chapters in this study examine these Stéphanois towns in the context of the arguments about the relationship between work structure, technological change, and strike militancy elaborated in Chapter One. The contribution of regional economic development to the outbreak of mass strikes is discussed in Chapter

Two. An overview of the relationships between work structure, technological change, and strike militancy in the three principal towns is the subject of Chapter Three. Chapters Four through Six focus more narrowly on the experiences of the individual towns and their workers.

NOTES

1. Louis Reybaud, *Études sur le régime des manufactures: Conditions des ouvrières en soie* (Paris: Michel Levy, 1859), pp. vii–ix.

2. An example of modern struggle over the issue of workers' control is found in Stanley Aronowitz's study, "Lordstown: Disruption on the Assembly Line," in *False Promises: The Shaping of American Working Class Consciousness* (New York: McGraw-Hill, 1973), pp. 21–50, and another is in two articles on the LIP strike in *Le nouvel observateur*, nos. 456 and 458.

American students of French working-class history have written some extremely sensitive studies of working-class life. Edward Shorter and Charles Tilly, *Strikes in France, 1830–1968* (London: Cambridge University Press, 1974), presents a panoramic view of protest for a century and a half. Three fine studies of artisanal life in the first half of the nineteenth century are: Robert J. Bezucha, *The Lyon Uprising of 1834: Social and Political Conflict in the Early July Monarchy* (Cambridge, Mass.: Harvard University Press, 1974); Christopher H. Johnson, *Utopian Communism in France: Cabet and the Icarians* (Ithaca, N.Y.: Cornell University Press, 1970); and William H. Sewell, Jr., "The Working Class of Marseilles under the Second Republic: Social Structure and Political Behavior," in *Workers in the Industrial Revolution*, ed. Peter N. Stearns and Daniel J. Walkowitz (New Brunswick, N.J.: Transaction Books, 1974), pp. 75–116. An invaluable and pathbreaking study of artisanal life in the late nineteenth century, a period which remains little studied, is Joan Wallach Scott, *The Glassworkers of Carmaux: French Craftsmen and Political Action in a Nineteenth-Century City* (Cambridge, Mass.: Harvard University Press, 1974).

Three other useful studies also merit mention. Alain Touraine's study of technological change in the Renault plant is a deservedly influential work: *L'Évolution du travail ouvrier aux usines Renault* (Paris: Centre nationale de la recherche scientifique, 1955). Peter Stearns, *The Lives of Labor* (New York: Holmes and Meier, 1975), looks at a whole variety of hitherto unexamined aspects of European working-class life. Michelle Perrot's *Les ouvriers en grève: France, 1871–1890*, 2 vols. (Paris: Mouton, 1975), which covers the first two decades of our period, is an incomparably rich source of information on working-class life and protest.

3. John U. Nef, *Industry and Government in France and England, 1540–1640* (Ithaca, N.Y.: Cornell University Press, 1957 [1940]). Nef noted, "Both by their influence on investment and by their influence on demand, the financial policies of the French kings served to discourage the rapid progress of mining and heavy manufacturing, and to foster skilled craftsmanship and fine art. They promoted quality at the expense of quantity" (p. 142).

Two helpful introductions to the study of industrial structure in England and

France are: Lucienne Cahen, "Évolution de la population active en France depuis cent ans d'après les dénombrements quinquennaux," *Études et conjonctures* 12 (May-June, 1953), 230–88, and Thomas A. Welton, "On Forty Years' Industrial Change in England and Wales," *Transactions of the Manchester Statistical Society, 1897–1898*, pp. 153–266.

Peter Stearns has written a provocative article on the subject of protest and industrial structure, "National Character and European Labor History," in *Workers in the Industrial Revolution*, ed. Stearns and Walkowitz, pp. 1–12. Adeline Daumard places the changing industrial structure in a national framework in "L'Évolution des structures sociales en France à l'époque de l'industrialisation (1815–1914)," *Revue historique* 502 (Apr.-June, 1971), 325–46.

4. G. N. Clark, *The Wealth of England from 1496 to 1760* (London: Oxford University Press, 1946), p. 170; Berrill, "Origins of the Industrial Revolution," *Past and Present* 17 (Apr., 1960), 79–80; François Crouzet, "England and France in the Eighteenth Century," in *Social Historians in Contemporary France: Essays from Annales* (New York: Harper and Row, 1972), pp. 59–86.

5. Tihomir J. Markovitch, "The Dominant Sectors of French Industry," in *Essays in French Economic History*, ed. Rondo Cameron (Homewood, Ill.: Richard Irwin, 1970), p. 235.

6. Armand Audiganne, "La crise du travail dans Paris," *Revue des deux mondes* 93 (May 15, 1871), 301.

7. Tihomir J. Markovitch, "Le revenu industriel et artisanal sous la monarchie de juillet et le Second Empire," *Économies et sociétés*, Ser. AF, 4 (Apr., 1967), 1–138.

8. On carriagemaking, see Chambre de commerce de Paris, *Statistique de l'industrie de Paris en 1860* (Paris: Chambre de commerce, 1864), pp. 815–17; Joseph Barbaret, *Le travail en France: Monographies professionnelles*, "Charrons et carrossiers," vol. 3 (Paris: Berger-Levrault, 1887); and Ministre de l'instruction publique, *Enquête sur la situation des ouvriers et des industries d'art* (Paris: Imprimerie nationale, 1884), p. 16.

The classic study of different systems of payment is David F. Schloss, *Methods of Industrial Remuneration* (London: Williams and Nargate, 1892).

9. Eric J. Hobsbawm, *The Age of Capital, 1848–1875* (New York: Charles Scribner's Sons, 1975), p. 45.

10. Paul Bairoch et al., *The Working Population and Its Structure*, Vol. 1 (Brussels: Editions de l'institute de sociologie de l'Université Libre de Bruxelles, 1968).

See also R. E. Tyson, "The Cotton Industry," in *The Development of British Industry*, ed. Derek H. Aldcroft (London: George Allen and Unwin, 1968), pp. 100–127.

11. Peter Kropotkin, *Fields, Factories, and Workshops* (New York: Greenwood Press, 1960 [1898]), p. 132.

12. *Ibid.*, p. 133.

13. M. Ducarre, *Rapport . . . sur les conditions du travail en France: Salaires et rapports entre ouvriers et patrons* (Lyon: Imprimerie Mougin-Rusand, 1877), pp. 165–66.

14. Lucienne Cahen, "La concentration des établissements en France de 1896 à 1936," *Études et conjonctures*, 9 (Sept., 1954), 846–47.

15. Camille Sabatier, "Le morcellisme dans l'industrie," *Revue d'économie politique* 21 (1907), 736–60.

The rising importance of consumers' goods was part of a worldwide trend; see

Charles Wilson, "Economy and Society in Late Victorian Britain," *Economic History Review*, Ser. 2, 18 (Aug., 1965), 183–98.

16. Markovitch, "Le revenu industriel et artisanal," p. 86.

17. C. K. Harley, "Skilled Labor and the Choice of Technique in Edwardian Industry," *Explorations in Economic History*, ser. 2, 11 (Summer, 1974), 391–414.

18. Office du travail, *Statistiques du recensement de la population, 1901* (Paris: Imprimerie nationale, 1906), vol. 4, pp. 193, 197.

19. Henry Steele, *The Working Classes in France: A Social Study* (London: Twentieth Century Press, 1904), pp. 16–17.

20. E. Levasseur, *The American Workman* (Baltimore, Md.: Johns Hopkins University Press, 1900), pp. 173–74. Levasseur visited America in 1893.

21. Eva McDonald Valesh, "Conditions of Labor in Europe," *American Federationist* 3 (May, 1896), 42.

22. Charles Limousin, "L'Instruction professionnelle et l'industrie nouvelle," *Journal des économistes* 48 (Oct. 1901), 23–24.

On the organization of work in French factories, see Bernard Mottez, *Systemes de salaires et politiques patronales* (Paris: Centre nationale de la recherche scientifique, 1966).

The kind of worker French industrialists were trying to create is described by Taine during his visit to Manchester: "The *phlegmatic*. This type is to be found everywhere but notably in cotton mills, and so far as the faces are concerned, all the workers up here belong to this type. The complexion is pale, the eyes dull, the expression cold and fixed; the movements are exact, regular and economical. For which reason they are excellent workers: there is nothing like a machine to operate a machine. French manufacturers tell me that French workers work perfectly well for the first hour, less well in the second, still less well in the third and so on in diminishing progression so that, during their last hour, they can do nothing right. Their muscular strength declines but above all their powers of attention" (Hippolyte Taine, *Notes on England* [London: Thames and Hudson, 1957], p. 227). Taine visited England between 1859 and 1862.

French theorists of industrial management were more concerned with order and the preservation of hierarchy than function. Fayol criticized Taylor for infringing on the chain of command in the factory; see Henri Fayol, *General and Industrial Management* (London: Pitman, 1948), pp. 69–70. The body of this book was developed from a lecture Fayol gave to the Association of Mining Industry in Saint-Étienne in 1908.

23. An interesting discussion of work organization in metalworking is found in Jean Vial, "L'ouvrier métallurgiste français," *Droit social* 13 (1950), 58–68.

24. "Artisanal" workers are defined as workers possessing a variety of skills who control the acquisition of these skills either through family groups or collective corporate organization. The definition of industrial worker follows from the definition of artisan. "Industrial" workers perform less skilled tasks which are often monotonous and repetitive, tasks which are often acquired "on the job" or in the employer-controlled training programs. Sumner Slichter, *Modern Economic Society* (New York: Henry Holt, 1928), pp. 28–121, and Touraine, *L'Évolution du travail ouvrier*, provide interesting discussions of the evolution of work structure. For a more thorough discussion of the definitions used in this study, see Michael P. Hanagan, "Artisan and Skilled Worker: The Problem of Definition," *International Labor and Working Class History* 12 (Nov., 1977), 28–31.

25. On the changing geography of nineteenth-century artisanal and industrial

working-class life, see Sam Bass Warner, Jr., *The Private City* (Philadelphia: University of Pennsylvania Press, 1968); Susan Eleanor Bloomberg, "Industrialization and Skilled Workers: Newark, 1826–1860" (Dissertation, University of Michigan, 1974); and John Taylor Cumbler, "Continuity and Disruption: Working Class Community in Lynn and Fall River, Massachusetts, 1880–1950" (Dissertation, University of Michigan, 1974).

On the culture of artisanal and industrial working-class life in the late nineteenth century, see Gareth Stedman Jones, "Working Class Culture and Working Class Politics in London, 1870–1900: Notes on the Remaking of the Working Class," *Journal of Social History* 7 (Summer, 1974), 460–508.

26. Limousin, "L'Instruction professionnelle," pp. 2–24.

27. Victor Griffuelhes, *Voyage révolutionnaire* (Paris: Marcel Rivière, 1910), p. 14.

28. Peter Stearns has emphasized textile militancy in *Revolutionary Syndicalism and French Labor: A Cause without Rebels* (New Brunswick, N.J.: Rutgers University Press, 1971), esp. Chapter Two.

On occupational strike rates, see Shorter and Tilly, *Strikes in France*, pp. 201, 221.

29. For female labor participation and strike rates, see Madeleine Guilbert, *Les femmes et l'organisation syndicale avant 1914* (Paris: Centre nationale de la recherche scientifique, 1966), pp. 12–14, 215.

30. Anthime Corbon, *Le secret du peuple de Paris* (Paris: Pagnenere, 1863), pp. 82–84.

31. On glassworkers, see Scott, *Glassworkers of Carmaux;* on shoeworkers, see Barbaret, *Le travail en France*, "Cordonniers."

32. A similar process is described in Irwin Yellowitz, "Skilled Workers and Mechanization: The Lasters in the 1890's," *Labor History* 18 (Spring, 1977), 197–213.

James Holt argues that employer resistance was a key force in explaining the relative weakness of American metal unionism in the late nineteenth century, in "Trade Unionism in the British and U.S. Steel Industries 1888–1912: A Comparative Study," *Labor History* 18 (Winter, 1977), 5–36.

Stearns has written an interesting article on the relative slowness with which French employers responded to worker militancy: "Against the Strike Threat: Employers' Policy towards Labor Agitation in France 1900–1914," *Journal of Modern History* 40 (Dec., 1968), 474–500.

33. A. Crouzel, *Étude historique, économique et juridique sur les coalitions et les grèves dans l'industrie* (Paris: Arthur Rousseau, 1887), p. 274. The "machine-breaking" movement in France was never as strong as in England, and it had almost completely disappeared by mid-century; see Frank E. Manuel, "The Luddite Movement in France," *Journal of Modern History* 10 (June, 1938), 180–211.

In general, American labor scholarship has tended to portray artisanal attempts at self-preservation as resistance to machinery and stressed the differences between artisan and industrial workers. Two widely influential examples of this tendency are John R. Commons, "American Shoemakers 1648–1895: A Sketch of Industrial Evolution," in *Labor and Administration* (New York: A. M. Kelly, 1913), and Sumner Slichter, *Union Policies and Industrial Management* (Washington, D.C.: Brookings Institution, 1941). Alan Dawley has shown how misleading is Commons's emphasis on the natural opposition between skilled and unskilled workers, in *Class and Community: The Industrial Revolution in Lynn* (Cambridge, Mass.: Harvard University Press, 1976).

34. On the origins of the European labor movement, see Walter Kendall, "The Rise of the Labour Movement," in Walter Kendall, *The Labour Movement in Europe* (London: Allen Lane, 1975).

On the results of the Paris Commune, see Jean Joughin, *The Paris Commune in French Politics 1871–1880*, 2 vols. (Baltimore, Md.: Johns Hopkins University Press, 1955), and Georges Lefranc, *Le mouvement syndical sous la troisième république* (Paris: Payot, 1967), pp. 13–27. A valuable introduction to the organization of repression in the Third Republic is A. Fryar Calhoun, "The Politics of Internal Order: French Government and Revolutionary Labor 1898–1914," 2 vols. (Ph.D dissertation, Princeton University, 1973).

35. For a basic summary of the labor laws of major European countries see, Gaston V. Rimlinger, "Labor and the Government: Comparative Perspective," *Journal of Economic History* 37 (Mar., 1977), 210–30. Rimlinger has also studied the effects of governmental regulation on miner protest, in "International Differences in the Strike Propensity of Coal Miners: Experience in Four Countries," *Industrial and Labor Relations Review* 12 (Apr., 1959), 389–403.

On the motives of Waldeck-Rousseau, see Pierre Sorlin, *Waldeck-Rousseau* (Paris: Armand Colin, 1966).

36. On the formation of Anglo-American craft unions, see Lloyd Ulman, *The Rise of the National Trade Union* (Cambridge, Mass.: Harvard University Press, 1955), and Eric J. Hobsbawm, "The Labor Aristocracy of Nineteenth-Century Britain," in *Workers in the Industrial Revolution*, ed. Stearns and Walkowitz, pp. 138–76.

To be sure, many of the same motivations which led to the formation of coalitions between artisanal and industrial workers in France were present even in the United States; see David Montgomery, "Workers' Control of Machine Production in the Nineteenth Century," *Labor History* 17 (Fall, 1976), 485–509, and John Amsden and Stephen Brier, "Coal Miners on Strike: The Transformation of Strike Demands and the Formation of a National Union," *Journal of Interdisciplinary History* 7 (Spring, 1977) 583–616. Conversely the tendency toward craft differentiation also existed in France; see Christian Gras, "L'Ouvrier mouleur à travers le journal de sa fédération: La Fonderie (1900–1909)," *Le mouvement social* 53 (Oct.-Dec., 1965), 51–68. While both tendencies existed in all three countries, in France the tendency toward industrial unionism and artisanal-industrial solidarity was dominant, while it seems to have been a minority influence within the American trade union movement.

For an even-handed comparison of the British and American trade union movements in the second half of the nineteenth century, see Philip S. Bagwell and G. E. Mingay, "Trade Unions," in *Britain and America 1850–1936: A Study of Economic Change* (London: Routledge and Kegan Paul, 1970), pp. 189–215.

37. On the logic of "artisanal" industrial unionism, see John T. Dunlop, "The Development of Labor Organization: A Theoretical Framework," in *Insights into Labor Issues*, ed. Richard A. Lester and Joseph Shister (New York: Macmillan, 1948). Arthur L. Stinchcombe discusses the environment for the formation of craft unions in "Social Structure and Organization," in *Handbook of Organizations*, ed. James S. March (Chicago: Rand-McNally, 1965), pp. 153–54.

38. Lipset and Rokkan have proposed an exciting model of European political

evolution in the nineteenth century and the origins of working-class parties; see "Cleavage Structures, Party Systems, and Voter Alignments: An Introduction," in *Party Systems and Voter Alignments: Cross-National Perspectives*, ed. Seymour Martin Lipset and Stein Rokkan (New York: Free Press, 1967), pp. 1–64.

In the case of France they overdraw the "isolation" of the working class. One of the more important questions of late nineteenth-century French political evolution is why the coalitions between working-class organizations and liberal middle-class "radicals" broke down. There was, after all, a liberal middle-class constituency in France which tried to appeal to the working class, in opposition to the majority regime of the conservative republicans; see two articles by Leo Loubère, "The French Left-Wing Radicals, Their Views on Trade Unionism, 1870–1898," *International Review of Social History* 7 (July, 1962), 203–30, and "Left-Wing Radicals, Strikes and the Military 1880–1907," *French Historical Studies* 3 (Spring, 1963), 93–105.

39. On American politics and the trade union movement in the late nineteenth century, see Dawley, *Class and Community*.

40. Office du travail, *Les associations professionnelles ouvrières*, 2 (Paris: Imprimerie nationale, 1901), 82.

41. Some descriptions of French artisanal life in the second half of the nineteenth century are: Georges Duveau, *La vie ouvrière en France sous le Second Empire* (Paris: Gallimard, 1946); Pierre Pierrard, *La vie ouvrière à Lille sous le Second Empire* (Paris: Bloud and Gay, 1965); and Jacques Rougerie, "Composition d'une population insurgée, l'exemple de la Commune," *Le mouvement social* 48 (July–Sept., 1964), 31–48.

42. Bernard H. Moss, *The Origins of the French Labor Movement: The Socialism of the Skilled Worker 1830–1914* (Berkeley: University of California Press, 1976). Two fine articles on the transition years between 1865 and 1880 are by Maxwell Kelso: "The French Labor Movement during the Last Years of the Second Empire," in *Essays in the History of Modern Europe*, ed. Donald C. McKay (New York: Harper, 1936) pp. 94–113, and "The Inception of the Modern French Labor Movement 1871–1879: A Reappraisal," *Journal of Modern History* 8 (June, 1936), 173–93, James C. Butler carries this theme into the later nineteenth century and focuses closely on the period between 1880 and 1906, in "Fernand Pelloutier and the Emergence of the French Syndicalist Movement 1880–1906" (Dissertation, Ohio State University 1960).

CHAPTER TWO

The Formation of The Stéphanois Working Class

I asked the way to the Forez; and, while talking with the landlady of an inn, was informed by her that it was a good country for workmen, that there were many forges in it, and a considerable amount of work to be done in iron. This panegyric cooled my romantic curiosity at once, and it seemed incongruous to look for Dianas and Sylvanders amongst a tribe of blacksmiths. The good woman who encouraged me in this manner, must have taken me for a journeyman locksmith.[1]

Rousseau was not alone in his conviction that metallurgy and romance could not abide together. More than a century and a half later, when the metalworking portion of the Forez had developed into the Stéphanois industrial region, potential tourists were being warned away for similar reasons. In 1890 an English guidebook noted that while the fifty-eight–kilometer road which followed the length of the Stéphanois valley passed within four kilometers of a fourteenth-century castle and an eighteenth-century chateau, the road itself was of "no interest," for "at night it is almost a continuous chain of lamps, so thickly is the district inhabited."[2] French guidebooks were still more blunt. In 1908 a French guidebook described the Stéphanois valley towns as

cities without history in this France where hundreds and thousands of little towns date back to the Romans, the Gauls, even to the early Celts. . . . Saint-Etienne is situated ten kilometers from the Loire, it has installed itself as best it could, following the demands of coalmining, possessing a cold and harsh climate, 523 meters high, on a meager, tributary river, the Furens, which, by chance, carries a Latin name, of which it is hardly worthy.[3]

Even a local poet lamented:

Here, along the valleys of the Ondaine, Furens, and the Gier, on this layer of coal . . . a supplicant humanity has set up its way of the cross, the stations of this *via dolorosa* are called: Firminy, Le Chambon, La Ricamerie, Saint-Etienne . . . Saint-Chamond . . . Rive-de-Gier!

Poor proletarian cities which have only your rags to display to visiting strangers. . . . Your names recall nothing but the memories of rebellion and slaughter. In our archives one scarcely finds a letter of nobility![4]

For the nineteenth-century seeker after royal ruins, Roman place names, or aristocratic remnants, the Stéphanois region had little to offer. Contrary to the guidebooks, the region did have a history, but it belonged more to the history of labor than to that of ruling elites. Since the sixteenth century, industrial development had transformed the Stéphanois region; highly skilled artisanal workers had settled in its cities and towns, and domestic industry spread through its countryside. Not only did the Stéphanois cities have a history but they possessed some spectacular scenery. The area's real attraction was to visitors looking for contemporary wonders produced by the rapid industrial development which occurred there between 1830 and 1890. In 1888 a visitor remarked on the terrible beauty of the Stéphanois towns by night:

> The spectacle . . . is fantastic. . . . Here and there, on the slopes, flames surge . . . from the unfinished combustion of the slag, thrown by the cartload at the side of the forges . . . it resembles the fires of the bivouac or the witches' sabbath. . . . By the light, in spite of the night, the industrial areas are clearly outlined, their streets aligned in a straight line, cut at right angles, mathematically, and, along the carbon-covered pavement, the flames of the blast furnaces. . . Everything here reveals work that is brutal, overwhelming, implacable, which does not accord the right to sleep.[5]

In the second half of the nineteenth century the Stéphanois region offered visitors a view of the heart of the contemporary industrial world. In that period urbanization and industrialization transformed the metalworking portions of the Forez into the industrial Stéphanois territory. This chapter attempts to answer some important questions about the formation of this industrial region. First, where did the urban industrial workforce come from and what type of work experience did migrant workers bring with them? Second, how did industrialization affect the local occupational structure and urban environment? Finally, how did Stéphanois workers respond to industrialization and urbanization?

The Pattern of Migration

Urban growth in the Stéphanois basin was possibly the most rapid in France during the first half of the nineteenth century, though the small size of basin cities in 1801 makes comparison difficult. A map of Stéphanois valley cities is shown in Figure 1. In 1801 the commune of Saint-Etienne, adjusted to its 1968 boundaries, had only 24,342 inhabitants, Rive-de-Gier had 4,263, Saint-Chamond, 4,977, Le Chambon-Feugerolles, 2,633, and Firminy, 1,713. By 1876 the population of Saint-Etienne had increased five times, the population of Firminy seven times, and the populations of Saint-Chamond, Rive-de-Gier, and Le Chambon-Feugerolles had tripled. Meanwhile, the average population of the twelve largest cities in France increased three times between 1801 and 1876.[6] Where did this enormous increase in the Stéphanois population come from?

Most of the urban population growth in the arrondissement of Saint-Etienne, an administrative area largely coterminous with our Stéphanois region, was due to an increase in local birth rates and to migration from rural areas within the arrondissement of Saint-Etienne or areas immediately adjacent to it. Population growth within the arrondissement accounted for 60 percent of the population increase between 1820 and 1876, the period of most rapid growth. In 1881, 54 percent of the population were living in their commune of birth and an additional 22 percent were born in the department of the Loire. Of the remaining 23 percent, by far the largest proportion came from the arrondissement of Yssingeaux in the neighboring department of the Haute-Loire.[7]

The origins of the Stéphanois industrial working class can be found in the industrial expansion which occurred in small Stéphanois towns and mountain villages in the two and a half centuries which preceded the Industrial Revolution. For centuries agricultural production in the area had been carried out by polycultural small proprietors. Beginning in the sixteenth century, and increasing at an irregular pace in subsequent centuries, a

Figure 1. Department of the Loire. The department of the Loire is divided into three arrondissements: Roanne, Montbrison, and Saint-Etienne. The map shows the four principal cantons of the Stéphanois coal basin: Le Chambon-Feugerolles, Saint-Etienne, Saint-Chamond, and Rive-de-Gier. The lower sketch shows the principal road from Firminy to Rive-de-Gier and illustrates the relative distance between major towns.

growing number of peasants began to supplement their incomes by engaging in manufacturing. In a recent study David Levine has shown the demographic consequences of rural industrialization in several preindustrial English villages; the spread of rural industry and the growth of population in the Stéphanois region seem to be similarly related.[8] Rural industrialization allowed many young peasants to marry earlier than they would have formerly, when they had to wait to inherit the family farm to obtain the income necessary to support a family. It also allowed many poor peasants to remain in the area and start families who would otherwise have emigrated. The industrialization of the countryside enabled this poor, mountainous region to support a far larger population than many richer agricultural areas, and so created the demographic preconditions for the rapid industrialization of the nineteenth century.

The existence of coal deposits on the valley floor and the presence of fast-flowing mountain streams created favorable conditions for all types of industry, and by the first half of the nineteenth century dozens of different industries existed in small mountain villages and valley towns. On the slopes of the Monts du Lyonnais, to the northeast of the valley towns, there were ribbonmakers, hemp dressers, linen cloth and table linen manufacturers, hatters, armorers, and ironmongers. In the long narrow basin that ran from Givors in the northeast to Firminy in the southwest were the nailmongers, knifemakers, locksmiths, edge toolmakers, glassworkers, ribbonmakers, and silk millers. In the foothills of Mont Pilat to the south and in the Monts du Forez in the southwest, there were lacemakers, nailmongers, knifemakers, paper manufacturers, and ribbonmakers.[9]

The small, nailmaking village of La Fayette in the Monts du Forez near Firminy provides a good example of Stéphanois rural industry. In the early nineteenth century the only road connecting the village with Firminy was a narrow mountain trail. Every week nailmakers had to take this trail to pick up a load of nailblanks and to deliver their forged nails to the local merchants who commissioned them. The more prosperous nailmakers owned mules that carried the iron packets for them, while the poorer strapped the heavy packets to their backs. Winter winds and snow often made this trip dangerous, yet the trade had continued, week by week, for over three centuries.

In the village of La Fayette, with its narrow, twisting, and uneven streets, were the workshops of the nailmakers. The typical workshop was both home and shop combined. It consisted of two stories, the first given over completely to the forge, the second possessing a bedroom and kitchen. In the shop the house timbers contained hundreds of differently shaped and sized nails, prototypes used to serve as models for the forger. Often these model nails represented the accumulated production of several generations of nailmakers, and an individual nailmaker would point out an odd-sized or strangely shaped nail, made by a grandfather, whose purpose was entirely forgotten. Frequently the second-floor bedroom also held a loom, and while the husband worked at the forge making nails, his wife worked on the loom weaving ribbons. While husband and wife each had their own distinct industrial vocation, they often shared pastoral responsibilities toward their few sheep or goats.[10]

The modern separation of city and country, worker and farmer, makes it easy to forget how often preindustrial manufacturing combined industry and agriculture. In many Stéphanois farming villages, rural metalworkers doubled as blacksmiths and dentists. Both in town and village, metalworkers celebrated the feast day of their patron, Saint-Eloi, but this celebration did not set them off from the nonindustrial population, for Saint-Eloi had been grafted on to the agrarian tradition. In many parts of France Saint-Eloi was invoked by farmers for protection against cattle diseases.[11]

It was the little metalworking and textile mountain villages and the small towns located in poor farming areas that were initially hit the hardest by the development of urban industry. The income from manufacturing, which had once been supplementary, had become necessary; further investment in agriculture was useless; and the small mountain villages and isolated towns had neither the resources nor the manpower to build and operate their own local factories. As a consequence, the younger men and women went to find work in the factory while their aged parents remained at home to tend the animals, cultivate their little plot of land, and continue on in domestic industry even when their earnings fell almost to nothing. Migrating young villagers were reluctant to try their luck in the Stéphanois capital, and most moved initially to the smaller valley towns which were nearer their villages; later they or their children might move to Saint-Etienne.[12]

The forces of Stéphanois rural life regrouped in the small, agricultural-industrial towns. Already by 1875, Victor Smith, a keen observer of Stéphanois rural life, concluded that Forézien rural traditions were most alive in the small towns, and "not very much [alive] in the countryside where isolation and misery join together to destroy every tradition which has need of association and minute expenditure."[13] The growth of the Stéphanois urban districts created a new demand for agricultural products, and the old rye- and potato-growing countryside began to shift to dairy production and truck farming; at the same time, domestic artisanal production gave way to factory industrial production.[14]

In the larger towns of between 2,000 and 5,000 inhabitants, textile employers, anxious to take advantage of the female labor force no longer engaged in domestic industry, established small factories. These farming and rural factory towns picked up the falling torch of Stéphanois rural life. In the 1890s folklorists, who were generally lamenting the decay of tradition in dying rural settlements, noted the reinvigorating effect of factory work on the small-town community. For example, Dunières, a small town in the arrondissement of Yssingeaux in the Haute-Loire, was one of the few places in the whole Stéphanois region which continued the once common May Day procession. In Dunières a May Day queen was elected from each local silk mill; the procession began at a factory gate at closing time and stopped at all the textile mills to pick up other contingents of queens and their several maids of honor.[15]

These small agricultural-industrial towns also contributed their share to the Stéphanois urban population. Indeed, the textile factories which functioned as retainers of the rural population also served as staging areas where young men and women were initiated into the ways of factory life. Having learned factory discipline in the small community, the worker could easily contemplate entering the urban labor market, which paid better and offered more opportunity. Whether pushed by the commercialization of local agriculture or pulled by relatively high urban wages, many young peasants with no industrial experience were also drawn to the city.[16]

The permanent migration of local rural workers to Stéphanois cities is undoubtedly of first importance in understanding the contribution of migration to the growth of valley cities, but it was not the only stream of migration. Another source of urban growth was long-distance "career migration" by skilled workers. The best example of this is the glassworkers of Rive-de-Gier, Saint-Galmier, and Saint-Etienne. At mid-century, many glassworkers had originated in the distant departments of the Nord and the Vosges, bringing their scarce skills to the expanding local glass industry. There are also traces of career migration in local metallurgy which drew on other established metalworking areas like the departments of the Saone-et-Loire and the Seine. Even among highly skilled workers such migration was probably infrequent, at most, occurring two or three times in a lifetime. Long-distance migration was no easy task, and, once established, skilled workers likely settled into their jobs unless major economic crisis put them again on the road.[17]

By all evidence, much more important than long-distance migration was short-distance migration. The statistics, which show an extremely high portion of the Stéphanois population living in their commune of origin, give a false impression of immobility. While they returned to their hometowns whenever they could, many Stéphanois workers were forced to move away to find work. Some short-distance migration was "circular" and was intended to only temporarily dislocate the worker. This was often the case in coalmining, where families sent young children to work in other occupations until they were old enough to be accepted in the mines. Petrus Faure, the future mayor of Le Chambon, son of a coalminer in La Ricamerie, was first sent to work as a shepherd in the countryside and then as a metalworker in Le Chambon, until he reached the age when he could enter the mines. Similarly, many farm girls were sent to work in the textile industry of Saint-Chamond until they had earned enough money for a dowry.[18]

But the most common of all forms of short-distance migration was the local migration of unemployed workers from one valley town to another. In the early nineties the construction of a tramway tying all the valley towns together powerfully encouraged this form of migration; the memoir literature illustrates its extreme frequency. In 1909 the young syndicalist Laurent Moulin was working in a metal plant in Le Chambon, the next year in a metal plant in Saint-Etienne, and in 1911 he was back in Le Chambon.[19]

Skill differences are important in accounting for intercity migration. Skilled workers were difficult to replace, and employers were inclined to keep them on during trying times when unskilled workers were let go. In contrast, unskilled labor was always plentiful, and an individual unskilled worker was easily replaced. For these reasons unskilled workers were more likely to migrate between cities and less likely to be integrated into stable, urban, working-class communities than skilled workers.

The movements of the famous anarchist Ravachol show the mobility of a young, unskilled worker. Born in 1850 in Saint-Chamond, Ravachol was the product of a common-law marriage between a textile mill girl and a skilled metalworker. Ravachol's mother was abandoned by his father within a few years of his birth. After spending several years in an orphanage, Ravachol was sent by his mother to work in the countryside, tending cattle. Later he was apprenticed to a firm of dyers in Izieux, near Saint-Chamond, but the dyer refused to teach him the craft, and he had still not mastered it when he moved back to Saint-Chamond after three and a half years. He returned just in time for the 1878 textileworkers' strike, and during this struggle he and several friends found work in Lyon. When the strike was over, he returned again to Saint-Chamond and worked in a textile plant there for a couple of years. Owing to his new-found anarchist convictions, Ravachol was fired. He then went to Saint-Etienne, where several years later he commenced on the first of the murderous expeditions which led to his celebrated trial and condemnation to death.[20] Ravachol was executed at Montbrison in 1892.

The Shape of Economic Development

Migrant workers entered cities that were also undergoing transformation. Three powerful waves of industrial change had left visible marks on late nineteenth-century Stéphanois valley communities. First, the protoindustrialization of the sixteenth through eighteenth centuries continued to influence the industrial structure of many cities. Then, in the first half of the nineteenth century the Industrial Revolution hit the area with full force. Finally, in the last quarter of the century the general advance of the local economy halted, and the Stéphanois economy became more specialized and integrated into the national economic system; this transition caused profound dislocations. The regional economic crisis led to a full-scale employer offensive against artisanal forms of organization.[21]

During the centuries in which industry penetrated the country-side, it also spread through the Stéphanois cities. By the early sixteenth century the small village of Le Chambon had become a center of the cutlery trade, Saint-Chamond a capital of the ribbon industry, and Rive-de-Gier the major coal-producing town. Much later, in the mid-eighteenth century, the glass industry abandoned its wood-burning ovens in the mountains for coal, and settled down in Rive-de-Gier.[22]

The most skilled artisanal industries settled in the valley cities. In part, governments forced them to settle there in order to more closely regulate them. But urban living suited the artisans' own needs. In the city skills could be easily transmitted, information exchanged about the condition of the trade, and craft communities created which could represent the artisans' political interests. Craft organizations flourished in these towns. In 1572 a *confrèrie* of Saint-Eloi was founded in Le Chambon, and during the same period the village church was rededicated to the metalworkers' saint. In 1601 Henri IV granted Chambonnaire master cutlers the right to form a *jurande* to administer their trade. *Compagnonnage* institutions also existed in cutlery and linked Chambonnaire cutlers to skilled artisans in other metalworking centers. In 1600 Henri IV also gave the silk millers of Saint-Chamond a *patente* confirming their "rules, articles, and statutes," and in 1617 the ribbonweavers obtained the same right. *Compagnonnage* organizations existed in both milling and ribbonweaving. Ripagérien coalminers were similarly organized and corporately celebrated the feast of their patron, Saint-Barbe.[23]

Preindustrial urban development had already traced the "line" pattern of the Stéphanois region which was to become even more evident in the nineteenth century. Partly the Stéphanois "road" cities were created by geographic conditions. The Stéphanois basin was formed by two connecting valleys named after their chief streams, the Gier and the Ondaine. In places the two valleys became very narrow; at Rive-de-Gier, there was only a fissure which widened considerably a few kilometers to the west at Saint-Chamond.

But there were other forces at work in the shaping of the Stéphanois conurbation. Cities grew up near the coal heads, which were dug irregularly along the valley and next to the energy-producing mountain streams where they merged into the Gier and Ondaine. The development of the railroad down the valley floor further promoted residential concentration on this thin strip of land. By the end of the nineteenth century an almost continuous main street ran the length of the valley. The well-known nineteenth-century Lyonnais urban planner, Tony Garnier, argued that industrial "road towns" like Le Chambon-Feugerolles and Rive-de-Gier were particularly favorable for industrial development because their outskirts contained the large spaces necessary to heavy industry, combined with access to transportation which facilitated industrial recruitment by shortening the journey to work.[24]

The presence of coal, water power, and a skilled and plentiful workforce all helped to make the Stéphanois area the "cradle of the French industrial revolution." In 1818 at Trablaine, near Le Chambon, an Englishman, James Jackson, introduced crucible steelmaking in France. French entrepreneurs followed in his footsteps, and in the years between 1820 and 1880 the Stéphanois region continued in the vanguard of French metallurgy. The first modern French blast furnace was built in the Stéphanois valley, as well as the original puddling and rolling mills. The Bessemer converter and the Siemens-Martin process entered France by way of this region, as did the first steam hammers.[25]

Urban artisanal industry reacted in a variety of ways to the expansion of heavy industry. Some artisanal industries such as glassmaking were stimulated by industrialization; the glass factory was closely tied to the cost of coal and it expanded as valley coal production increased. Other urban artisanal industries adapted themselves successfully to industrial change. Under the pressure of mechanized competition Chambonnaire cutlery disappeared, but many artisanal cutlers switched over to filemaking, an artisanal occupation which demanded similar skills. Although Chambonnaire filemakers produced for a national market, their proximity to the rapidly expanding Stéphanois metal industry, a major consumer of files, was an important factor in their successful growth.[26]

The disappearance of artisanal industry in one large valley town, Saint-Chamond, was the result not of industrialization but of urban centralization. Saint-Chamond had formerly shared the silk ribbon trade with Saint-Etienne, but by 1850 the dramatic expansion of the ribbon industry resulted in its centralization in Saint-Etienne. A new textile specialty, braidmaking, gradually replaced ribbons as the town's major textile industry. Local ribbon merchants gradually began to invest in braid manufacture, and this industry, which employed unskilled workers, almost exclusively replaced artisanal ribbonmaking.[27]

In the age of the Industrial Revolution in the Stéphanois region, both urban industrial production and urban artisanal production grew together. While the production of valley coal increased ten-fold between 1818 and 1868, so did the production of ribbons. The ribbon industry, which remained dominated by artisanal production methods until World War I, was the largest single employer in the region throughout the entire period. Metalworking and mining only followed at a considerable distance.[28]

Heavy metalworking was the entering wedge of industrial production in the Stéphanois region. While artisanal industry tended to specialize and concentrate in individual towns—glassmaking in Rive-de-Gier, filecutting in Le Chambon, and ribbonweaving in Saint-Etienne—metalworking had similar characteristics in all of these towns. First, from its beginnings in 1818, steel was the major valley metal product, although between 1820 and 1870 wrought iron production also increased dramatically. Second, most Stéphanois valley metal towns possessed factories engaged in both metal production and steel fabrication. As a result, heavy metalworking in every town required roughly the same proportion of skills. Finally, Stéphanois metalworking was large-scale production; at mid-century, when a plant which employed several hundred workers was considered large in most of France, there were plants which employed more than a thousand workers in half a dozen Stéphanois towns.[29]

Under the pressure of rapid industrialization and mushrooming urban growth, the physical environment of Stéphanois cities badly deteriorated. Travelers' descriptions of Rive-de-Gier and Saint-Chamond are reminiscent of Engels's portrait of Manchester in 1840. The routine of daily life in valley cities required accommodation to almost continual loud noise. Barron's guide to France catalogued the "hammer's resonance, the machine's whistle and bellow, the whistle's gasp, the collision of iron and steel . . . the dull and terrible blow of the steam hammer."[30] To which Fournier added "the oven's roar . . . the rattle of the glassworkers' canes, the hum of the looms. . . ."[31]

Coal-burning factories polluted the air, and industrial dyes and waste products killed the streams. Ardouin-Dumazet observed that smoke was "the plague of Rive-de-Gier. There are beautiful gardens surrounding the city owned by the forge masters, but the foliage and the flowers are covered with soot, one cannot pick a rose without dirtying oneself."[32] He described the water of the Ondaine as a "stream of ink," and Fournier characterized the Gier as "polluted . . . martyred."[33]

Not to be daunted, advocates of industrial progress pointed to the bright side of industrial pollution. James Condamin, the representative of an old family of Saint-Chamonnais industrialists, noted philosophically:

> After having served industry [textile dyes] are thrown into the Gier which they color the most diverse shades, this causes bitter complaints from inhabitants of the river banks and farmers. . . . But if one thinks of the services these [dyes] have already rendered, and if one takes into account the new services, not the least significant, which they will render still, after they have left the workshops, it will be necessary to recognize that the particular interest must yield to the general. These waters, in effect, saturated with acid and tannic material, are anti-microbe in the highest degree.

Condamin also invoked science against those who complained about the quality of the air: "While the smoke from our forges blackens our houses and fills our apartments with soot, at the same time it saturates the air with tar atoms whose inhalation is beneficent and healthful. . . . It is necessary to reflect several times before complaining about the inconveniences entrained by our large industries. . . ."[34]

Unfortunately for Condamin's argument, it seems clear that the Industrial Revolution did not bring an infusion of "beneficence and good health" to the valley cities. Between 1835 and 1845, during the high tide of industrial transformation, death rates in the cities were exceptionally high, one-third higher than in the mountain areas. Within the department of the Loire only the agricultural Forézien plains in the arrondissement of Roanne had comparable death rates, and this was due to their disease-ridden marshes.[35] Tenements in Rive-de-Gier, hemmed in by narrow valleys, were forced to abut on the polluted Gier, and this town was particularly susceptible to cholera and typhoid.

Between 1876 and 1894 a great industrial depression swept the whole continent of Europe. In a sense the Stéphanois region never recovered from this depression, which revealed structural faults in the local economy. For one, after mid-century, powerful economic forces were acting to move steel plants out of coal areas and relocate them in ore-producing areas; in France this meant that steel moved east. Just as important, in the late nineteenth century coalmining technologies opened up large new coalfields in the departments of the Nord and Pas-de-Calais, and these fields soon outstripped the Loire. In fact, important sections of the Stéphanois coal basin were nearing exhaustion; by 1890 almost all the coal mines in Rive-de-Gier, once the principal coal-producing town in the area, were shut down. Finally, during the Second Empire the Loire lost its advantage in transportation. The first railroads in France were built in the arrondissement of Saint-Etienne in the thirties; as the French railway network filled out during the fifties and sixties, the Loire lost its advantage over other regions.[36]

The weaknesses of the Stéphanois economy revealed by the "great depression" resulted in the departure of the mass steel industry from the valley towns and their increasing specialization in high-quality steel production. Except for the large steel company at Terrenoire, all the local firms survived the crisis; at Terrenoire the blast furnaces were closed down and the population of the town decreased by a third between 1886 and 1896, from 6,500 inhabitants to 3,900. The remaining companies escaped the worst because during the Second Empire, between 1851 and 1870, the concentration and centralization of the steel industry had created large national companies which owned many plants scattered throughout France. These companies increasingly shifted mass steel production to their newer plants in the east.[37]

The effect of the shift in the mass steel industry away from the Loire was to encourage the consolidation of the position of the small minority of skilled workers who had endured the dramatic change of the Industrial Revolution. Even large steel companies could not afford to simply close down huge factories worth millions of francs. Instead, they converted their factories to production of steel of high quality, which allowed them to take advantage not only of high-grade Stéphanois coal but also of the existing large stock of skilled labor. Although skilled metalworkers were a small part of the total Stéphanois metal workforce, it would have been very difficult to find or train several thousand new workers in a short time to replace them.[38] High-quality steel production demanded a larger skilled working class than the more mechanized, mass steel industry, and so the conversion of the steel industry helped to preserve the relatively highly skilled character of Stéphanois steel manufacture. At the same time, the presence of high-quality steel attracted the metal fabrication industry, which employed mostly semiskilled workers. Metal fabrication was the only segment of Stéphanois metalworking which continued to expand rapidly in the years after 1890.

While the industrial conversion which followed in the wake of economic depression did not result in massive skill dequalification, it did mark the beginning of a frontal assault on local artisanal industry which was to continue through World War I. For local industrialists the great years of lush profits were over, and a new era of careful cost-cutting opened. The decline of Stéphanois coal put local glassmakers at a disadvantage compared with those in the Nord, and Ripagérien glassmakers began to demand higher productivity from their workers. Increased competition in the file trade encouraged Chambonnaire employers to experiment with mechanization. In quality steel, industrialists began to search for ways to exert more control over their skilled workers.[39]

Even in the still expanding ribbon industry, the growing pressure on artisanal forms of organization made itself felt. In 1900 ribbonworkers struck to establish a minimum piece rate. Both small masters and workmen united against the low wages offered by the increasing number of large-scale manufacturers. Small masters were being wiped out by the increasing division of labor introduced by merchant capitalists. A student of the 1900 strike, Jean Lorçin, has characterized it as "a typical example of the looking back, the Stéphanois duplication of Lyonnais events already old by half a century and beyond, to the medieval notion of just price characteristic of the corporatist tradition of the artisans."[40]

Worker Organization and the Growth of Protest

In the city artisanal workers were brought face to face with the industrial juggernaut. Rural artisans were powerless to defend their trade against an invisible urban competitor. But urban artisans were more strategically located; they were able to see with their own eyes the changes that were going on, for they were personally subjected to them. Because they were part of the industrial machine, they were able to resist it.

In the years before World War I the working class in the Stéphanois cities acquired a reputation for militancy. In 1912 a student of French strike conflicts, Léon de Seilhac, characterized the valley towns as

> the great road of rebellion which is at the same time one of the most well travelled roads in France. This road which goes from Saint-Etienne to Firminy passes by La Ricamerie and Le Chambon, the distances are short on this great road where mine shafts and large metallurgical factories swarm. If a strike broke out at Firminy, there was an immediate exodus towards Saint-Etienne, and tumultuous demonstrations . . . on the road forced all the factories to close and emptied the mines.[41]

But the road shape of Stéphanois valley towns is hardly sufficient to explain the mass actions of a working class that was one of the best organized in France. In 1901 the department of the Loire had the fourth largest number of union members, expressed as a percentage of its total labor force, of any department in France; in 1911 it ranked seventh. The vast majority of unionized workers in the department of the Loire were in the arrondissement of Saint-Etienne.[42]

The only available evidence on the unionization rates of different occupational groups in the arrondissement of Saint-Etienne is for 1896 (see Table 2). It shows the highest rates for ceramics and glass, then mining, then metalworking, followed by wood and construction, trailed by textiles, printing, and leather, and, at the tail, chemicals, garments, and transport. There is some evidence that skilled occupations had higher unionization rates than unskilled. Glassworkers, construction workers, miners, printers, and ribbon-weavers were all artisanal workers. Some may question the classification of miners as "artisans," but most adult underground workers in the Stéphanois region, indeed in most of Europe and America in the nineteenth century, could be characterized as possessing a variety of important skills and belonging to a worker-controlled work group. On the other hand, most garment workers and chemical and paper workers were semiskilled or unskilled. In the Stéphanois region most "chemical" workers worked in a gas generating plant, garment workers were machine

Table 2

Labor Force and Union Membership in the Arrondissement of Saint-Etienne, 1896

Industry	Labor Force	Union Membership	Percent of Labor Force Unionized
Ceramics and Glass	2,381	400	17
Chemicals and Paper	890	0	0
Garments	6,185	71	1
Leather	1,380	45	3
Metalworking	20,005	2,097	10
Mining	18,938	2,484	13
Printing	708	35	5
Textiles	29,086	1,556	5
Transport	3,484	0	0
Wood and Construction	6,855	498	7
Unclassified	—	155	—
Total	89,912	7,341	

operators with a few tailors thrown in, and railway workers, except for a small periphery of engineers and mechanics, performed station work and maintenance.[43]

While artisanal industries lead the way, at first sight, the clear pre-eminence of predominantly semiskilled metalworking over predominantly artisanal construction and textiles seems to make generalization difficult. In a large part this difference is accounted for by the extremely decentralized forms of work organization in ribbonweaving. Many ribbonweavers rented workshop-apartments, owned their own looms, and employed their own families, aided at most by several other wage workers. Squeezed by competitive pressure, these small worker-employers were quite capable of uniting with their workers in opposition to the large industrialists, but they did not go so far as to join trade unions. Also, while the great majority of Stéphanois textile workers were artisanal weavers, this figure includes several thousand unskilled braidmakers and factory operatives who were completely un-unionized.[44]

Almost as important in explaining the difference in unionization rates between metalworkers and textile and construction workers are the inflated membership figures for the metalworkers of Rive-de-Gier. In Chapter Six we will look at this group in considerable detail. For now the important point is that 850 Ripagérien metalworkers are listed as being union members during a period when this extremely short-lived union had suffered a grave defeat and was rapidly collapsing. By this time, metal union membership in Rive-de-Gier was almost certainly much nearer the 85 members shown in 1900 than the 1,600 reached very briefly during the height of the strike in 1894.

Although a metal and textile proletariat developed in the Stéphanois valley towns, the mainstays of regional worker militancy were still the old artisanal working classes with roots in the valley towns that stretched back before the Industrial Revolution. Glassworkers, fileworkers, coalminers, and ribbonweavers swelled the rolls of trade union organizations while metalworkers in large industry and braidmakers remained aloof.

Participation in May Day strikes is one good indicator of worker militancy. While large numbers of workers in newly urbanized industries participated occasionally in the May Day actions, it was the workers in the long-time urban-centered and organized trades who were the backbone of the movement. This survey of May Day observance is based on the prefect's yearly report to the Minister of the Interior. These reports show that artisanal workers played an active role in every single May Day in the region, while industrial worker attendance was more variable. In the nineties May Day observance was almost completely confined to the miners of Grand-Croix, La Ricamerie, and Lorette and the glassworkers of Rive-de-Gier, both groups of skilled workers. The miners' union organization was the first in the region to stop work on May 1.[45]

In 1905 participation in May Day protest began to increase as unions of skilled workers, the dyers, masons, and construction workers, all voted to join the miners in their strike. In 1906 semiskilled metalworkers did join in beside striking miners, dyers, weavers, construction workers, typographers, and tramway employees, but in 1907 the metalworkers were described as extremely reluctant to participate. In 1908 the prefect noted few metalworkers in the ranks of the strikers. In the tumultuous 1909 demonstrations metalworkers marched alongside artisanal workers, but in the almost equally riotous 1911 demonstrations they are again mentioned as nonparticipants.[46]

A quick look at the nature of protest in the Stéphanois region shows that workers did indeed express their opposition to the powerful forces molding their urban and industrial world. By and large, the protesting workers were not the proletarians created by industrial transformation. These proletarians engaged in protest irregularly; the ongoing basis of worker militancy was the old-established artisanal worker, whose urban traditions and skills effectively enabled him to make a stand.

This broad survey of the origins of the Stéphanois working classes and their response to industrialization and urbanization suggests some questions for further investigation. First, how did industrial concentration and the growth of cities affect the nature of work? What did the transition from domestic work and small workshops to factories mean in terms of industrial discipline, working conditions, and wages? The militancy of Stéphanois artisans, glassworkers, ribbonweavers, coalminers, and others has been described, as well as the more erratic participation of industrial workers, in this case mostly metalworkers. How can this disparity between artisanal and industrial workers be explained? What caused the fluctuating militancy of industrial workers? Subsequent chapters will explore these questions.

NOTES

1. J. J. Rousseau, *Confessions* (New York: E. P. Dutton, 1931 [1770]), p. 149.
2. Augustus J. C. Hare, *South-Eastern France* (London: George Allen, 1890), pp. 158–59.
3. Onésime Reclus, *La France à vol d'oiseau*, 2 (Paris: Flammarion, 1908), 406.
4. M. Fournier, *La vallée ardente: Scenes de la vie populaire* (Saint-Etienne: Libraire Dubouchet, 1938), pp. 8–9.
5. Louis Barron, *Les fleuves de France—La Loire* (Paris: Renouard, 1888), p. 70.
6. Population figures for Stéphanois cities were taken from *Les villes françaises: Saint-Etienne et son agglomeration* (Paris: La documentation française, 1973), pp. 24–27. French census figures for the 1891 national comparison were found in Adna Ferrin Weber, *The Growth of Cities in the Nineteenth Century: A Study in Statistics* (New York: Columbia University Press, 1899), p. 239.
Some overviews of the process of proletarianization are: Louis Chevalier, "Origines rurales du prolétariat des grandes villes," in *Villes et compagnes: Civilisation urbaine et civilisation rurale en France*, ed. Georges Friedman (Paris: École pratique des hautes études, 1952), pp. 153–78; the presentations by Eric J. Hobsbawm, "The Formation of the Industrial Working Class: Some Problems," and by Albert Soboul, "Aux origines de la classe ouvrière industrielle parisienne," in the report of the *Third International Conference of Economic History—Munich 1965* (Paris: Mouton, 1968); and Charles Tilly, "Sociology, History, and the Origins of the European Proletariat," address presented to the American Historical Association annual meeting, 1976.
7. Jacques Schnetzler, "L'Évolution démographique de la région de Saint-Etienne de 1876 à 1946," *Études foréziennes* 4 (1971), 157–96; Michele Tomas, "L'Origine de la population de Saint-Etienne," in *Les villes du Massif central* (Paris: Centre d'études foréziennes, 1971), pp. 50–70.
8. David Levine, *Family Formation in an Age of Nascent Capitalism* (New York: Academic Press, 1977).
Some other important discussions of the process of protoindustrialization and demographic change are: the article by Rudolf Braun in *Historical Studies of Changing Fertility*, ed. Charles Tilly (Princeton, N.J.: Princeton University Press, forthcoming); Wolfram Fischer, "Rural Industrialization and Population Change," *Comparative Studies in Society and History* 15 (Mar., 1973), 158–79; and Franklin F. Mendels, "Protoindustrialization: The First Phase of the Process of Industrialization," *Journal of Economic History* 32 (Mar., 1972), 241–61.
9. Jacques Schnetzler, "Un demi-siècle d'évolution démographique dans la région de Saint-Etienne, 1820–1876," *Études foréziennes* 1 (1968), 165–66.
10. Albert Boissier, "Essai sur l'histoire et sur les origines de l'industrie du clou forgé dans la région de Firminy," *Revue de folklore français* 12 (Apr.-June, 1941), 65–101.

11. See C. Leroy, "Le culte de Saint-Eloi en Artois et dans le Nord de la France," *Revue de folklore français* 5 (1934) 217–52, and Albert Boissier, "Quelques notes sur les Maréchaux ferrants de la région de Firminy (Loire)," *Revue de folklore français* 10 (Apr.-June, 1939), 62–64.

12. At least this pattern of migration from village to small town to larger city has been suggested by the study of one Stéphanois village, Marlhes; see James Lehning, "Peasant Families and Rural Industrialization: The Village of Marlhes, 1840–1914" (Ph.D. dissertation, Northwestern University, 1977).

13. Victor Smith, "Chants du Velay et du Forez—Chants de saints et de damnés," *Romania* 4 (1875), 437–52.

14. Pierre Bozon, "L'Agriculture dans un milieu industralisé et urbanisé: La vallée du Gier (Loire)," *Revue de géographie de Lyon* 47 (1972), 227–57.

15. On Dunières's May celebrations, see Germaine Brizard, "Chansons populaires du Velay and du Forez—Traditions populaires chantées," *Revue de folklore français* 1 (May-June, 1930), 125–26, and Victor Smith, "Chants de quêtes—Noëls du premier de l'an—Chants du mai," *Romania* 2 (1873), 59–71. A treasure trove of folklore material is Eugen Weber, *Peasants into Frenchmen: The Modernization of Rural France 1870-1914* (Stanford, Calif.: Stanford University Press, 1976).

16. On migration in European and French history, see J. P. Poussou, "Les mouvements migratoires en France," *Annales de démographie historique—1970* (Paris: Mouton, 1971), pp. 11–79, and Charles Tilly, "Migrations in Modern European History," Working Paper no. 145, Center for Research on Social Organization.

17. Yves Lequin, "La formation du prolétariat industriel dans la région lyonnaise au XIXᵉ siècle: Approches méthodologiques et premiers résultats," *Le mouvement social* 97 (Oct.-Dec., 1976), 121–37.

18. Petrus Faure, *Un témoin raconte* (Saint-Etienne: Dumas, 1962).

19. Jean-Paul Martin, "Le syndicalisme révolutionnaire chez les métallurgistes de l'Ondaine 1906–1914" (Unpublished mémoire, Université de Saint-Etienne, 1972), p. 250.

20. Jean Maitron, ed., *Ravachol et les anarchistes* (Paris: Julliard, 1964).

21. For a general introduction to French and Stéphanois industrial transformation, see Arthur Dunham, *The Industrial Revolution in France 1815–1848* (New York: Exposition Press, 1955), and Maxime Perrin, *Saint-Etienne et sa région économique: Un type de la vie industrielle en France* (Tours: Arrault, 1937).

22. James Condamin, *Histoire de Saint-Chamond et de la seigneurie de Jarez depuis les temps les plus reculés jusqu'à nos jours* (Paris: Alphonse Picard, 1890); L.-J. Gras, *Essai sur l'histoire de la quincaillerie et petite métallurgie* (Saint-Etienne: Théolier, 1904); Robert Lacombe, "Le choc de la révolution industrielle sur une petite ville du Lyonnais—Rive-de-Gier," *L'Ethnographie*, n.s., 64 (1970), 1–25.

23. Petrus Faure, *Histoire de la métallurgie au Chambon-Feugerolles* (Le Chambon-Feugerolles: Jué, 1931); Condamin, *Histoire de Saint-Chamond*.

24. Tony Garnier, *Une cité industrielle: Étude pour la construction des villes*, 2 vols. (Paris: Massin, n.d.), esp. his introduction.

25. L.-J. Gras, *Histoire économique de la métallurgie de la Loire* (Saint-Etienne: Théolier, 1908).

26. On Chambonnaire filemakers, see Camille Pagé, *La coutellerie*, vol. 3 (Chattelrault: H. Rivière, 1898), and Michael P. Hanagan, "The Logic of Solidarity: Social Structure in Le Chambon-Feugerolles," *Journal of Urban History* 3 (Aug., 1977), 409–26.

27. On ribbonmaking, see L.-J. Gras, *Histoire de la rubanerie et des industries de la soie à Saint-Etienne* (Saint-Etienne: Théolier, 1906); E. Dubois and A. Julian, "Industrie de la rubanerie à Saint-Etienne," in *Les moteurs électriques dans les industries à domicile*, vol. 3 (Brussels: Office de publicité, 1902); Paul Pic and Justin Godart, "Industries de la rubanerie de Saint-Etienne," in *Le mouvement économique et social dans la région lyonnaise*, vol. 1 (Lyon: A. Storck, 1902); and Reybaud, *Études sur le régime des manufactures*.

28. Perrin, *Saint-Etienne et son agglomeration*, pp. 10–22.

29. Lucien Thiollier, *La chambre de commerce de Saint-Etienne et les industries de sa circonscription 1833–1890*, (Saint-Etienne: Théolier, 1891), p. 95.

30. Barron, *Les fleuves de France*, p. 70.

31. Fournier, *La vallée ardente*, pp. 7–9.

32. M. Ardouin-Dumazet, *Voyage en France*, no. 11 (Paris: Berger-Levrault, 1897), pp. 4–6.

33. Fournier, *La vallée ardente*, pp. 7–9.

34. Condamin, *Histoire de Saint-Chamond*, p. 649.

35. On Stéphanois mortality rates, see Pierre P. Guillaume, "La situation économique et sociale du départment de la Loire d'après l'enquête sur le travail agricole et industriel du 25 mai 1848," *Revue d'histoire moderne et contemporaine* 10 (Jan.-Mar., 1963), 5–34. On urban conditions in Saint-Etienne, see Claude Chatelard, "La misère à Saint-Etienne de 1870 à 1914," *Études foréziennes* 4 (1971), 139–56.

36. For the economic forces behind the movement of the Stéphanois steel industry, see Walter Isard, "Some Locational Factors in the Iron and Steel Industry since the Early Nineteenth Century," *Journal of Political Economy* 56 (June 3, 1948), 318–28. On the evolution of the Stéphanois transport system and coal mines there are two detailed studies by Gras, *Histoire économique générale des mines de la Loire*, 2 vols. (Saint-Etienne: Théolier, 1922), and *Histoire des premiers chemins de fer français et du premiers tramways de France* (Saint-Etienne: Théolier, 1924).

37. On the effect of the "great depression" in the Stéphanois region, see Perrin, *Saint-Etienne et sa région économique*.

For a discussion of concentration in French metalworking, see Bertrand Gille, "Esquisse d'une histoire de syndicalisme patronale," *Revue d'histoire de la sidérurgie* 5 (1964), 119–32, and two articles by J. B. Silly, "La concentration dans l'industrie sidérurgique en France sous le Second Empire," *Revue d'histoire de la sidérurgie* 3 (Jan.-Mar., 1963), 19–48, and "Les plus grandes sociétés métallurgique en 1881," *Revue d'histoire de la sidérurgie* 4 (1963), 20–35.

38. On the division of labor in metallurgy, see Louis Reybaud, *Le fer et la houille* (Paris: Michel Levy, 1874), p. 149.

39. Chapters Four, Five, and Six discuss these transformations at greater length.

40. Jean Lorçin, "Un essai de stratigraphie sociale: Chefs d'atelier et compagnons dans la grève des passementiers de Saint-Etienne en 1900," *Cahiers d'histoire* 13, no. 2 (1968), 181–82.

41. Léon de Seilhac, *Les grèves du Chambon* (Paris: Arthur Rousseau, 1912), pp. 5–7.

For the relationship between proletarianization and protest in another European region, see Louise A. Tilly, "The Working Class of Milan 1881–1911" (Ph.D. dissertation, University of Toronto, 1973).

42. Guilbert, *Les femmes et l'organisation syndicale avant 1914*, pp. 30–33.
43. For the labor force breakdown in the arrondissement of Saint-Etienne, see Office du travail, *Résultats statistiques du recensement des industries et professions . . . 1896*, 4 vols. (Paris: Imprimerie nationale, 1899–1901). For union members, see Office du travail, *Annuaire des syndicats, 1896* (Paris: Berger-Levrault, 1896).
44. Lorçin, "Un essai de stratigraphe sociale."
45. Archives nationales (AN), "Célébrations du 1er mai en France et à l'étranger, 1898–1901," AN F/7 12527–29.

A background on the May Day movement is provided in Maurice Dommanget, *Histoire du premier mai* (Paris: Editions de la Tête de Feuilles, 1972); see particularly his chapter "Le réveil français de 1905–1906," pp. 215–45. For background on the May Day movement in the Loire, see Petrus Faure, *Histoire du mouvement ouvrier dans le département de la Loire* (Saint-Etienne: Dumas, 1956), particularly "Les premiers mais 1905–1906–1909," pp. 222–29, and "Le premier mai 1911," pp. 232–34. The best summary of the events of May 1, 1906, in the Loire are the reports in *L'Humanité* from Apr. 28 to May 4, 1906, written by its correspondent, Fernand Faure, a leading Stéphanois socialist.

46. "Célébrations du 1er mai en France et à l'étranger, 1903–1911," AN F/7 12530–34.

CHAPTER THREE

Economic Structure and Strike Activity

The worker is no longer anything but a manual laborer.
If our fathers, in earlier times,
Knew how to create masterpieces
The times are no longer the same for the sons.
Our ancestor devoted his mind
To the work that he perfected.
But now the machine is established;
The Worker-Artist disappears.[1]

From the song "Les Travailleurs
de la Loire," c. 1903

Before narrowing in on the individual towns, an examination of the economic environment within which local strikes occurred would be useful. Chapter One argued for the importance of changes in work structure and worker resources on the formation of strike coalitions. This chapter takes a broad preliminary look at how well our arguments fit with the major changes in the Stéphanois industrial and economic environment which took place between 1870 and 1914. It first sketches the broad outlines of the relationship between strikes and changes in technology, comparing each of the Stéphanois towns, and then examines the relationships between strikes and changes in regional work organization and standard of living. Later chapters will fill out this outline in greater detail for each of the individual cities. Chapter Two showed how a Stéphanois region was created within which many thousands of industrial workers and artisans toiled and protested, living together in small "road" towns, building their own trade union organizations, and participating in mass strike actions. This chapter will describe the evolution of local strike behavior and examine its relationship to the evolving social and economic conditions of working-class life in the Stéphanois region as a whole.

Strike Activity in Three Stéphanois Towns

If technological change did indeed influence strike actions, as suggested earlier, there are several ways in which aggregate strike activity might show its influence. First, technological change determined the industrial composition of each of the towns, and if there is a difference in artisanal and industrial workers' patterns of strike activity, overall strike statistics for the individual town should reflect this difference. Second, major technological changes occurred in each of the towns at different times, and if threatened artisans tend to promote strike militancy, periods of technological change should correspond to periods of strike militancy.

In order to compare overall strike differences, three indices of strike activity were chosen: median duration, average number of workers per strike, and number of strikes per 100,000 workers. The computation of the average strike size and median duration was relatively easy, but there were serious obstacles in the way of computing the measure of frequency. The statistic of strikes per 100,000 workers is valuable because it standardizes the number of strikes with respect to the size of the urban population. There was no difficulty in obtaining the absolute number of strikes in each town, but, unfortunately, continuous data on the size of the work-force are not readily available at the communal level. To get some estimate of the relationship between the number of strikes and the size of the workforce, information for a midpoint year, 1891, a year for which information on workforce composition exists at the communal level, was used as the average for the entire period. With this estimate the number of yearly strikes per 100,000 workers could be calculated for each city. This figure is represented in Graphs 1–3; it is an approximation and only used for lack of a better estimate.[2]

In order to facilitate a comparison of the strike pattern in the different cities over the period 1870–1914, the three principal measures of strike activity have been combined into a three-dimensional diagram. The vertical axis on the diagram shows the average number of strikers per strike, the horizontal axis shows the average duration, and the lateral axis shows the absolute number of strikes. Together these three dimensions form a rectangle, and

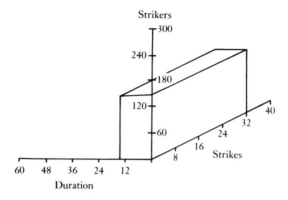

Graph 1. Strikes in Saint-Chamond, 1870–1914.

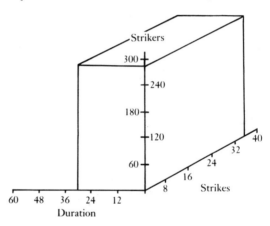

Graph 2. Strikes in Le Chambon-Feugerolles, 1870–1914.

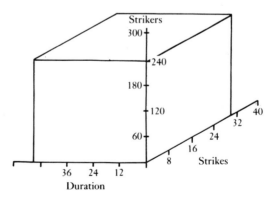

Graph 3. Strikes in Rive-de-Gier, 1870–1914.

artisanal—industrial

the shape of each rectangle represents the long-run strike pattern of each town.

The shape of long-term strike activity in the three towns should provide some clues about the overall influence of work structure on worker militancy. The most noticeable single feature of a comparison of strike activity among the three towns is the relatively small size of the Saint-Chamonnais rectangle. All three measures of strike activity show that strikes were smaller in the predominantly industrial Saint-Chamond than in the other two cities. This provides a preliminary confirmation of the interpretation of the "catalytic" role of artisanal workers, which leads us to expect that a town with few artisanal workers would be the most poorly mobilized.

The shape of strikes in Le Chambon, the predominantly artisanal town, and in Rive-de-Gier, the artisanal-industrial town, is also intriguing; their diagrams show the large average strike size and long median duration of strikes in both towns. The duration of strikes in Rive-de-Gier is somewhat longer than those in Le Chambon, which has a larger average strike size. Both towns have a strike size and duration far above national averages. This suggests that important confrontations between workers and employers occurred in these towns, which both had important numbers of artisanal workers. Overall strike patterns should give more plausibility to the argument that there is a connection between artisanal worker militancy and mass strike actions.

Now that the long-term characteristics of strike activity in each of the three towns for the whole period 1870–1914 have been examined, a look at the evolution of strike activity and technological change during these years is in order. (See Graphs 4–6, which show the number of strikes, their total duration, and the number of strikers in each town during five-year periods between 1870 and 1914.) The graph for Saint-Chamond shows a progressive decrease in strike size and an increase in the number and duration of strikes. The largest mass strikes took place in the years between 1877 and 1879, when the city still had a substantial population of artisanal dyers. The small size and long duration of Saint-Chamonnais strikes in the later years suggest that the triumph of industrialization in Saint-Chamond confined strikes to a small artisanal periphery.[3]

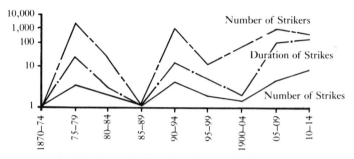

Graph 4. Strikes in Saint-Chamond.

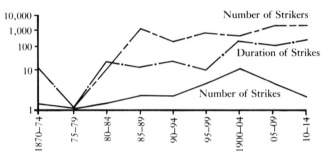

Graph 5. Strikes in Le Chambon-Feugerolles.

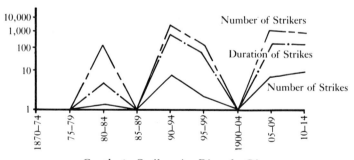

Graph 6. Strikes in Rive-de-Gier.

In the years after 1880 Saint-Chamond lost the reputation for militancy that it had once possessed. As far back as 1789 Saint-Chamonnais artisans had played a leading role in revolutionary politics; there was local agitation in 1848, and Louis Napoleon was never popular there. In 1877 a secret police agent reported "stirrings of the proletariat in Saint-Etienne, Roanne and Saint-Chamond. Three cities are at the head of the workers' movement in the Loire: Saint-Etienne, Saint-Chamond and Roanne: They are the only cities so far where a trade union movement has arisen."[4] By the end of the nineteenth century Saint-Chamond had acquired such a reputation for conservatism that the usually well-informed Petrus Faure could remark, "Even in a region as industrialized as Saint-Chamond strikes have never been very numerous. This is due chiefly to the state of mind of the population where extremist political ideas have never penetrated."[5]

The graph of Le Chambon-Feugerolles shows a very different trend. The numbers of workers involved in strike activity increased dramatically toward the middle and end of the period 1870–1914, the duration of strikes increased, and the number of strikes declined. Between 1905 and 1914 Le Chambon became a center of mass strike activity. The growth of strike militancy in Le Chambon coincided with the introduction of the first mechanized file factory and the increasingly rapid pace of mechanization in the file trade between 1906 and 1914. During these years Le Chambon-Feugerolles, or "Red Chambon" as it came to be called, which had no prior history of worker militancy, became a renowned center of militant syndicalism.[6]

The high point of strike activity in Rive-de-Gier occurred in the middle of the period 1870–1914, in the years between 1890 and 1894, but there was another important upsurge of strike activity between 1905 and 1914. Artisanal glassmaking was the single largest employer in the city, and a major concern of glassworkers in the upsurge of 1891 and 1894 was the partial mechanization of the bottle trade caused by the introduction of the Siemens continuous-flow glass oven in 1878. It may seem strange that it took almost fifteen years before Ripagérien glassworkers felt the effects of mechanization, but in 1878 the Ripagérien glassworks were the first in France to introduce the Siemens oven, which increased the productivity of the individual glassworker tremendously. Only as the invention spread throughout the entire French glass industry did the resulting overproduction and unemployment finally affect the Ripagérien glassworkers. The strike upsurge of 1906–14 also coincided with a wave of mechanization in the plate glass industry.[7]

The Rise of a New Industrial Work System

The rise of the strike form of worker protest, as the previous discussion suggests, is related to the spread of a new industrial work system which sharpened the distinction between employer and worker, imposed a new discipline on the workforce, and threatened the position of artisanal workers. By the end of the nineteenth century work in large-scale industry was performed by full-time workers in a factory for full-time employers. In heavy industry, at least, all forms of subcontracted labor, whether the "putting out system" or the labor contractor who led his own independent "gang" within the factory, had disappeared. In 1850 the new industrial work system had made little headway in the Stéphanois region, but sixty years later it dominated the local economy. This new industrial system, which provided the background for the rise of strike militancy, had its own distinctive wage structure and an entirely new work environment.

The modern industrial system of time and work discipline is so much a part of contemporary society that it takes an effort to recall how recent are its origins. Denis Poulot, a worker and foreman who described working-class life in the Parisian metal trades in the 1860s, reminds us how different was the world of the mid-century metalworker. Poulot describes the conversation in a wine shop on the rue des Poissonniers, near the Hotel de Ville; this shop was nicknamed the "senate" because it was the exclusive meeting place of highly skilled metal forgers—the owner himself was once a metal forger. The café was an almost direct descendant of the *mère* of the *compagnonnages*. Several older workers were gathered around the bar boasting of their skills to a young, newly arrived worker from the provinces. One forger, nicknamed "Beam Welder," began to describe the greatest feat of his life and the source of his nickname, the story of how he became the first French forger to weld the sideframe of a locomotive. He explained to the young man that the engineers were baffled, when he suddenly volunteered that he and his friends could accomplish the task. He bragged about the anxiety of the engineers when, on the day that he had promised to finish the job, he arrived much later than expected, drunk with his friends. He described how the task was finally accomplished. Although Poulot mocks the man's alcoholic bravado, he does not deny the outlines of the story.[8]

Except for the magnitude and novelty of the particular task, Poulot's metal forger was in fact describing the routine work system in machine construction as a whole. In 1874 Louis Reybaud described this "task" system in the Stéphanois valley in some detail. When a large metal object, an armor plate or prow for a ship, had to be fashioned, engineers would make their needs known and accept bids from individual workers. The low bidder hired other workers to help him, and his "gang" carried out the work according to the directions of its leader. Some gang leaders paid their workers a straight daily wage and kept the profits for themselves. Others assigned their workers a proportion of the agreed-upon price, paid them a small daily wage, and when the task was finished, distributed their profits according to the assigned proportions. Sometimes "task work" lasted a few days, sometimes weeks or even months. Reybaud noted that in the Stéphanois valley task work was very popular among both workers and employers and was widespread in every aspect of heavy metalworking.[9] Puddlers and molders decided how many assistants they needed, hired whomever they wanted, and worked as they saw fit.

The task system helped industrialists solve the problem of discipline which arose as the scale of industry increased. Before the rise of the large-scale metal construction industry, artisanal employers had worked alongside small groups of workers, some of whom were personal friends, others of whom were relatives. The basic problem posed for employers by the increased size of industry was how to supervise effectively large numbers of highly skilled workers. The task system basically extended the old artisanal system by subdividing the work among teams of highly skilled workers who supervised their associates. Many contemporaries were enthusiastic about this system because they believed that through "subcontracting" the artisanal system of organization could be continued in large-scale industry.[10]

Increasingly, however, employers became dissatisfied with the task system. In 1870 J. Euverte, a Stéphanois industrialist who had had some experience at Le Creusot, wrote disparagingly of this system:

> When an industrialist decides to organize an enterprise thus, when he decides to abandon a third part of his authority and a third part of his opportunity for profit, it is because he is making the best of a bad situation, because he recognizes the impossibility of carrying out work or having it carried out in the most favorable conditions. . . . It is then that the "entrepreneur" presents himself. Nearly always he comes from the workshop he is given to supervise, he knows thoroughly all its abuses which, often enough, he has contributed to implanting in the factory. He makes a deal with the industrialist which at first seems advantageous to the latter . . . but [the entrepreneur] knows better than anyone that the going price is higher than it should be in a well directed factory.

Euverte accused the task workers of abusing their fellow workers and sometimes beating them. This surely happened under the task system, just as it happened in the English factories where workers supervised their own children. But there were sharp limits on the authority of the subcontractor, who ultimately depended on his reputation to recruit skilled workers to his gang. Euverte's major complaint seems to be the employer's loss of control: "The industrialist has relations only with the entrepreneur, he doesn't know anything about those working for him, he remains totally ignorant of their situation."[11] In 1901, when Charles Benoist surveyed Stéphanois metalworking, he found no trace of the task system.

The new industrial system that developed in the Stéphanois region between 1870 and 1900 had three essential components which together severely restricted the skilled worker's autonomy. First, there was an unending series of technical innovations. A new semiskilled worker appeared in the factory, and many of the highly skilled jobs that remained were specialized and compartmentalized. Second, most skilled workers lost the right to determine their own work methods or hire assistants. Workers were expected to report to work on time and leave on time, and entry to plants was restricted to workers hired by the employer. Third, a new individual piece-rate system developed and, along with it, a vast increase in the power of the foreman. The real basis of the foreman's power was his ability to set the piece rate for each worker. This required a foreman who knew a great deal about the work process and who could judge the performance of individual workers. Under this new industrial system the power of the employer, through his delegate the foreman, reached onto the shop floor. Later on, in the early twentieth century, as workers' skills were further undermined, the piece system itself began to be gradually replaced by a system of time payment, which resulted in a decline in the authority of the foreman.[12]

The rise of the new system of work organization facilitated the rise of strike militancy by restricting workers' power to peacefully influence the work structure. The old system provided many informal methods for enforcing workers' demands. Under the task system wages were determined by competitive bidding among skilled workers, and if workers could agree among themselves, they could impose a high price on their employer. Poulot notes that metalworkers often beat up workers who submitted low bids. Similarly, if a gang's leader paid low wages or mistreated gang members, they could simply join another gang or designate a new leader. The new system, based on increased compulsion, offered less room for informal pressure. If workers did not like their foreman, if they resented work conditions, if their wages were too low, they had only two alternatives: leave the factory or strike. No good estimates on job turn-over in the Stéphanois region exist, but workers increasingly began to employ the strike weapon.

The new industrial work system also caused changes in working hours, working conditions, and labor discipline. The new work situation became a target of worker protest, and it played an important role in shaping the environment in which workers organized. Workers lost the right to regulate their time at work. Under the domestic and task systems workers had fixed their own work schedules; under the new system the employer stepped onto

the workshop floor to regulate the workers' use of time. The
regulation of the workday became a source of conflict between
worker and employer.

Industrialization in the Stéphanois region did not greatly affect
the length of the working day; already in 1848 those metalworkers
working in an employer's shop and all miners worked a ten-hour
day. Artisanal ribbonmakers regularly worked a fifteen-hour day,
but they were only employed eight months out of the year. In the
years between 1850 and 1890 the increased pull of the factory, the
expansion of coalmining, and the decline of the task system brought
a large number of Stéphanois workers under the ten-hour regime.
In some of the newly created highly skilled jobs, such as puddling
or working the blast furnace, where an expensive oven was in
continuous use, the length of the workday was extended to twelve
hours, but in glassmaking, where a continuous-flow oven was also
introduced, workers succeeded in reducing the work day to eight
hours. The major industrial sector in which hours were drastically
increased was textiles. Employers were able to do this because
textile work was completely unskilled and employed women
and children—the groups least financially and organizationally
equipped to defend themselves against employer mistreatment.[13]

The major changes in the length and regulation of the workday
in the Stéphanois region were the result of legislation. In 1886 an
eleven-hour limit on child and female labor was voted by the
chamber of deputies, and in 1892 women and children were
prohibited from doing night work. Strike actions were sometimes
necessary to enforce these laws. In 1892 a strike broke out among
Saint-Chamonnais female braidmakers, who protested against the
attempt to impose on them a complicated shift system whose
purpose was to circumvent the legislation against night work. The
new shift system required that each braidmaker work four and
one-half hours on the day shift and the same number of hours on an
evening shift, but the new shift system extended the length of the
workday by requiring workers to journey back and forth to work
twice a day or to remain at the factory for an interval of thirteen and
one-half hours. The brief strike of Saint-Chamonnais braidmakers
forced factory inspectors to take action. As a result the two-shift
system was abandoned.[14]

As mentioned in Chapter Two, on May Day, 1906, a powerful strike movement of both artisans and industrial workers developed in the Stéphanois region around the theme of the eight-hour day. While it was ultimately unsuccessful, it represented the major attempt of nineteenth-century Stéphanois workers to influence the length of the workday. The 1906 movement developed under many of the same conditions which Bienefeld found among English workers demanding a reduction in hours. Artisanal workers threatened by technology, who generally did not join in wage disputes, were enthusiastic about attempts to reduce the workday. Bienefeld argues that for threatened artisans a reduction in the length of the workday represented another way of restricting the supply of skilled labor. The interests of local workers were upheld by the CGT when in its call for May Day, 1906, it stressed the slogan of the eight-hour day.[15]

Furthermore, the concentration of work in factories and the growing role of the foreman meant that workers lost control of their physical work environment. Formerly, when workers had worked at home or in the factory with their own tools and at their own rhythm, they had been able to shape their own work environment. Because of this individual autonomy, it is difficult to characterize early work conditions. Some home workshops were dark and dangerous while others were clean and wholesome. In any case, the new factory discipline imposed a uniform environment on all workers. Stéphanois industrialists do not seem to have been very sensitive to the question of work conditions. Petrus Faure, who had worked in several industrial establishments in the Stéphanois region, reported:

> [In heavy metallurgy] . . . the ovens were heated with coal and all day they emitted unhealthy fumes which filled the workshop.
> Wash basins and showers did not exist and large oil lamps furnished the only light in winter.
> . . . In the bolt workshops hygiene was not better. . . . Machine tools were run by workers seated next to coal stoves.
> . . . [the air was] unbreatheable.[16]

Still, in the years before 1914 changes in work conditions were not a principal demand in Stéphanois strike conflicts.

Work discipline itself was occasionally an issue in strike conflict.

Strikes over work discipline took several forms. Strikes against foremen often concealed protests against work discipline. In Le Chambon-Feugerolles in 1909 a foreman in a small metal shop nailed shut a window through which workers ordered snacks from a sidewalk vendor, and workers responded by striking for his dismissal. Occasionally workers defended a lenient foreman. In 1898 in Rive-de-Gier sheet-metalworkers demanded the firing of a worker who had reported a popular foreman for drinking in a café during work hours. Strikes against work discipline also took place over work rules. In 1893 plate-glassworkers in Rive-de-Gier refused to adopt a new scheme for the organization of work teams which an employer introduced.[17]

Given the great loss of worker autonomy caused by the rise of this new industrial system, it is surprising that there were not more strikes over questions of industrial discipline. Of the ninety-eight strikes which took place in our three cities during the years between 1871 and 1914, the formal demands of ninety can be found in the departmental archives. Less than 15 percent of these strikes had demands which protested against work discipline. There were several reasons for the relatively small number of such strikes. First, French employers were particularly known for their resistance to any challenge to their authority on the shop floor, and workers, realizing that strikes over work issues had little chance of success, turned to other demands. Workers often decided that wage increases were easier to win and channeled their anger where it was most likely to be successful. Second, workers protested against the employer's discipline by forming trade unions and trying to involve the trade union in the administration of work organization. While these strikes were often fought over the question of trade union recognition, an important component of union strength in skilled trades came from its defense of more autonomous forms of work organization.

The Structure of Wages

The evolution of the structure of work had the most far-reaching effects on the structure of wages. The increasing mechanization of industry decreased the proportion of the most highly skilled workers employed in industry, while the wages of these workers either stagnated or declined during the years between 1890 and 1914. At the same time a new class of semiskilled workers appeared, whose wages were substantially higher than those of unskilled workers. This group played an increasingly large role in Stéphanois industry, and its influence on the local wage structure was disproportionate to its numbers. The large number of highly skilled workers in the Stéphanois region had never had much effect on the local wage structure because, however high their wages, the exclusive character of the craft limited admission to only a few. The appearance of the semiskilled worker had considerably more influence on the local wage structure because it was relatively easy to acquire the basic skills to enter the industry. All local industries which employed adult men thus had to be competitive with the wages of semiskilled workers.

In 1887 Emile Chevalier noted the general tendency for the wages of less skilled workers in France to rise faster than the wages of the more skilled. Gerard Weill has shown that in the course of the nineteenth century the wage differentials between skilled and less skilled occupations tended to decrease.[18] This same tendency can be found in the Stéphanois region and is largely a result of the changing structure of work and the decreasing demand for artisanal labor. While some skilled groups such as the artisanal subcontractor disappeared entirely, almost everywhere in the Stéphanois region the wages of the remaining highly skilled jobs stagnated while those of the less skilled workers increased. In 1870 many skilled workers earned very high wages. In 1874 a puddler received two and one-half times the wages of a semiskilled forger; in 1902 the ratio was closer to two to one. Puddlers would have been foolhardy to attempt any increase in wages because, during this same period, the opportunities for employment in puddling were diminishing. At the same time the relative decline in the position of the puddlers hardly left them in desperate financial straits or even seriously threatened their superiority over semiskilled workers.[19]

From the point of view of the industrial worker, the evolution of heavy industry took a particularly fortunate direction in the Stéphanois region; in many other areas of southeast France, such as Roanne or Vienne, artisanal industries gave way to a low-wage industrial economy, but in Saint-Etienne a relatively high-wage industrial economy developed. Table 3 shows the three largest components of the economy of Saint-Etienne in 1896, the average daily wage these sectors of the economy paid, and the average male wage in all of France. These averages are based on wage reports assembled from all over France—only the exceptionally high wage structure of Paris was excluded. Although the low-paying textile industry was present in the Stéphanois region, high-wage industries like mining and particularly metalworking played the dominant role. Mining and heavy metalworking, which together employed 39.0 percent of all Stéphanois workers, were industries whose average wage was higher than the national average, while textiles, which employed 32.3 percent of all workers, paid wages below the national average. Table 3 also allows a comparison of the role that textiles, metalworking, and mining played in the arrondissement of Saint-Etienne and the neighboring arrondissement of Roanne. The contrast is clear between the high Stéphanois wage structure and the much lower Roannais wage structure.[20]

The arrondissement of Saint-Etienne is an exception to the rule that large cities tend to have a higher wage structure than small towns. Table 4 shows the division of metalworking, textiles, and mining between the city of Saint-Etienne and the rest of the arrondissement of Saint-Etienne. The low-paying textile industry

Table 3

Wage Structure, 1896

	Population Engaged in Industry (as percentage of workforce engaged in industry and transport)		Average Daily Wage (average paid in French industry excluding Paris)
	Arrondissement of Saint-Etienne	Arrondissement of Roanne	France
Mining	17.9%	0	Miner—4.1 francs
Textiles	32.3	67.0%	Spinner—2.9 francs
Metalworking	22.2	3.1	Forger—4.2 francs
Total	72.4	70.1	Average Male Wage— 3.9 francs

Table 4

Wage Structure in the Arrondissement of Saint-Etienne, 1896

| | Population Engaged in Industry (as percentage of workforce in arrondissement engaged in industry and transport) | | |
	Saint-Etienne	Arrondissement	Total
Mining	34.9%	65.1%	100.0%
Textiles	46.7	53.3	100.0
Metalworking	30.6	69.4	100.0
All Industry	41.8	58.2	100.0

was more concentrated in the city of Saint-Etienne, which was a center of artisanal ribbonmaking, while the higher-paying industries like metalworking and mining were more concentrated in the valley towns.[21]

Not only was Stéphanois industry composed of high-paying industries, but local wages for these industries were higher than the national average. Table 5 compares the wage rates for all of France with those in the Stéphanois region in 1896.[22] Wages were uniformly higher in the Stéphanois region, particularly in textiles where ribbonworkers were among the highest-paid textile workers. The Stéphanois region was also one of the most important centers of mining and heavy metalworking in all of France, and its large mines and forging mills could afford to pay more than the smaller enterprises scattered throughout France.

Evidence also suggests that the distribution of skills within industry favored Stéphanois workers. The industrial survey of 1896 selected scattered enterprises throughout France and listed the distribution of skills within various industries and their wages.[23]

Table 5

Daily Wages, 1896

	Saint-Etienne	France (excluding Paris)
Miner	4.24 francs	4.10 francs
Spinner	3.50 francs	2.90 francs
Forger	4.50 francs	4.20 francs
Carpenter	4.50 francs	4.40 francs
Joiner	4.50 francs	4.00 francs

In general, both the machine construction and steel production industries in the Stéphanois region employed higher proportions of skilled workers than comparable industries in other regions. This was due to the increasing concentration of Stéphanois metalworking on the production of quality steel and its products, which demanded a high proportion of skilled workers.

Table 5 also shows evidence of "wage rollout" in the Stéphanois region. "Wage rollout" is the influence on the local labor market caused by the presence of a high-wage industry in the local economy. Skilled workers who were working in the Stéphanois outside of the three major industries, such as carpenters and joiners, also had higher wages than the national average. Wages of Stéphanois construction workers were also influenced by the metal wage structure. It took several years of apprenticeship to become a construction worker, and few young men were likely to enter a trade which paid less than metalworking and demanded more training. The most detailed study of French wages made in the pre-1914 period, the inquiry organized by the London Board of Trade in 1906, provides additional evidence of wage rollout. It showed that not only were Stéphanois metalworkers among the highest-paid French metalworkers, but Stéphanois construction workers were among the highest-paid construction workers.[24]

In sum, the evolution of the Stéphanois wage system was characterized by the creation of a new category of semiskilled worker which absorbed some displaced artisans and a great many unskilled workers into its ranks. This development had a significant effect in increasing the will and the ability of industrial workers to organize. Their increased financial resources made them able to afford strike actions and made them potential allies of threatened artisans.

The Standard of Living

How the wage differential between artisanal and industrial workers decreased during the years between 1870 and 1914 has already been shown, but it is also important to examine the changes in wages of Stéphanois workers as a whole during this period. How did the standard of living of Stéphanois workers change in the years between 1870 and 1914, and how did the changes in the standard of living affect strikes? In order to study real wages, it is necessary to undertake the tedious but essential task of examining their two chief components, prices and wages. How did the cost of living in the Stéphanois region change in the years between 1870 and 1914? How did the wages of different groups change in relation to price increases?[25]

During the years between 1870 and 1914 the Stéphanois region was renowned for its low cost of living. In 1874 Louis Reybaud noted:

> Nowhere else are the resources more abundant than in the central region of France; here nature shows itself prodigal of its wealth. The whole basin which climbs from Givors to Saint-Etienne and prolongs itself on one side toward the great mountain chains of the Auvergne and on the other towards the rich growing areas which border the Loire, this basin is, by itself, largely self-sufficient, and still its zone of supply is insignificant compared to that which surrounds it. There is no product of the sun or the farm which is not present there in the most abundant proportions. . . . Thus consumable goods are there, in general, moderately priced and of an excellent quality. This does not include bread whose price, within one or two centimes, everywhere conforms to the prices of the large markets; but for the other commodities the margin is noticeable; provisions are less expensive than elsewhere. It is particularly in the direction of the Midi that the differences are evident; in some cases [the differences] . . . rise to 20% or 25%.[26]

The low cost of living in the Stéphanois region continued throughout the whole period. In 1896 a government study ranked the department of the Loire the seventeenth lowest in France for the cost of food and heating required to support a working-class family. The 1906 British Board of Trade study, which examined working-class living conditions in thirty large French cities, found three—Saint-Etienne, Brest, and Belfort—to have the lowest food costs for working-class families.[27]

In order to obtain a broad view of changes in Stéphanois cost of living in the years between 1870 and 1914, let us examine changes in the prices of bread and meat, the two largest components of the working-class budget. The estimates of Stéphanois food prices

1884–1908 are from the *Statistique agricole annuelle*, those of 1872–84 and 1908–13 from the *Statistique générale de la France*. There was some difference in the number of cities that each reported and the two estimates are not identical, as the figure for 1908 shows. The *Statistique agricole* included several Stéphanois towns, while the *Statistique générale* was based mainly on Saint-Etienne. Of the three qualities of bread generally obtainable, the price of second-quality bread was used. "Meat" includes pork, veal, beef, and mutton but not horsemeat, fowl, or sausage. In order to calculate the price index, estimates of worker food consumption are necessary. Unfortunately, sufficiently detailed budgets for Stéphanois industrial workers do not exist; for lack of better, the average budget of French skilled workers, who received between 30 and 38 francs, the range of the salary of Stéphanois metalworkers, was used. The estimate of the budget used was developed as the result of an extensive series of questionnaires sent out by the British Board of Trade, and this compilation of budgets is probably the most accurate estimate of French working-class consumption habits in the prewar years.[28]

Graph 7 shows the changes in the price index of Stéphanois bread and meat prices over two-year periods between 1870 and 1913. Prices fluctuated considerably during the period. They were highest in 1870–76 at the very beginning of the period and in 1908–13 at the very end. The periods 1883–86, 1891–94, and 1898–1906 were times of low or declining prices, while the years 1886–90 and 1894–98 were years of moderately high or increasing prices. Although our index is much less sophisticated, its slope resembles the "indice ouvrier A" calculated by Jeanne Singer-Kérel for the cost of living in Paris, based on the prices of 213 commodities.[29] The major differences are that fluctuations in bread and meat prices are much sharper than those in Singer-Kérel's index. In particular, the rise in 1894–98 is much less noticeable. These differences can easily be explained by the crudity of our calculations. In fact, there are a great number of relatively stable commodities which played an important role in the working-class diet, such as potatoes and vegetables, which are entirely omitted. Their inclusion would certainly lessen the fluctuations.[30]

Let us look more closely at the period between 1900 and 1913,

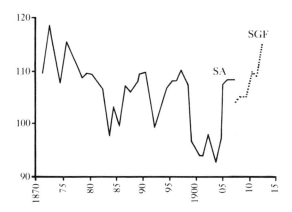

Graph 7. Stéphanois Price Index, 1870–1908 (bread and meat in Saint-Etienne worker's budget in 1907).

for this period has been the subject of conflicting analyses. Peter Stearns has maintained that the years between 1900 and 1910 were years of stagnation or rising inflation while the years between 1911 and 1914 were years of relative stability. Both Jeanne Singer-Kérel and Jean Lhomme have made exhaustive studies of the cost of living for this period, Singer-Kérel for Paris, Lhomme for all of France. Both have found that prices fell between 1900 and 1906 or 1907, began a moderate rise between 1906 or 1907 and 1911, and then rose dramatically between 1911 and 1914. Table 6 illustrates the Stéphanois cost of living in the years between 1900 and 1908; it is based on the prices of twelve commodities weighted according to the Board of Trade survey of 1906.[31] It shows that the cost of living in the Stéphanois region in the years between 1900 and 1908 was essentially similar to the findings of Lhomme and Singer-Kérel.

Similarly, several French government studies confirm the evidence of our index of bread and meat prices that the years between 1911 and 1914 were years of inflation in the Stéphanois region. Inflation seems to have spread particularly rapidly in 1911, although it proceeded at an uneven pace in the Stéphanois towns. A French government study found that between the first and last

Table 6

Cost of Living Index, 1890–1908

Year	Saint-Etienne (1900 = 100)	France
1890	103	105
1895	104	101
1900	100	100
1901	99	94
1902	98	92
1903	101	100
1904	96	98
1905	100	94
1906	107	93
1907	109	98
1908	110	100

quarters of 1911 its food price index had increased by over 10 percent in Saint-Chamond, 5 percent in Le Chambon, and had decreased slightly in Rive-de-Gier. A comparison of food prices in the three cities between 1911 and 1913 showed that the price of beef and bread had continued to rise but the prices of butter, eggs, potatoes, and milk had stabilized.

All the indexes of food consumption so far considered make no allowance for alcohol consumption. This is a significant omission because it was an important item in the Stéphanois worker's budget and because its price declined in the years between 1890 and 1914. The Stéphanois region was one of the great wine-consuming regions of France. A Stéphanois miner's family studied by one of Le Play's followers spent 20 percent of their budget on alcohol. Although this might well have been an extreme case, in 1911 only eight departments in France had a per capita annual wine consumption higher than the 1.6 hectoliters of the Loire. In that same year per capita wine consumption in Saint-Etienne was 2.49 hectoliters, the highest of any large city in France. The price of this important component of the Stéphanois worker's budget declined considerably in the years between 1890 and 1914. Although government taxes occasionally bedeviled the wine producer, the introduction of new wine-making methods after 1880 was the cause of this long-term decline.[33]

But alcohol consumption was more than an item in the worker's budget. It also represented the new luxury made possible by a high standard of living and the expansion of an important leisure-time institution, the café, among the mass of French workers. The English economic historian A. F. Dingle has suggested that the rise of alcohol consumption and the pub in late nineteenth-century England represented an increase in worker consumption made possible by the increase in the worker's standard of living. According to Dingle, a rising standard of living allowed English workers to consume more luxuries in their free time, and the liquor industry, through the spread of the pub, was the first large industry to adapt itself to the increase in workers' buying power. Michael Marrus has argued that parts of this argument might well apply to France, and the Stéphanois case supports his argument. The Stéphanois region with its high standard of living was one of the highest alcohol-consuming areas in France. Also, alcohol consumption in the Stéphanois was associated with the presence of the café. In 1895 a doctor estimated that there was one café for every fifty-five inhabitants of the Stéphanois region. High alcohol consumption and the large number of cafés are important symbols of the high standard of living of Stéphanois workers.[34]

Summarizing the influence of the cost of rent on the cost of living is difficult because rents varied considerably among the three towns, and there are few reliable comparisons of intracity rents during this time period. As early as 1875 government surveys picked up complaints about the high cost of rent in Saint-Chamond. A 1902 study found that average rents varied between 50 and 65 francs a month for working-class families in different small towns around Rive-de-Gier and Saint-Chamond, while the average cost of boarding houses for individual workers varied between 60 and 80 francs in all three towns. Rents in all three towns were considerably lower than those in Saint-Etienne, which in 1906 had among the lowest rents of any large city in France. In 1911 the average cost of rent for two rooms plus kitchen for a working-class family was 200 francs in Saint-Etienne, 100 in Rive-de-Gier, 160 in Saint-Chamond; and 125 in Le Chambon. For five rooms plus kitchen average costs were 450 francs in Saint-Etienne, 200 in Rive-de-Gier, 320 in Saint-Chamond, and 400 in Le Chambon. Unfortunately, it is not possible to estimate changes in the cost of rent over the years between 1870 and 1914.[35]

Our evidence indicates that changes in the cost of living had little influence on strike activity in the years between 1870 and 1914. Militant strike actions took place between 1892 and 1894, when the cost of living was falling, and between 1906 and 1911, when it was rising. Correlations between prices and the number of strikes and strikers in the three towns give similar results. The correlation coefficient for the number of strikes in all three towns over two-year periods between 1870 and 1908 and the index of bread and meat prices is negative and weak, − .1423, while that between the number of strikers and bread and meat prices is positive and weak, + .1005. Correlation between strikes and strikers in individual towns and bread and meat prices are similarly weak and inconclusive. None of these results is significant at the .05 level. These conclusions are similar to those of Andréani for the whole of France in the years between 1890 and 1914.[36]

The absence of a direct relationship between strikes and the cost of living is not surprising. Under some conditions workers are more able to adjust their wages to rising prices than others. For instance, increases in the cost of living are likely to occur during periods of economic expansion when they are often more than counterbalanced by increases in wages, but increases in the cost of living may also occur during periods of economic decline when wages tend to decrease. In order to determine whether changes in the cost of living influence strike actions, it is necessary to examine changes in nominal wages and economic conditions.

Table 7 shows an index of nominal wages of carpenters and forgers in the Parisian and the Stéphanois regions between 1853 and 1911.[37] Although there is only fragmentary information on Stéphanois wages between 1876 and 1895, there is some indication that local wages evolved at a different pace than Parisian wages. The greatest Stéphanois wage increases came between 1896 and 1911, while the greatest Parisian increases came between 1853 and 1896. The wages of Stéphanois forgers and carpenters seem to have increased most rapidly between 1906 and 1911 while the wages of Parisian workers were declining or stabilizing.

In order to examine the relationship between changes in nominal wages and the cost of living, two different budgets were used. Worker preferences with regard to different kinds of meat and the total amount of bread and meat in the budget changed over the fifty

Table 7

Wage Index in Paris and Saint-Etienne

Year	Forger (1896 = 100)		Carpenter (1896 = 100)	
	Paris	Saint-Etienne	Paris	Saint-Etienne
1853	63	80	59	67
1855–57	—	89	59	78
1860	75	78	59	—
1871	81	100	71	100
1876	81	—	71	—
1882	88	89	106	111
1886	88	—	100	—
1892	94	—	100	—
1896	100	100	100	100
1901	106	111	106	111
1906	125	122	94	120
1911	125	144	106	155

years encompassed by this study, and so two budgets were used, one at the beginning of this period and the other at the end. For the early period the budget of a working-class family whose head of household was involved in metalworking located in Herimoncourt in the Doubs was used. Although the size of this family was smaller than the average Stéphanois working-class family, conditions in the region seemed very similar to those in the Stéphanois region at mid-century. For the later period the 1906 survey was used. Thus two very different budgets were used for different periods: one in the early period for workers in a similar area and profession, another in the later period based on a national average for a similarly paid work group.[38]

In sum, evidence on changes in real wages between 1870 and 1914 does not support the argument that strike militancy was provoked by a declining or stagnating standard of living. The real wages of Stéphanois metalworkers between 1890 and 1914, the years of greatest strike militancy, were the highest that semiskilled metalworkers had ever received and, despite the rise of inflation, were rapidly increasing. Table 8 shows a small decline in real wages in 1906, which was the first year of rapid inflation, but by 1911 Stéphanois metalworkers had not only regained their losses

Table 8
Real Wages for a Forger in Saint-Etienne, 1853–1911

Year	1858 Budget	1906 Budget
	(1853 = 100)	
1853	100	100
1855	82	78
1872	88	98
1884	89	98
1895	91	100
1900	114	119
1906	111	114
1911	126	131

but significantly increased their real wages. The major strike wave of the early nineties seems to have occurred during a period of wage increase, as did the growing strike militancy between 1900 and 1911. Unfortunately data on wages are too irregular to make a more precise comparison, and our conclusions must remain tentative. Nevertheless, our study of the Stéphanois region concurs with other regional studies such as that of Barral on the Isère and Dupeux on the Loir-et-Cher.[39] Evidence about both prices and wages shows that Stéphanois strike conflicts occurred against a background of a rising standard of living.

The changing social environment in the Stéphanois region in the years between 1870 and 1914 had a powerful influence on the development of regional strike activity. Changes in work structure and technology stimulated artisans to enter into strike actions. The introduction of a new work system which limited the autonomy of industrial life weakened the internal mechanisms which workers had used to bargain peacefully with their employers. And, finally, the appearance of a new, relatively high-paid category of semi-skilled workers and their increasing standard of living created allies for threatened artisans who had the financial resources to carry out strike actions.

NOTES

1. J. F. Gonon, *Histoire de la chanson stéphanoise et forézienne* (Saint-Etienne: Imprimerie cooperative, union typographique, 1906), p. 480.
2. The design for Graphs 1–3 was taken from Shorter and Tilly, *Strikes in*

France, who use it to depict the "shape" of French strikes. Material on strikes in the three towns can be found in the Archives départementales de la Loire (ADL) in the series 92/M and in the yearly annual of the Office du travail, *Statistique des grèves* (Paris: Imprimerie nationale, 1890–1914). The industrial census of 1891 contains estimates of the industrial composition of each town; see ADL 54/M/8.

The most influential attempt to estimate long-term patterns of technological change in France is the work of François Simiand, *Le salaire, l'évolution sociale et la monnaie*, 3 vols. (Paris: Alcan, 1932). Like Schumpeter's great work, *Business Cycles*, 2 vols. (New York: McGraw-Hill, 1939), Simiand's work presumes the existence of long-term economic cycles described by the Russian economist N. D. Kondratieff in "The Long Waves in Economic Life," *Review of Economic Statistics* 17 (Nov., 1935), 105–15. Kondratieff waves have never been accepted by American economists and have recently come under attack in Europe; see George Garvey, "Kondratieff's Theory of Long Cycles," *Review of Economic Statistics* 24 (Nov., 1943), 203–30, and Maurice Lévy-Leboyer, "L'Héritage de Simiand: Prix, profit et termes d'échange au XIXe siècle," *Revue historique* 243 (Jan.-Mar., 1970), 77–120. The collapse of the theory of long-term economic cycles seriously damages Simiand's argument and throws his periodization of economic history into question.

3. For more detailed information on Saint-Chamonnais strikes, see Chapter 5. Detailed information on the great 1878 strike, which involved both threatened dyers and women braidmakers, can be found in the Archives de la préfecture de police in Paris, July 4, 1878, BA 171.

4. Archives de la préfecture de police, Agent 47, Mar. 31, 1877, BA 1476; Maurice Durousset, "La vie ouvrière dans la région stéphanoise" (DES, Université de Lyon, 1960).

5. Faure, *Histoire du mouvement ouvrier*, p. 455.

6. For more information on Chambonnaire strikes, see Chapter 4 and Petrus Faure, *Le Chambon rouge* (Le Chambon-Feugerolles: Editions du syndicat unitaire des métaux, 1929).

7. For more information on Ripagérien strikes, see Chapter 6. On technological change in French glassmaking, see Scott, *Glassworkers of Carmaux*.

8. Denis Poulot, *Le sublime* (Paris: Lacroix and Verboeckhaven, 1872), pp. 169–75.

9. Reybaud, *Le fer et la houille*, pp. 144–47.

10. On the "task system" and "subcontracting" in metalworking, see Mottez, *Systemes de salaires*, and Katherine Stone, "The Origins of Job Structure in the Steel Industry," *Review of Radical Political Economics* 6, no. 2 (Summer, 1974), 61–97.

11. J. Euverte, "De l'organisation de la main-d'oeuvre dans la grande industrie," *Journal des économistes* 19–20 (Sept., 1870), 354–56.

12. On the introduction of the foreman system in France, see Mottez, *Systemes de salaires*.

On the relation of subcontracting and the foreman system, see David Nelson, *Managers and Workers: Origins of the New Factory System in the United States, 1880–1920* (Madison: University of Wisconsin Press, 1975).

13. The most thorough study of the duration of factory work in France is Charles Rist, "La durée du travail dans l'industrie française," *Revue d'économie politique* 61 (1897), 371–95. Citing mainly examples from the textile industry, Rist argues that industrialization caused a great lengthening of hours in French

industry. If so, France provides a contrast to England, where M. A. Bienefeld has shown that hours were lengthened only in a few industries; see *Working Hours in British Industry: An Economic History* (London: Weidenfeld and Nicolson, 1972). The length of the workday in the Stéphanois region seems similar to Bienefeld's findings for English workers. Guillaume has found that the ten-hour day predominated among Stéphanois metalworkers in 1848; see "La situation économique et sociale du département de la Loire." It seems to have remained largely unchanged throughout the whole of the prewar period. On glassworkers' and metalworkers' hours in 1894, see the report of Apr., 1894, ADL 10/M/102, and for 1901 see Charles Benoist, "Le travail dans la grande industrie," pt. 2, *Revue des deux mondes* 14 (June, 1903), 637–66.

14. A detailed description of the 1892 strike is ADL 91/M/49.

15. Bienefeld, *Working Hours in British Industry.*

16. Faure, *Un témoin raconte*, p. 21.

17. On the 1893 and 1898 strikes in Rive-de-Gier, see ADL 92/M/50 and ADL 92/M/80; on the 1909 strike in Le Chambon, see ADL 92/M/50.

18. On decreasing wage differentials, see Emile Chevalier, *Les salaires au XIXe siècle* (Paris: Arthur Rousseau, 1887), and Gerard Weill, "Le rôle des facteurs structurels dans l'évolution de rémunérations salariales au XIXe siècle," *Revue économique* 10, no. 2 (Mar., 1959), 237–67.

Most French students of the decline of wage differentials emphasize the role of trade unions; while this may be the case in the twentieth century, it is doubtful in the nineteenth century. There is no need to believe that French unionism was particularly "weak" to question whether it could be responsible for such widespread and important phenomena. See André Tiano, "L'Action des syndicats ouvriers," *Revue française de science politique* 10, no. 4 (Dec., 1960), 912–30; André Marchal, "Réflexions sur une théorie économique du développement," *Revue économique* 2 (Feb., 1951), 45–61; and Jules Vuillemin, "Les syndicats ouvriers et les salaires," *Économie appliquée* (Apr.-Sept., 1952), 261–336.

19. On the decreasing wage differential in American metalworking, see Stone, "Origins of Job Structure in the Steel Industy"; on Stéphanois puddling, see Reybaud, *Le fer et la houille*, p. 146, and Benoist, "Le travail dans la grande industrie," pt. 2, p. 653.

20. On the industrial composition of the Stéphanois and Roannais population in 1896, see Office du travail, *Résultats statistiques du recensement des industries et professions . . . de 1896*, vol. 4 (Paris: Imprimerie nationale, 1901); on the national average of wages in spinning and forging, see Bureau de la statistique générale, *Annuaire statistique, 1961—Rétrospectif* (Paris: Imprimerie nationale, 1961); and for the average wage in mining, see François Simiand, *Salaire des ouvriers des mines de charbon en France* (Paris: Cornely, 1907).

21. For the departmental breakdown of industry, see Office du travail, *Résultats statistiques . . . de 1896.*

22. *Bureau de la statistique générale, Annuaire statistique, 1961—Rétrospectif*, p. 253.

23. Office du travail, *Salaires et durée du travail dans l'industrie française* (Paris: Imprimerie nationale, 1896), 3, 84–85, 96–107.

24. On the phenomenon of "wage rollout," see Wilbur R. Thompson, *A Preface to Urban Economics* (Baltimore, Md.: Johns Hopkins University Press, 1965), pp. 67–74. The 1906 Board of Trade survey was supervised by the father of British budget analysis, Seebohm Rowntree; see "Cost of Living in French Towns," *House of Commons Sessional Papers*, vol. 91 (1909).

25. The relationship between living standard and strikes in late nineteenth-century France is a subject of controversy among contemporary historians and economists. In a recent book Peter Stearns has produced evidence that a declining standard of living between 1900 and 1910 created an environment favorable to strikes, while other studies by Edgard Andréani and Edward Shorter and Charles Tilly have found that strikes during this period were likely to occur during periods of rising standard of living. See Stearns, *Revolutionary Syndicalism and French Labor*, esp. Appendix A; Edgard Andréani, *Grèves et fluctuations: La France de 1890 à 1914* (Paris: Editions Cujas, 1968), pp. 111–51; and Shorter and Tilly, *Strikes in France*, pp. 76–104.

26. Reybaud, *Le fer et la houille*, p. 148. There are some provocative studies on the relationship of worker movements to economic cycles: Jean Bouvier, "Mouvement ouvrier et conjonctures économiques," *Le mouvement social* 48 (July-Sept., 1964), 3–30; Eric J. Hobsbawm, "Economic Fluctuations and Some Social Movements since 1800," *Economic History Review* ser. 2, 5 (1952), 1–25; and Michelle Perrot, "Grèves, grévistes et conjoncture: Vieux problèmes, travaux neufs," *Le mouvement social* 63 (Apr.-June, 1968), 109–24.

Owing to the dramatic changes in Stéphanois industrial structure, it is hard to discern business cycles in the period between 1870 and 1914. The changing nature of the metal industry breaks the period in two parts: the years between 1870 and 1890, a period of growth in the steel-producing industry, and the years between 1890 and 1914, a period of decline in steel production and the rise of machine construction. It is possible to trace a metalworking business cycle between 1890 and 1914, but this short period makes comparison difficult. The correlation between two-year averages of strikes in the three towns and the production of metal goods between 1870 and 1914 is very weak, as is the correlation between metal goods and strikers in the three towns, and none of the correlations for any of the towns is significant at the .05 level.

An excellent study of the French metal industry and economic change between 1890 and 1914 is Lucien Brocard, "La grosse métallurgie française et le mouvement des prix de 1890 à 1913," *Revue d'histoire économique et sociale* 10 (1922), 303–506.

27. Office du travail, *Salaires et durée du travail*, vol. 4; "Cost of Living in French Towns," p. xxiv.

28. The graph of bread and meat prices is based on the *Statistique générale de la France* for the periods 1872–84 and 1908–13, and on the *Statistique agricole annuelle* for 1884–1908. The figures for 1872–1908 can be found in L.-J. Gras, *Histoire du commerce locale* (Saint-Etienne: Théolier, 1910), while the figures for 1908–13 were found in the Bureau de la statistique générale's *Statistique générale de la France* (Paris: Imprimerie nationale, 1908–14). The Board of Trade budget is found on p. xviii of "Cost of Living in French Towns."

29. Jeanne Singer-Kérel, *Le coût de la vie á Paris de 1840 á 1954* (Paris: Armand Colin, 1961), p. 89.

30. Gras notes that during the years between 1884 and 1904 the price of potatoes, pasta, rice, and vegetables remained stable in the Stéphanois region while the price of oil, sugar, coffee, and jams fell, because of the lowering of tariffs; see *Histoire du commerce locale*, pp. 648–49.

31. Peter Stearns's argument that the standard of living of French workers declined between 1900 and 1910 has little support either among scholars or in the literature of the period. Albert Aftalion did state that prices rose faster than wages

in the period, but this was more a passing remark than a seriously argued position; see "Le salaire réel et sa nouvelle orientation," *Revue d'économie politique* 26 (1912), 541–52. Maurice Halbwachs suggested not so much that the buying power of workers was declining as that their choices were improvident and their family life decaying; see *Évolution des besoins dans les classes ouvrières* (Paris: Felix Alcan, 1933). Almost the only scholar to endorse Stearns's view is Jacques Rougerie, who makes this argument to support the existence of Kondratieff waves, in "Remarques sur l'histoire des salaires à Paris au XIXᵉ siècle," *Le mouvement social* 63 (Apr.-June, 1968), 71–108.

Claude Chatelard has written a dissertation arguing that the standard of living of workers in the city of Saint-Etienne declined between 1870 and 1914: "*La misère à Saint-Etienne entre 1870 et 1914*" (DES, Université de Lyon, 1966). Although his evidence is somewhat selective, Chatelard may, in fact, be right. The wages of ribbonworkers and miners, two mainstays of the economy of Saint-Etienne, were declining, but this decline of living standard was in every way exceptional and hardly reached outside the city. Chatelard's strongest case is that the quality of urban life in Saint-Etienne declined during this period as housing stagnated, but it is unclear how much of the "growth" in misery is due to increased reporting. The quality of urban life in cities like Rive-de-Gier and Saint-Chamond was low throughout the nineteenth century, although there is no evidence of decline.

Studies of the French standard of living are on shaky ground until more is known about unemployment. All commentators agree that the existing statistics are unreliable. See Jacques Néré, "Une statistique du salaire et de l'emploi en France," *Revue d'histoire économique et sociale* 2 (1955), 224–30, and Charles Rist, "Relations entre les variations annuelles du chômage, des grèves, et des prix," *Revue d'économie politique* (1912), 748–58. Only Andréani has incorporated unemployment estimates into his calculations, and his results are not very different from Singer-Kérel or Lhomme; see *Grèves et fluctuations*.

It is possible that the consumption of meat did decline a little in this period, but—shades of the English standard of living controversy—this shift probably indicated a change in consumer preference toward increased consumption of sugar, coffee, and fruit. See Jean-Claude Toutain, "La consommation alimentaire en France de 1789 à 1964," *Cahiers de l'ISEA*, vol. 5, no. 11 (Nov., 1971). Aggregate consumption figures can be very misleading.

One of Stearns's strongest arguments is that, given the poor quality of French measurements of standard of living, the general decline in workers' living standards in Europe at the time should lead us to expect France to share in this trend. But the recent work of E. H. Phelps Brown and Margaret H. Browne establishes rather conclusively that there was no trend in European wages during this period; see *A Century of Pay* (New York: St. Martins Press, 1968).

Our 1890–1908 price index includes the prices of bread and meat in our earlier price index plus seven items in the budget of the Lycée of Saint-Etienne. The twelve commodities are: bread, beef, veal, mutton, fresh pork, poultry, *charcuterie*, butter, eggs, milk, cheese, and sausage.

32. For changes in the cost of living in 1911, Bureau de la statistique générale, *Bulletin de la statistique générale*, vol. 1 (Jan. 1912), and, for a comparison of the cost of living in 1911 and 1913, vol. 2 (Aug. 1913–July, 1914).

33. Le Play's Stéphanois miner is cited in C. Dauphin and P. Pezerat, "Les consommations populaires dans le seconde moitié du XIXᵉ siècle à travers les

monographies de l'école de Le Play," *Annales: Économies, sociétés, civilisations* 30 (Mar.-June, 1975), 537–52.

For figures on wine consumption in the Stéphanois region in 1911, see Bureau de la statistique générale, *Annuaire statistique—1911* (Paris: Imprimerie nationale, 1912), pp. 252–53.

34. A. F. Dingle, "Drink and Working-Class Living Standards in Great Britain 1870–1914," *Economic History Review*, ser. 2, 25, no. 4 (Nov., 1972), 608–22; Michael Marrus, "Social Drinking in the Belle Epoque," *Journal of Social History* 7, no. 2 (Winter, 1974), 115–41.

A Dr. Merlin estimated the ratio of inhabitants to cabarets as 62 to 1 in Saint-Etienne, 47 in Firminy, 46 in Saint-Chamond, and 55 in Rive-de-Gier; see Gras, *Histoire du commerce locale*, pp. 406–7.

The high alcoholic consumption of highly skilled workers was long ago noted by Joseph Lefort in his study, *Études sur . . . les classes ouvrières: Intemperance et misère* (Paris: Guillaumin, 1875). Lefort concluded: "Let us note that drunkenness in our country is frequent among the construction workers, housepainters, tailors, and shoemakers, the artist-workers (*arts et métiers*), and those who are nomads, the carpenters, shoemakers, and forgers. This predilection is encouraged by Monday unemployment as well as facilitated by their elevated wages and the nature of their work which in certain trades occupies the workers only part of the week and leaves them the remainder to spend in the cabaret . . ." (pp. 83–84).

35. "Enquête de 1871–1875," report of the Chambre consultative de Saint-Chamond, AN C3022. Information on 1900 rents is found in Office du travail, *Bordereaux des salaires pour diverses catégories d'ouvriers en 1900 et 1901* (Paris: Imprimerie nationale, 1902), p. 206, and on 1911 rents in *Bulletin de la statistique générale*, vol. 1 (Oct. 1911–July, 1912). A comparison of Stéphanois rents with those of other large cities in 1906 appears in "Cost of Living in French Towns," p. xxxiii.

36. Andréani, *Grèves et fluctuations*, p. 165. The correlation between strikes and prices in individual towns is: Le Chambon .4746, Rive-de-Gier .0610, and Saint-Chamond .1863; between strikers and prices, Le Chambon .0706, Rive-de-Gier −.0102, and Saint-Chamond .2309.

37. Information on Parisian wages appears in Rougerie, "Les salaires à Paris." On Stéphanois wages, information was found in: Bureau de la statistique générale, *Statistique de la France—Prix et salaires à diverses époques*, ser. 2, vol. 12 (Nancy: Berger-Levrault, 1863), *Statistique de la France—Résultats généraux de l'enquête . . . 1861–1865* (Nancy: Berger-Levrault, 1873), *Statistique de la France —1872* (Paris: Imprimerie nationale, 1872), and *Statistique de la France—1884* (Paris: Imprimerie nationale, 1884); Office du travail, *Salaires et durée du travail*, vol. 4, *Bordereaux des salaires . . . 1901*, *Salaires et durée du travail . . . en 1906* (Paris: Imprimerie nationale, 1907), and *Salaires et coût de l'existence . . . en 1910* (Paris: Imprimerie nationale, 1911).

38. The Herimoncourt budget is by Charles Robert, "Monteur d'outils en acier," *Les ouvriers des deux mondes* 2, no. 16 (1858), 285–311.

Real wages are calculated according to the formula

$$\frac{\text{Nominal Wage Index}}{\text{Cost of Living Index}} \times 100$$

39. Pierre Barral, *Le département de l'Isère sous la troisième république 1870–1940* (Paris: Armand Colin, 1962) pp. 159, 227; Georges Dupeux, *Aspects de l'histoire sociale et politique de Loire-et-Cher 1848–1914* (Paris: Mouton, 1962), pp. 290–92.

CHAPTER FOUR

Artisans and Industrial Workers in Rive-de-Gier, 1871–1914

Comrades whose brains
Are planning a new world.
Let us struggle that the factory may be,
One day, a temple for the spirit
Which contemplates science and love.[1]

From the Roannais workers'
song, "The Factory"

Dramatic changes occurred in the social environment of Stéphanois workers in the years between 1871 and 1914: a new factory discipline was introduced, old crafts were threatened by mechanization, and a new proletariat was created. Mass strikes broke out as workers resisted these changes. An analysis of the mass strike process in one small Stéphanois town, Rive-de-Gier, can contribute to an understanding of the mechanisms at work on a larger scale. In the years between 1870 and 1914 the economy of Rive-de-Gier was divided between two contrasting major industries. One was metalworking, an industrial trade which employed 1,700 workers, and the other was glassmaking, an artisanal trade which employed 2,200 workers.[2] Rive-de-Gier was also a center of worker militancy and mass strike actions of artisanal and industrial workers.

The history of a late nineteenth-century working-class town like Rive-de-Gier offers many examples of strike conflicts. As Tables 9–11 show, between 1885 and 1914 metalworkers and glassworkers were involved in several bitter struggles. In order to carefully study the dynamics of Ripagérien mass strike actions, one local strike, the 1893 metalworkers' strike, was selected for detailed study. This strike, the largest which took place in the town in the years between 1871 and 1914, happened during the five-year period 1890–94, when the city's strike activity crested.[3]

Table 9

Number of Strikers (Glassworkers and Metalworkers)
in Rive-de-Gier, 1885–1914

	1885–89	1890–94	1895–99	1900–1904	1905–9	1910–14
Metalworkers	0	1,672	0	0	122	37
Glassworkers	0	3,277	36	0	802	505

Table 10

Duration of Strikes (in Days) in Rive-de-Gier, 1885–1914

	1885–89	1890–94	1895–99	1900–1904	1905–9	1910–14
Metalworkers	0	78	0	0	20	20
Glassworkers	0	645	43	0	313	226

Table 11

Worker-Days Lost in Strikes in Rive-de-Gier, 1885–1914

	1885–89	1890–94	1895–99	1900–1904	1905–9	1910–14
Metalworkers	0	100,320	0	0	846	414
Glassworkers	0	308,030	1,548	0	117,442	42,535

The 1893 metalworkers' strike was of sufficient size and significance to merit national attention. The rebellion, which involved all 1,700 metalworkers and lasted two months, was cited as an important example of industrial workers' militancy. In the Chamber of Deputies Jean Jaurès challenged the government's handling of the strike and demanded that the prefect behave in a more evenhanded manner.[4]

The strike in Rive-de-Gier was only one of a series of massive strikes in the early 1890s in France. The years between 1890 and 1894 were years of dramatically increased strike protest, and "strike waves" swept France in 1890 and 1893.[5] During the period 1889–93 French socialist parties first appeared on the political map of the Third Republic; large numbers of socialist deputies were elected in 1893. The early nineties were years of working-class political optimism. There was reason to believe that the state might soon come to the aid of hard-pressed artisanal and industrial workers. In 1891 a coalition of well-known radical socialists and independent socialists announced their intention to press for and implement a program of legal limitation of the workday, protection for working women and children, laws on factory safety, arbitration, workmen's compensation, old age pensions, public assistance reform, and government-guaranteed trade union freedom.[6] So striking Ripagérien workers could feel that national authorities would not be totally unsympathetic to their strike goals and that their newly formed socialist party had a real chance to win recognition for local workers' demands.

On the surface, the metalworkers' 1893 strike might be distinguished from other contemporary strikes by its exclusively industrial character. Shorter and Tilly have demonstrated that artisanal workers played an important role in strikes during this period, and the Ripagérien metalworkers were overwhelmingly semiskilled workers.[7] But this initial impression is misleading; in fact, careful inspection reveals that the strike was an impressive example of artisanal worker solidarity with industrial workers. Artisanal workers did not strike alongside industrial workers, but they provided essential support to striking workers. Artisanal workers joined in solidarity because, owing to their artisanal work structure, they were able to develop a militant trade union movement. Industrial workers needed these skilled workers' assistance, since their own industrial work structure put powerful obstacles in the way of worker organization. Also, artisanal union organizations decided to aid embattled industrial workers because artisans felt their own collective interests were at stake in the industrial workers' struggle.

Worker Solidarity and Strike Action: Rive-de-Gier, 1893

The glassworkers' union took a leadership role in the 1893 metal strike from its inception. Presiding at the initial mass meeting, called to decide whether all the town's metalworkers would go out on strike in solidarity with the workers of the Marrel metal plant, was Gaudin, the ex-president of the glassworkers' union, who began with a short speech encouraging the metalworkers.

The order of speakers at the meeting was a tacit recognition of glassworkers' leadership of the metal union. Gaudin was followed by Vinay, another glassworker who spoke for an hour. He began by announcing that in order to encourage the metalworkers' resistance, the glassworkers' union had appealed to the glassworkers' federation for aid. He then added that as a delegate of the glassworkers' union he was authorized to donate 500 francs to the metalworkers. After a long and fiery speech he concluded with the declaration that from that moment, the glassworkers would impose a 2 percent deduction on their salaries which would be contributed to the metal strike. Vinay estimated that the deduction would produce 5,000 francs a month for the metalworkers. During the wave of applause which followed, another glassworker union leader, Philloux, took the platform and attacked the mayor of Rive-de-Gier, M. Brunon. He lectured the metalworkers to beware of this radical politician, who was also a large metal manufacturer. Philloux was followed by several metalworker speakers. After this meeting the metalworkers voted almost unanimously to go out on strike.[8]

This meeting was only the first of a series in which glassworkers' union leaders influenced the conduct of the metal strike. Of the thirteen metalworkers' mass meetings about which there are detailed police reports, all but one included a major speaker from the glassworkers' national union.[9] A month after the strike had begun, in fact, the head of the glassworkers' national union federation addressed the metalworkers and expressed his strong support.

Individual rank-and-file glassworkers joined their leaders in aiding the metalworkers. According to newspaper reports, glassworkers were an important component of the February 18 demonstration which supported the metal strike, and the newspaper accounts are reinforced by police records; of the nine workers with known occupations who were arrested for threatening nonstrikers or insulting policemen, six were glassworkers and three were metalworkers.[10]

The glassworkers also provided indispensable financial support for the two-month-long metal strike. Not only did the glassworkers' union contribute substantially to the metalworkers' strike fund, but it was also able to persuade the glassworkers' federation

Table 12

Strike Contributions from Metalworkers and Glassworkers in Rive-de-Gier

	Glassworkers		Metalworkers		Others	
	Francs	Percent	Francs	Percent	Francs	Percent
Metalworkers' Strike, 1893 (N = 25,818)	7,298	28.3	4,832	18.7	13,687	53.0
Glassworkers' Strike, 1894 (N = 110,240)	87,453	79.3	2,064	1.9	20,723	18.8

Table 13

Strike Contributions by Geographic Distribution, Rive-de Gier

	Local		Regional		National	
	Francs	Percent	Francs	Percent	Francs	Percent
Metalworkers' Strike, 1893 (N = 25,818)	14,900	57.7	5,634	21.8	5,194	20.1
Glassworkers' Strike, 1894 (N = 98,538)	20,909	21.2	12,470	12.7	65,185	66.2

and its member unions to contribute. Tables 12 and 13 compare the occupational and geographic distribution of the contributions to the metalworkers' strike of 1893 and the large glassworkers' strike which followed a year later. Of the 25,818 francs raised for the 1893 strike, 28.3 percent came from glassworkers, 18.7 percent came from metalworkers, and 53.0 percent came from other sources. Interestingly, glassworkers donated more money to the metalworkers' strike than did other metalworkers. Glassworkers' generosity can partly be explained by their stronger national organization. Table 13 shows the larger role which national-level organizations played in the 1894 glass strike than in the 1893 metal strike. The glassworkers' national union and its affiliated branches were much stronger than its affiliated metalworkers' counterpart.

In fact, almost all the money donated to the metalworkers' 1893 strike by non-regional, nonlocal organizations was donated by the glassworkers' federation and its affiliates.[11]

Trade Union Organization in Rive-de-Gier

Glassworkers were able to aid the metalworkers effectively because they were organized into strong trade unions, both locally and nationally. The growth of union strength in the Ripagérien glass trades dates back to 1890, when the existing local union transformed itself by lowering its dues and opening its membership to all the workers in the skill hierarchy.[12] This local union upsurge was part of a national expansion of glassworkers' unionism.

The secret of trade union strength in Rive-de-Gier was its militant discipline. A newspaper labeled it "very severe." The local police commissioner in 1894 reported on the union organization: "It is now very nearly a universal obligation in this profession to be a union member. If he is not, the worker exposes himself to lively reproaches from his colleagues and sometimes even violence. The particular work conditions of the glassworkers makes the 'boycott' very successful against workers opposed to the idea of unionism."[13] Glassworking demanded close collaboration among fellow workers, and an uncooperative worker could easily be made to appear incompetent in the presence of his employers.

The local glassworkers' union had gained quite a bit of strike experience in the years between 1890 and 1893. In these years it led four strikes and systematically confronted every major bottlemaker in the city. While it was not always successful, it did succeed in establishing a factory committee in every important local glass factory. These committees were charged with setting up shop rules and settling wage disputes. The Ripagérien factory committee system was the envy of glassworkers throughout France and strongly influenced the demands of metalworkers in their 1893 strike. By 1893 the glassworkers' union was strong enough to begin using May Day to demonstrate its strength. Representatives of the union approached every employer asking for permission to take May Day off; sometimes it was granted, sometimes refused. In any case, permission hardly mattered because all glassworks were emptied on May 1, 1893.[14]

In contrast to the glassworkers' union, the local metalworkers' union organization desperately needed outside aid. It is difficult to get any perspective on the metal union organization because within seven months of its formation it was fighting for its life. While the union gained the adherence of the majority of metalworkers, it had no strike fund or experienced leadership.[15] The short-term problems of the metal union were quite serious. The majority of metal employers were agreed that the union must be destroyed, and the manager of the largest plant in town, Marrel Brothers, had provoked the 1893 strike with the express intention of destroying the union in his plant.[16]

Work Structure and Strike Militancy: The Glassworkers

Glassworkers were able to aid the metalworkers effectively because they were organized into a strong trade union. The sympathy of the glassworkers' union would have counted for nothing unless backed by experienced trade unionists whose organizational discipline and financial ability were well known. The glassworkers' ability to build a powerful union organization was strongly facilitated by the nature of the work they performed. Even though they worked inside a large factory, Ripagérien glassworkers were artisans; that is, the work they performed was highly skilled, and they possessed a variety of difficult skills acquired in apprenticeship programs controlled by the workers. As members of an artisanal occupation, glassworkers earned a high family income and belonged to a strong informal work group; high income and a cohesive work group provided the basis for a powerful glassworkers' trade union organization.

There were three major divisions of artisanal glassmaking in Rive-de-Gier; different artisans were skilled in the manufacture of bottles, windows, and crystal. These skills were not interchangeable and workers seldom passed from one division of the trade to another. Bottle manufacturing involved the largest number of workers; in 1893, 59.7 percent of glassworkers were employed in the production of bottles, 30.3 percent in windows, and 9.7 percent in crystal.[17] Some highly skilled workers in crystal and window-making had their own separate unions loosely affiliated with the central glass union, but the majority of Ripagérien glassworkers belonged directly to the central union, the Chambre syndicale des ouvriers verriers de Rive-de-Gier.[18] Although all artisanal glassworkers participated in strikes between 1890 and 1894, the bottleworkers were the most combative division of the glass industry during those years.

The character of the glassworkers' union was entirely determined by artisanal glassworkers. Only about half the workers in the glass industry were included in the artisanal skill hierarchy; only those involved in the skill hierarchy plus the *porteurs* were eligible for membership in the glassworkers' union. The artisanal skill hierarchy included all those who were or would become glassblowers (*souffleurs*). It included the *souffleur*, his assistant the *grand garçon*, and the *gamin*. The *porteur* usually had little chance of becoming a glassblower, nor did the machinists or packers. The skilled glassworkers' union encouraged the other unskilled groups to form their own union. An unskilled glassworkers' union existed briefly between 1892 and 1895, but played no role in the metalworkers' strike of 1893.

Glassworkers' skills enabled them to earn the wages necessary to support a solvent union movement. Any method of calculation reveals that artisanal glassworkers were an exceptionally highly paid working-class group. A look at bottleworkers' wages is particularly informative because they composed a large percentage of the total workforce in glass. All wage estimates for bottleworkers are approximate because wages were based on team output, which varied considerably. Bottleworkers worked in teams of four, and each member of the team had his own pay scale. In 1894 the *souffleur* received between 8.50 and 9.00 francs a day, the *grand garçon* between 4.25 and 4.50, the *gamin* 2.25 francs, and the *porteur* 1.25. Highly skilled glassworkers were also entitled to free lodging and free heating. Glassworkers who did not live in the employer-owned housing received 70 francs a month in compensation. Including monthly compensation for rent, most glassblowers would have received betwen 11.50 and 12.00 francs for an average working day.[19]

These calculations somewhat exaggerate glassworkers' earnings because they do not account for the frequent periods of unemployment of glassworkers or the short worklife of glassblowers. Several periods of anticipated unemployment for glassworkers occurred every year, such as the *fours morts*, which lasted four or five weeks while the oven was repaired. Glass employers often took advantage of this hiatus to get rid of their excess inventory; and when the market was slow, the dead season could last much longer. Furthermore, glassblowing was a physically disabling profession. Constant proximity to a fiery oven weakened the worker's eyes while glassblowing took its toll on his lungs. A man who became a *souffleur* at twenty-five was fortunate to continue in that position until he was fifty. Frequently, incapacitated glassblowers were "retired" to work alongside young boys as packers. If a glassblower did not possess some savings, his old age was likely to be spent in dire poverty.[20]

In addition to the income of the adult male glassworkers, glassmaking contributed to the family income insofar as it allowed children to find work at an earlier age than in many working-class occupations. In an 1891 sample of Ripagérien families, 30 percent of all the families with a glassworker head of household had another member of the family in the glass trade. Glassworkers usually initiated their male children into the trade as soon as they could legally do so. At twelve a male child could begin to contribute to the family income.[21] This perhaps helps account for the story told by Guillaume Roquille, a local working-class poet, that glassworkers in particular boasted of their ability to produce male children.[22]

The relationship between glassmaking and women's work is much less clear. There was little employment for women in Rive-de-Gier. Several nineteenth-century authors argued that the high wages of glassworkers allowed their wives to stay at home and thus discouraged potential employers of female labor from opening factories in that area; 82.5 percent of all glassworker families in the 1891 sample had a female who is identified only as "housekeeper." A frequently repeated nineteenth-century saying ran: "Rive-de-Gier is hell for horses, a purgatory for men, and a heaven for women."[23] Horses endured hell in the mines, men suffered from fire and brimstone in the glassworks and mines, and women, presumably, had a "heavenly" time staying at home.

The "high wages" argument seems inadequate when we look at the actual situation of all Ripagérien working-class women; miners' wives, whose husbands earned much lower wages than glassworkers, also stayed at home. An alternative explanation, suggested by Louise Tilly, is based on the nature of men's work.[24] It is possible that even if women had wanted to work to supplement the family income, they would not have had the free time to do so. Both mining and glassmaking employed men and young boys working in shifts. Someone was needed at home to feed family members working at different hours and to help coordinate their different schedules for working, dressing, and spending leisure time. To the extent that family employment in glassmaking placed extraordinary demands on women inside the home, it restricted their participation in the outside labor force.

But more important than wages in explaining the strength of glassworkers' unionism was the close-knit, informal work group which characterized day-to-day occupational experiences. In order to maintain their high wage levels, glassworkers had to work together as a team. The *gamin* gathered the glass on the cane, the *grand garçon* shaped it in preparation, and the *souffleur* blew it into its required shape. The *porteur* then carried the glass bottle to the annealing oven. Figure 2 shows the process. Glassworker teams predominated in both large and small factories. The only difference between the large Richarme works, which employed 1,061 bottleworkers, and the small Société anonyme des verriers, which employed 236 workers, was the number of ovens in the plant and their size. In 1894 the Richarme works, one of the largest glass factories in France, had four ovens with a total space for fifty-six separate teams of artisanal glassworkers. Glassworkers in the Richarme plant worked in three eight-hour shifts, and in that time 168 different glassblowing teams worked in this factory.[25]

The artisanal glasswork team encouraged the growth of strong informal relations which were the basis for the glassworker union's solidarity. Glass production depended on the smooth coordinated action of every member of the work unit. That, in turn, created an

Figure 2. The skill hierarchy in glassmaking, 1862: La compagnie générale de la Loire et du Rhône in Rive-de-Gier. Source: *L'Illustration*, Sept. 6, 1862.

informal but impenetrable system of workers' control over the pace and rhythm of work; work patterns corresponded closely to the needs and personal situation of the glassworker team. In 1924 a study of English artisanal glassworkers by the Industrial Fatigue Research Board showed that the production rate of glass teams changed substantially over days, weeks, and months, reflecting changes in the stress levels and morale of team members.[26] There was little management could do to supervise this work group because it was almost impossible for an outsider to judge team performance on any individual task. The observations of crystal-glassworkers by W. F. Whyte apply equally well to bottleworkers:

> Time and motion studies in the blowing room would have faced unusual technical problems. The industrial engineer could observe and time each movement made, but how could he determine how many movements were necessary? This applied to the movements a man made in working the glass, and even more to the warming in periods. An additional warming in or two could add markedly to the

duration of a work cycle, and yet how could the industrial engineer say just how many times a piece needed to be warmed in? The servitor or gaffer [rough equivalents to the *grand garçon* and the *souffleur*] made this judgement by the appearance or feel of the glass, based on long years of experience. If the men were required to speed up their pace, they could spoil piece after piece, and it would be impossible for management to prove it had been done on purpose.[27]

Glassworker tradition also acted to protect the unity of the work group, for tradition asserted the inviolability of the glassworkers' team as a unit. Informal craft rules regulated the promotion and replacement of team members. Each glassworking team had its own members and designated replacement; the employer who ignored these customs risked serious trouble. When in 1892 the manager of a glassworks replaced a drunken glassblower with a *grand garçon* who was not the designated replacement for that team, the result was a three-month strike of bottleworkers.[28]

The solidarity of the work team was reinforced by ties of kinship and apprenticeship. For centuries glassworkers had initiated their sons into the glass trade. In 1894 a visitor, Ardouin-Dumazet, remarked on the glassworkers' "privileges," which prohibited "employers from hiring workers outside the city or taking apprentices from among those who are not glassworkers."[29] Only in emergencies, during periods of rapid expansion or when dozens of glassblowers left town together to seek employment in a newly established glassworks, were outsiders initiated into the trade. In 1894 a glassworker's son ususally began as a *gamin*; it took about ten years for a *gamin* to become a *souffleur*. In 1894 the average *gamin* in the Richarme works had been there for 3.6 years, the *grand garçon* for 7.7 years. The *gamin* and the *grand garçon* each had his own interest in cultivating relations with the *souffleur* because only he could teach them the advanced stages of their craft. Moreover, a *souffleur* could effectively punish a refractory young apprentice by dismissing him from his team.[30]

Further, the cohesive work group formed around the glass oven continued to exist after the artisanal glassworkers had completed their eight hours in the factory. Indeed, a tightly knit artisanal glassworker community existed in Rive-de-Gier. Residential prox-

Figure 3. Nineteenth-century housing for glassworkers, 1974.

imity encouraged informal contact. Artisanal glassworkers were thrown together in large company-owned tenement houses, a legacy of the days when the housing shortage created by the rapid growth of an industrial workforce induced employers to construct lodging for their workers. A Ripagérien novelist, M. Fournier, writing in the early thirties, describes these tenements (see Figure 3) in the years before World War I and the collective experience of the journey to work in the early morning:

> They walked on the left past a long grey wall, which appeared horribly sad to Jacques, passed before several houses, all constructed on the same plan, a stairway, facing the street, concealed the facade. Here lived the glassworkers.
>
> On the stairs, some mattresses, some bundles of straw, were exposed to the sun. On a clothes line hung in strange poses, some shirts, some solid blue pants and some enfants' bonnets. At this hour, the stairs were too narrow to contain the flood of *gamins* who

poured out like an avalanche from the upper stages. They yelled, swore and threatened, rattling the wooden steps with their wooden shoes. . . .[31]

On occasion, residential proximity threw glassworkers not only into social contact with one another but into actual physical contact; mornings en route to the glassworks demonstrated informal sociability with a vengeance.

Tenements formed the core of both the eastern and southwestern neighborhoods where the glassworkers lived. By 1894 the number of glassworkers had long surpassed the vacancies in these tenements, and the majority of glassworkers lived in nearby apartments.[32] Table 14 shows these two glassworker concentrations. The southwest section of Rive-de-Gier was close to the Richarme works; the northern half of the eastern section was the historic glassworkers' *quartier*. (See Figures 4 and 5). In the eighteenth and early nineteenth centuries several important glassworks had been concentrated in this part of the eastern section. Although these works had long been abandoned, the area was still a center of glassworker habitation.[33] It was also a center of militant trade unionism. In 1907, when a *bourse du travail* was finally established at Rive-de-Gier, it was located in the rue de la Barrière, which was historically part of this *quartier*.

Table 14

Residential Patterns in Rive-de-Gier, 1891
Individual Sample of Glassworkers and Nonglassworkers

Rive-de-Gier	Glassworkers		Nonglassworkers	
	Number	Percent	Number	Percent
Western Section	2	2.2	178	12.3
Northern Section	3	3.3	206	14.2
North-Central Section	18	19.6	222	15.3
Eastern Section	29	31.5	207	14.3
South-Central Section	7	7.6	217	15.0
Southwestern Section	29	31.5	185	12.8
Countryside	1	1.1	159	11.0
Unidentified	3	3.3	76	5.2
N	92		1,450	

Index of Dissimilarity = 40.2

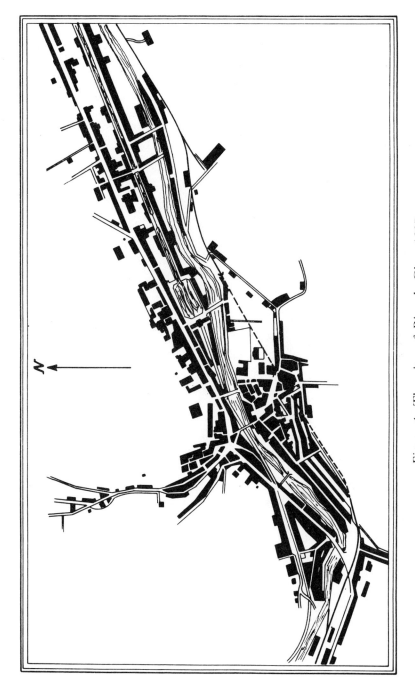

Figure 4. The city of Rive-de-Gier, 1887.

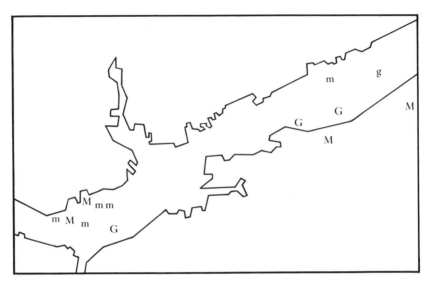

Figure 5. Location of industry (G for glassworks, M for metalworks).

One of the distinguishing characteristics of the centers of glassworker habitation was their narrow streets.[34] The narrowness of the streets was due partly to their age; the glassworkers' sections were among the oldest portions of the city. But also these pinched alleys were probably the result of the instructions of the glass manufacturers who had constructed most of the buildings. Before the age of the Siemens oven, when glassworkers might be called to work at any time of the day or night, there was a serious danger that workers leaving or entering the heated glassworks would catch pneumonia in the cold streets. The narrower the streets, the less was the chance of exposure to the elements (see Figure 6). Cramped streets encouraged informal contact among glassworkers. Figure 7 shows the *bourse du travail* built in 1907, commanding the glassworkers' trench-like precincts like a fortress.

The geographic concentration of glassworkers facilitated contact with workmates outside the job. In 1895 there was one cabaret for every fifty-five inhabitants of the city, and Ripagérien workers spent most of their leisure time in cafés.[35] Among glassworkers,

Figure 6. Nineteenth-century glassworkers' *quartier* in the southeast section of Rive-de-Gier.

Figure 7. The *bourse du travail* in the rue de la Barrière.

who·were particularly famous café customers, the situation in the 1890s was much as it had been in the 1850s when Guillaume Roquille described window-glassworkers:

> restaurateurs as well as café owners
> Welcome happily the men of this profession
> Ah! what well known customers are these window glassworkers!
> They do not amuse themselves by emptying a few liters [of wine]
> Or eating lamb; instead it is fowl and wild game,
> They demand the best of the dove-cot;
> At the café, they want beer after fine-quality coffee.

He continued, describing the bottleworkers:

> There are the cane handlers: The bottlemakers.
> Their customers' taste and mores are similar [to those of the window-glassworkers]
> Except that these latter [the bottlemakers] prefer good wine
> To beer, liqueurs, and other liquids . . . [36]

Many of the customs of the glass trade which existed in the immediate prewar period presumed a commonly shared leisure time. A new apprentice was expected to buy a drink, the *bienvenue*, for his new team members, and in return he was offered a puff on the *jacob*, the glassworkers' traditional clay pipe. M. Fournier describes a drinking place near the Richarme works: "In a narrow, obscure room, tiny tables were lined up. Every table was occupied by a young glassworker, cane changer, *porteur* or *gamin*."[37] As he walked past the café district on payday, the young protagonist of Fournier's novel could hear "a raucous voice which was singing. The child pricked his ears. He recognized the song of the glassworkers: *Je suis compagnon, Je suis sans ouvrage*."[38]

In the early 1890s, politics was a favorite pastime of artisanal workers, and there was a close connection between the leisure institutions of glassworkers and union politics; barroom conversations must often have turned to job questions. Most glassworkers' union meetings took place in cafés. In the early eighties, M. Negrel, a glassworker who ran a bar, was the leader of the Ripagérien socialist party. Another café owner, Pierre Blanc, played a prominent role in union and socialist politics in Rive-de-Gier; in 1907 he was elected head of the *bourse du travail*. Workers could talk confidentially in the café, for the police were not normally able to enter unobserved.[39] A fragmentary police report probably gives an accurate sense of café politics. In 1911 a police agent gave this account of an anarchist group meeting at the café Garod: "The group ordinarily meets at Garods. They meet there whenever they have the spare time, except in 'emergency' cases, there are no specified days or hours. It is rather a 'hang out' (*fréquentation*) for men with similar affinities, all others are excluded. Wives, mistresses, children, friends are, naturally, all admitted. They get together like a family group and leave together like a family group. . . . Discussions are not always courteous and the particular 'opinions' of these men vary every few days."[40]

The Formation of a Working-Class Coalition

Why did glassworkers, who moved in a very self-contained world of occupation-centered cafés and trade union politics, rush to the aid of metalworkers who did not belong to this world? To suppose that because artisanal workers possessed considerable collective strength they were bound to come to the aid of industrial workers would be naive. Everywhere in nineteenth-century industry technological change was enabling semiskilled workers to replace highly skilled artisans. Why did artisanal workers not delight in the discomfiture of a group of workers who might one day replace them?

Interoccupation solidarity was based on the common interests of artisanal and industrial workers. First, the growing threat of technological obsolescence caused the Ripagérien glassworkers to turn to politics and trade unionism to defend their privileged position. According to police reports, the glassworkers largely financed the socialist candidate for deputy in 1893 and played an important role in organizing a "new crusade" to enroll local workers in trade unions.[41] As they developed political demands, glassworkers began to realize the need to coalesce with metalworkers. At the same time the glassworkers' hardening commitment to trade unionism caused them to view with alarm the open anti-unionism of the metal barons. In 1893 *Le réveil des verriers*, the official newspaper of the glassworkers' national union, widely read by local glassworkers, carried an article on the subject of "worker solidarity" which observed, "Yesterday, it was the turn of the miners of Carmaux, tomorrow, it may be our turn. It is imperiously necessary that everyone understand, once and for all, that trade unions are sisters, as workers are brothers, that when one of them feels the oppressors' scourge, all are menaced with the same lot. . . ."[42]

The glassworkers aided the metalworkers in the 1893 strike because they believed they had genuine interests at stake in its successful outcome. Glassworkers' interests were shaped by the nature of the crisis which threatened them; mechanical innovations in the glassmaking process created overproduction and industrial concentration. Throughout most of the nineteenth century the relative scarcity of artisanal glassworker skills had ensured that glassworkers could move from one area of France to another and be reasonably sure of finding work. As Joan Scott has shown in *The Glassworkers of Carmaux*, the overproduction created by the new technology acted to fasten previously mobile glassworkers to a permanent settlement in a particular community. Thus glass-workers acquired a real interest in the conditions of local trade unions and politics.[43]

Rive-de-Gier was the first glassworkers' town to feel the effects of the new technology. In 1877 Petrus Richarme entirely rebuilt his works and introduced the Siemens continuous-fusion oven into France. Before the use of the Siemens oven, the young *appeloux* would run into the street at any hour of the day or night to announce that the glass was ready for working, and to call the workers to the factory. With the use of the Siemens oven, it was possible to plan on regularized, continuous glass production, spread over an entire twenty-four-hour period.[44] Glassworker delegations to the Paris exhibitions of 1878 and 1889 warned that the new technology of glassmaking, introduced into the Richarme works, seriously threatened the position of the artisanal glass-worker.[45] The new process tripled worker productivity, which resulted in a dramatic increase in the supply of glass bottles. The price of bottles began to drop, and small glassworks which could not afford to mechanize had to shut their doors.

The glassworkers of Rive-de-Gier were among the first to settle down and become permanent members of a community. Once Ripagérien glassworkers had been renowned for their mobility; glassworkers born in one department might move several times before settling down in a different department. By 1894 the vast majority of Ripagérien glassworkers in the Richarme works had been born in the department of the Loire or departments adjacent to it (see Table 15). The percentage of native-born glassworkers in the Richarme works at Rive-de-Gier was higher than at the Verrerie Sainte-Clotilde in Carmaux; this suggests that the glassworkers of Rive-de-Gier might have settled down earlier than those of Carmaux. If so, it is partly explained by the fact that the Ripagérien glassworks were mechanized seven years before those of Carmaux.[46] The uneven economic development of Ripagérien glassmaking was another contributing factor. In the early seventies Rive-de-Gier had been the capital of French glassmaking; by the early nineties the rise of the coalfields in the Nord and Pas-de-Calais and the decline of Stéphanois coal caused the most rapid economic development in glassmaking to occur in the Nord. As a

Table 15

Workers in the Richarme Glassworks by Department of Birth, 1894

	Loire	Adjacent Departments	France	Foreign	Uniden-tified
Souffleurs (N = 164)	64.2%	21.9%	11.6%	0	2.4%
Grand Garçons (N = 173)	72.3	20.8	1.7	1.2	4.0
Gamins (N = 168)	69.0	10.7	5.4	9.5	5.4
Total Population, 1891	74.4	15.3	8.3	2.0	0

consequence, Rive-de-Gier no longer served as a pole of attraction for migrating glassworkers.

Like the glassworkers of Carmaux, the glassworkers of Rive-de-Gier turned to trade unionism to defend their interests. Glassworkers hoped to regulate glass production through their union and made stringent requirements for admission to the trade. The 1891 strike in Rive-de-Gier had partially achieved this goal. During the strike workers had established committees which had considerable power within the factory. A *Le temps* article by Tuiebault-Sisson on the metal strike noted:

> The greater part [of the glass employers] have been forced to accept union commissions in their factory, commissions charged with making rules . . . about the interior administration of the factory. In the question of wages the commission always intervenes to discuss directly with the employers. . . . It polices the factory, inflicts fines, by itself or upon the complaint of an employer and, ultimately, decides whether a worker should be fired. It assigns a position to each worker and, at will, increases or limits his daily production.[47]

By 1891 the union had everywhere succeeded in establishing factory committees which set up shop rules and settled wage disputes. In 1892 *Le réveil des verriers* published an article by a Ripagérien glassworkers' leader, Pierre Vinay, entitled "The Limitation of Production." Vinay argued that "the regulation of production is certainly the essential question that interests us most."[48]

The establishment of factory committees and the regulation of production naturally aroused the opposition of the glass employers. From the moment of the committees' appearance in 1891 until their disappearance in the wake of the disastrous strike of 1894, the activity of these shop floor organizations was a source of growing tension. Three large strikes of glassworkers (two in 1891 and one in 1893) centered around the committees' actions. Each incident increased the employers' antagonism to these organizations and strengthened the glassworkers' determination to defend them. It was apparent to everyone that the glass employers had not accepted the principle of shop floor representation and that they would act to abolish it at the first opportunity. The bitterness of employer opposition is best demonstrated by the willingness of the largest glass employer in town to shut down his plant for a full 317 days in 1894 in an ultimately successful attempt to destroy these representative organizations. Meanwhile, the employers' hostility constantly reminded the glassworkers of their precarious position and encouraged the workers to search for allies in the coming struggle.

Because of the growing importance of the trade union in the glassworkers' lives and the union's insecure position, glassworkers became interested in the fate of all local unions. The metalworkers' demand for shop floor representation won glassworkers' sympathy. The attempt of the metal employers to destroy the metalworkers' union concerned workers in glass because they feared it would intimidate all local workers and create an atmosphere hostile to trade unionism. A Ripagérien glassworker, appealing to his union's national federation for aid to the metalworkers, described glassworker sentiments this way:

". . . [the metalworkers'] . . . cause is so just that it is necessary that they triumph at any price, otherwise their defeat would be a ten year set back for the locality and, perhaps, lead to the complete disorganization of all the local trade unions. The *chambre syndicale des verriers en bouteilles* certainly thinks so. . . ."[49]

Another reason that glassworkers supported the metalworkers is because the metalworkers represented a pivotal political constituency which could be an important source of support in local elections. Interest in political campaigns on the part of the glassworker leadership marked a real break with tradition. Although a few workers in glass had been politically active in Rive-de-Gier for decades, the great majority of them only began to enter local politics when they began to expect to spend most of their lives there.

Moreover, trade union activity in Rive-de-Gier inevitably brought workers into conflict with the existing local political parties, which were dominated by employers. Indeed, strike actions between 1890 and 1893 led to a whole series of confrontations beween the glassworkers' union and elected republican politicians. During the glassworkers' strike of 1891 M. Brunon, mayor of the city and a metal employer, denied the union permission to hold a mass meeting in the municipal concert hall. In 1891 the republican deputy and glass employer, M. Richarme, had gone into court to have striking workers thrown out of his company-owned tenements. During their strikes the glassworkers felt that they had been unfairly treated by the local *juge de paix* and the prefect. And they were probably right, for in his memoirs the prefect noted the inability of the national government to give clear guidelines for dealing with local strikes, adding that "I was forced to seek advice elsewhere. I found more useful support from Monsieur Montgolfier, the steel master."[50]

Glassworker union leaders and many of their constituents believed that an unsympathetic local political structure was responsible for their poor treatment, and many metalworkers began to share their convictions. In 1892 the city council of Rive-de-Gier scornfully rejected the local trade unions' request for a municipal subsidy to establish a *bourse du travail*. This enraged many workers, and the *commissariat spécial* reported to the prefect:

> . . . the governmental party [in Rive-de-Gier, the liberal republicans] does not even have the ability of the Catholics to dam up the workers' movement for its own purposes. . . .
> . . . they should hasten to create a *bourse* if they do not want to suffer a truly crushing defeat in the next elections. The metalworkers still preserve a little confidence in the governmental party and if they wish to maintain this they should cede a little to their [the metalworkers'] platonic views of worker unanimity. . . .[51]

By 1893 the glassworkers' union had begun to develop its own political demands; Ripagérien glassworker leaders specifically demanded that the existing child labor laws be strengthened and enforced. Child labor was important in glassmaking, where two members of the work team, the *porteur* and the *gamin*, were usually under eighteen. Control of admission into the trade was a key aspect of the glassworkers' program for regulating production. Indeed, while an important minority in the national glassworkers' federation wanted to allow no more than one son of a glassworker's family to enter the trade, the majority agreed that no child under twelve should be allowed in the factory. So the glassworkers' union actively fought for the enforcement of the legal prohibition on child labor before twelve years of age.[52]

Glassworkers' union leaders charged that the existing government inspectors winked at irregularities and were encouraged to do so by local politicians. The most serious violators of the child labor laws in Rive-de-Gier were Italians. While Italians were seldom admitted into the higher ranks of the skill hierarchy, their presence in large numbers as *porteurs* and, less frequently, as *gamins* was considered a threat to the regulation of the trade. By 1894 the majority of *porteurs* were young Piedmontese. The glassworkers charged that most of them were "rented" children, children rented from their parents by a *padrone* who brought them in gangs to work in France. Most of these children were very young or they would have been able to find more remunerative work elsewhere. It was easy for the *padrone* who brought children in from a foreign country to obtain forged birth certificates, although this was not always necessary. According to the glassworkers' union leaders, the most common form of evasion was for the employers to simply evacuate underage children while the inspectors "politely" waited in their offices. The glassworkers demanded that an officially recognized committee of workers be set up which would investigate alleged violations.[53]

Thus the outbreak of the metalworkers' strike in 1893 only a few months before the departmental elections provided the leaders of the glassworkers' union with an excellent opportunity to accomplish some of their political goals. Glassworker and metalworker trade union leaders from Rive-de-Gier and miners' leaders from nearby Grand-Croix were, after protracted negotiations, able to agree on a candidate: Edmund Charpentier, a moderate socialist lawyer from Limoges. In the 1893 election the metalworkers and the glassworkers faced a common enemy; the announced liberal republican candidate was the large metal employer, M. Brunon.[54]

Much of the tone of the emerging Ripagérien socialist movement was set by the terms of local political debate. In the 1860s, in opposition to the policies of Louis Napoleon, the metal barons of the Stéphanois region had identified themselves with the republican opposition. Throughout the seventies the mass of metalworkers remained loyal to the republican programs enunciated by their employers. The moderate socialism that developed in Rive-de-Gier under the aegis of the glassworkers' union emphasized commitment to republican ideals while attempting to expose the undemocratic social policies of the republican industrialists. During the 1893 strike bitter editorials appeared in the socialist press denouncing the republican candidate: "If this pseudo-republican M. Brunon, put his action in accord with his electoral promises and had, as he would have us believe, recognized the well-founded demands of the workers, then it follows that his factory instead of being shut down like those of his reactionary colleagues, would now be in full production."[55] The strike strengthened the ties between glassworkers and metalworkers, and both unions worked together to secure Charpentier's election in September, 1893. He was the first socialist deputy elected from the district and was sworn in just in time to support the Ripagérien glassworkers in the climactic strike which began in March, 1894.

The 1894 strike demonstrated that the glassworkers had been prudent to prepare themselves for a fight. Unfortunately, all their maneuvering and coalition-building were of no avail; even the best-organized working-class group was vulnerable to fierce and determined employer assault. The glassworkers' strike of 1894 was an impressive example of skilled worker solidarity in adversity, for even after ten months the desperate glassworkers remained united. Their strike was defeated not by internal collapse but by the importation of strike breakers from outside the country. In all of France, despite the unemployment created by mechanization, qualified workers could not be found to take the glassworkers' jobs. Ultimately the employer turned to the numerous unemployed

German glassworkers, who had no fraternal contact with their French counterparts. In the face of increasing numbers of foreign workers, and continued employer intransigence, the glassworkers' union assembled its members one last time and voted in a disciplined manner to return to work.[56] Never again would the strike activity of Ripagérien glassworkers attain the size or duration of the early nineties.

Work Structure and Strike Militancy: The Metalworkers

The splendid unity of the glassworkers in the 1894 strike illustrates the strong sense of occupational identity inspired by an artisanal work structure. In contrast, the organization of work in heavy metal did not spur the formation of the informal work groups which crystallized collective consciousness. Work structure in the metal industry explains why the support of artisanal glassworkers was so crucial to the mobilization of industrial metalworkers.

The disappearance of artisanal forms of work organization in metalworking had undermined the social basis for a strong and inclusive trade unionism. In 1891 there were only a handful of artisanal metalworkers to be found at work in Rive-de-Gier; the great majority of Ripagérien metalworkers performed minute and monotonous tasks. The shift from artisanal to industrial work in local metalworking had taken place largely unnoticed in the years between 1860 and 1875, when the repressive regimes of Louis Napoleon and President MacMahon had made worker protest difficult. The transition to industrial work had meant a decline in workers' wages and the destruction of the skilled work team; the net effect of this change was to discourage strong trade union organization.

Rive-de-Gier had once possessed a large artisanal metalworker community. In the early seventies when Louis Reybaud visited Rive-de-Gier, both artisanal and industrial metalworking existed side by side; the technical transformation of large-scale forging was not then complete. As mentioned in Chapter Three, Reybaud was struck particularly by the "task system" of labor contracting in the Ripagérien mills. Under the "task system" the artisanal metalworker was part worker, part contractor. The skilled forger negotiated each job with the employer, and, once a price was agreed upon, the worker brought in the skilled men to help him carry it out. Although the system was already in decline when Reybaud observed it in the seventies, some skilled forgers still found steady employment at task work, and a very few, highly skilled metalworkers earned as much as skilled glassworkers.[57] The worker-poet Guillaume Roquille, a tinsmith, was a product of this artisanal milieu. Roquille composed many of his poems in cafés, and his poems celebrate the drinking customs and barroom repartee of the skilled male metal worker.[58] But by 1890 the skilled metal artisan had practically vanished from the local scene.

By 1893 Rive-de-Gier had become the main Stéphanois center for forging steel, and most Ripagérien metalworkers were involved in some way in the forging process, which was one of the most rapidly changing branches of metalworking. In the first part of the nineteenth century an integrated steel industry had begun to develop in Rive-de-Gier. This changed in 1867, when the Marrel brothers expanded their works by building a huge forging plant on the edge of town; by 1893 the Marrel plants employed 42.1 percent of the metal workforce. The evolution of the Association des forges et aciéries de la marine reinforced this trend. In 1874 this company moved its headquarters from Rive-de-Gier to Saint-Chamond, where it constructed its Bessemer converters. Only its forging operations continued in Rive-de-Gier. The smaller producers followed the lead of the larger in converting to forging.[59]

During this period the press and the steam hammer were making constant inroads in the forging trade. In 1893 a student of the metal strike, Tuiebault-Sisson, noted:

> Industrial progress has nearly completely substituted mechanized work for hand work in forging. The term "forger" remains; the thing has disappeared. What relation can be seen between the individual who maneuvers a steam hammer and the robust, hardy fellow who hammered the red hot ingot on the anvil with such force? In order to accomplish this task it was necessary to be dextrous, to have some professional training, to possess a strength which was not accumulated in a day; a long apprenticeship was necessary and the labor was exhausting. In order to maneuver a steam hammer, and produce, in infinitely less time, enormous pieces of steel, what is necessary? An

apprenticeship of eight days, and a half a dozen unskilled workers led by a good foreman.[60]

By 1893 Ripagérien metalworkers were predominantiy semi-skilled and were paid accordingly. There were a few skilled workers, puddlers and foundrymen, who were paid high wages, but most workers received between 4 and 6 francs a day. In 1892 the most common single worker was the "forger," who received 4.5 francs a day. There was also a large number of unskilled workers who received only 3.0 francs a day.[61]

And the relatively low wages of local metalworkers were not supplemented by opportunities for family employment; in most cases, the wages of the adult male metalworker were the sole income of metalworking families. There were sixty-four families with metalworker heads of households in our 1891 family sample of the Ripagérien population. Of these families, 67.2 percent depended exclusively on the wages of the head of the household for their total income, while only 17.8 percent of the families with metalworker heads had another member employed in the metal trade. Only a few families (7.8 percent) had members, usually children, who were able to find employment in the glassworks. Very few married women worked; 82.8 percent of metal households had female members who are identified only as "housekeepers."[62]

One reason that Ripagérien metalworkers were unable to organize as effectively as glassworkers was their lower wages; it was hard for metalworkers to support ongoing organization and harder still to use their paltry savings to sustain a strike. Another reason for their inadequate organization was the weakness of the metal work group. Skilled and unskilled metal workers had little chance to meet one another on the job, and the close-knit work group of the glassworkers was altogether absent. In the medium-sized Marrel plant in Rive-de-Gier (see Figure 8), each group occupied its own separate section of the main factory building. The large ten- and twenty-five-ton steam hammers were located in the large forging shop; smaller steam hammers and hand forging went on in the large southern extension of this shop. The more skilled work was carried on in the corners of the building where the fitting shop and the turners' workshop for cannons and bands were located.

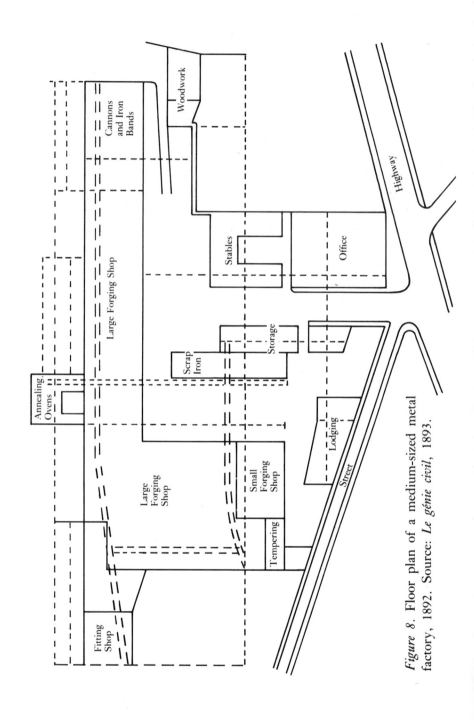

Figure 8. Floor plan of a medium-sized metal factory, 1892. Source: *Le génie civil*, 1893.

Figure 9. A large metal plant: Marrel Frères, c. 1910.

In the larger Marrel plant on the outskirts of Rive-de-Gier, each category of metalworker was employed in a separate building (see Figure 9). The big building in the foreground was the forging center. Medium-sized steam hammers were located in the front and gigantic fifty- and hundred-ton hammers were in the rear of the building. The more skilled workers were in the rear buildings; adjusters and turners worked in the right and left background buildings, puddlers and foundrymen in the center background complex of buildings.[63]

Forging was the branch of heavy metalwork which particularly inhibited on-the-job contacts among workers. The noise of the large hammers was absolutely deafening. In the early nineties the large steam hammer dominated heavy forging, the size of the hammers grew every year, and the Marrel plant possessed some of the largest steam hammers in France; their sounds could be heard all over Rive-de-Gier and the whole factory shook when the large hammers were in use. The reverberation of hese hammers often damaged delicate machinery. It was not until the press replaced the large hammer after 1900 that workers could begin to hear one another in the large forging workshop. The same principle applied to small forging, which was done by individual workers distributed along a row of small forging machines.[64]

Unlike glassworkers, metalworkers were not concentrated in distinct residential neighborhoods; they were scattered all over the city. Insofar as they participated in neighborhood social life, they were thrown into contact with other classes and occupational groups. A standard measure of segregation, the index of dissimilarity, was more than four times higher for glassworkers than for metalworkers. In 1891 there was no statistically significant difference between metalworkers' residential patterns and those of the larger population (see Table 16). Workers in metal lived in the predominantly glassworkers' section and in the small shopkeepers' and miners' sections.[65]

The financial weakness of the metalworkers and their lack of a cohesive work group clearly affected the outcome of the 1893 metal strike. Despite the considerable financial support given by the glassworkers, the metalworkers were still financially weak. The total sum raised by the striking metalworkers in 1893 was less than a quarter of that raised by the striking glassworkers in 1894. Given their lower salaries and weak organization, the two-month strike was as totally exhausting for the metalworkers as was the 317-day strike for the glassworkers.

The absence of informal factory work groups and residential

Table 16

Residential Patterns in Rive-de-Gier, 1891
Individual Sample of Metalworkers and Nonmetalworkers

Rive-de-Gier	Metalworkers		Nonmetalworkers	
	Number	Percent	Number	Percent
Western Section	14	13.7	164	12.1
Northern Section	13	12.7	193	14.2
North-Central Section	10	9.8	212	15.6
Eastern Section	14	13.7	193	14.2
South-Central Section	20	19.6	197	14.5
Southwestern Section	13	12.7	172	12.7
Countryside	15	14.7	144	10.6
Unidentified	3	2.9	73	5.4
N	102		1,358	

Chi-square = 5.32, p < .70
Index of Dissimilarity = 10.8

community contributed to disunity among metalworkers. Although the strike had begun with almost universal support, the consensus soon began to break down. While the majority of metalworkers demanded official recognition for their union organization, an important minority began to seek a compromise and to break away from the metal union. These dissenting workers, many of whom had never joined the union in the first place, wished to accept the wage increases offered by the employers and refused to continue on strike to defend the existence of the union. In part, these differences originated in disagreements about strategy and, in part, they were due to the machinations of the employers, but underlying these factors was the lack of cohesion of the metal workforce, which prevented the creation of a unified work group capable of enforcing collective decisions. In any case, the metalworkers' strike of 1893 ended with an important minority of the workers returning to work against the wishes of the union leadership.[66] The effects of industrial and artisanal work structure on worker militancy are revealed most clearly in the telling contrast between the discordant industrial metalworkers in 1893 and the solidary glassworkers in 1894.

The defeats of 1893 and 1894 were serious but not fatal for the Ripagérien trade union movement. In 1906 glassworker unionism began to revive, particularly among the window-glassworkers, and several strikes broke out. Yet neither the strike movement nor union organization ever reached the heights of the earlier period (see Graph 8). The artisanal windowworkers were a much smaller group than the artisanal bottleworkers, and windowworker strikes had much less influence on local strike activity and political life. However, in the strikes of 1910 and 1911 window-glassworkers resisted technological change just as bitterly as the bottleworkers had in 1894.[67]

The roots of glassworker solidarity in Rive-de-Gier are to be found in workers' attempts to defend their skill group and their trade union. Artisanal glassworkers in Rive-de-Gier were much better able to defend their interests than industrial metalworkers. In cases where glassworkers' and metalworkers' interests coincided, glassworkers were powerful allies.

The case of Rive-de-Gier shows that a mixture of artisanal and

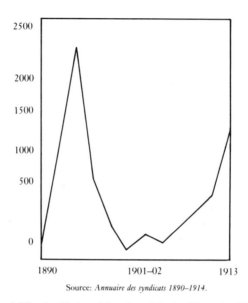

Source: *Annuaire des syndicats 1890–1914.*

Graph 8. Total Trade Union Membership in Rive-de-Gier, 1890–1913.

industrial workers could lead to a powerful explosion. But the precise role of artisans and industrial workers in the mass strike process still needs clarification. In a mixed artisanal-industrial town artisans provided working-class leadership, but the reasons for their authority need to be better understood. Perhaps the more politically experienced Ripagérien artisans were only preaching to the already converted. In the absence of articulate artisanal spokesmen, industrial workers might have evolved their own leadership which could have prepared them to carry out a sustained struggle in spite of their poverty and disorganization. Strike actions in Rive-de-Gier bear the mark of artisanal influence and blur our perceptions of industrial workers. If industrial workers were thrown on their own resources, how would these workers have shaped strike actions? What were the characteristics of industrial worker organization and social life? In order to answer these questions, it will be necessary to turn to the predominantly industrial town, Saint-Chamond.

NOTES

1. Gonon, *Histoire de la chanson stéphanoise*, p. 461.
2. For information on the occupational structure of Rive-de-Gier in 1891, see

ADL 54/M/18; for detailed breakdowns of the metal labor force in 1893, see ADL 92/M/45; and for detailed breakdowns of the glass labor force, see ADL 92/M/52.

3. The major source of information on Ripagérien strikes was the official government publication from the Office du travail, *Statistique des grèves* (Paris: Imprimerie nationale, 1890–1914) and the series 92/M—Grèves in ADL. There were only two strikes listed in the departmental archives not listed in the government publication: a strike of glassworkers in 1890 (AN F/12 4667) and another strike of glassworkers in 1907 (ADL 92/M/143). A useful summary of local glassworker strike activity can be found in L.-J. Gras, *Histoire des eaux minérales du Forez, suivie de notes historiques sur l'industrie de la verrerie en Forez et en Jarez* (Saint-Etienne: Théolier, 1923).

Local strike activity did not suddenly begin in 1890; there was a small strike of metalworkers in Rive-de-Gier in 1882 (ADL 92/M/18 and AN F/12 4685) and a number of glass strikes in Rive-de-Gier in 1847 and 1852 (AN BB/18 1530/A24469 and AN BB/18 1450n 3485). Most of the nineteenth-century Stéphanois miners' strikes had a Ripagérien contingent; see Gras, *Histoire économique générale des mines de la Loire*, and Durousset, "La vie ouvrière," pp. 258–59. On the history of Ripagérien mining in the first half of the nineteenth century, see A. Meugy, *Histoire des mines de Rive-de-Gier* (Paris: Edouard Cornely, 1847).

4. Jean Jaurès, "La grève de Rive-de-Gier," *Discours parlementaires*, 1 (Paris: Edouard Cornely, 1904), 390–402.

5. Shorter and Tilly, *Strikes in France*, pp. 105–7.

6. Georges Weill, *Histoire du mouvement social en France 1852–1910* (Paris: Felix Alcan, 1911), pp. 285–87.

7. Shorter and Tilly, *Strikes in France*, pp. 224–27.

8. Several reports of this meeting are in ADL 92/M/44.

9. ADL 92/M/44–47.

10. Notice of arrests was published in *Le stéphanois*.

11. A fairly complete list of contributors to the metalworkers' strike fund was published every day or so in *Le stéphanois* between Jan. 11 and Mar. 23, 1893.

12. According to Pierre Vinay, speaking at the second glassworkers' national convention held in Lyon, *Fédération des verriers de France, Congrés national, Lyon, 1–6 Septembre 1891* (Lyon: Coffer Fabier, 1892), p. 36.

13. *Le temps*, Feb. 28, 1893; *commissariat spécial*, July 10, 1894, in ADL 92/M/54.

14. On May Day, 1893, in Rive-de-Gier, see the report of the police commissioner in ADL 10/M/89.

15. On the state of the metalworkers' organization in 1894, see ADL 93/M/66.

16. An excellent summary of the metal strike can be found in Office du travail, *Statistique des grèves*, 1893, pp. 337–54.

17. On the structure of Stéphanois glassmaking, see ADL 92/M/52. On the differences between the various types of glassmaking, see Georges Bontemps, *Guide du verrier* (Paris: Libraire du dictionnaire des arts et manufactures, 1868), p. 178, and Warren C. Scoville, *Revolution in Glassmaking* (Cambridge, Mass.: Harvard University Press, 1948), pp. 13–29.

Four very helpful descriptions of French glass technology between 1870 and 1894 are: L. Appert and J. Henrivaux, *La verrerie depuis vingt ans* (Paris: E. Bernard, 1894); Eugène Peligot, *Le verre, son histoire, sa fabrication* (Paris: G. Masson, 1877); Pierre Pelletier, *Les verriers dans le Lyonnais et le Forez* (Paris: by the author, 1887); and A. Sauzay, *La verrerie depuis le temps les plus reculés jusqu' à nos jours* (Paris: Libraire Hachette, 1884).

18. Information on Ripagérien glassworkers' unions can be found in Office du travail, *Annuaire des syndicats* (Paris: Imprimerie nationale, 1890–1914).

19. According to Gras, the president of the chamber of commerce, skilled glassworkers received between 250 and 300 francs per month in 1891 in addition to their rent; see Gras, *Histoire des eaux minérales*, p. 218. A much lower figure is given in two separate prefectoral reports, ADL 92/M/52 and ADL 10/M/102, which estimate between 8.50 and 9.00 francs, per day. The government reports are more consistent with national data on glassworkers' wages as presented in Scott, *Glassworkers of Carmaux*, and are the basis for the present calculations.

On Ripagérien glassworkers' wages in the first half of the nineteenth century, see Armand Audiganne, *Les populations ouvrières et les industries de la France dans le mouvement social du XIXe siècle* (Paris: Capelle Libraire, 1854), 1, 314–15. On the origins of French glassmaking, see F. G. Dreyfus, "L'Industrie de la verrerie en Bas-Languedoc de Colbert à la révolution industrielle du XIXe siècle," *Annales du Midi* 63, (Apr., 1951), 43–70, and Warren C. Scoville, *Capitalism and French Glassmaking, 1640–1789* (Berkeley: University of California Press, 1950). A related study of some interest is Robert H. McNulty, "Common Beverage Bottles; Their Production, Use and Forms in Seventeenth and Eighteenth Century Netherlands," *Journal of Glass Studies* 13 (1971), 91–119, and 14 (1972), 141–48.

20. On the *four mort* and yearly glassworker employment in Rive-de-Gier, see AN F/7 12766. On the health of glassworkers, see Léon and Maurice Bonneff, "Les travailleurs du feu," in *La vie tragique des travailleurs* (Paris: Marcel Rivière, 1914), pp. 48–90, and Dr. Defferney, *Des souffleurs de verre, hygiène, maladies et accidents*, vol. 5 of *Mémoires couronnés et autres mémoires publiées par l'académie royale de medicine de Belgique* (Brussels: Henri Manceaux, 18803.

21. Manuscript census, Rive-de-Gier, 1891, ADL 49/M/314. These figures are the result of a 10 percent sample of all Ripagérien households; some households could not be assigned a definite occupation. Everyone in the 1891 census was asked to give his occupation, but dozens of workers in the sample simply responded "manoeuvre," i.e. "manual laborer," an occupational designation common to both glass and metal industies. "Manoeuvres" were not counted as belonging to either occupation.

22. Guillaume Roquille, "Rive-de-Gier," *Poèmes français et patois* (Saint-Etienne: Imprimerie de la Loire républicaine, 1883), p. 253.

23. Several mid-nineteenth-century authors quote this saying: Audiganne, *Les populations ouvrières*, 1, 321–22; Roquille, *Poèmes français*, p. 239; and Reybaud, *Le fer et la houille*. Between 1854 and 1888 miners' daily wages increased from 3.43 francs a day to 4.62 francs, both about half the glassworkers' contemporary wages; see Gras, *Histoire économique générale des mines de la Loire*, p. 793.

24. Louise Tilly, presentation to the Seminar in Comparative History, University of Michigan, Sept., 1975.

25. A description of work in the Ripagérien glassworks in the early nineties can be found in ADL 92/M/52 and in Léon de Seilhac, *Une enquête sociale: La grève de Carmaux et la verrerie d'Albi* (Paris: Perrin, 1897), pp. 29–31.

26. E. Farmer, "A Comparison of Different Shift Systems in the Glass Trade," Industrial Fatigue Research Board, Report no. 24, Medical Research Council, 1924.

27. William Foote Whyte, "Teams of Artisans," in *Men at Work* (Homewood, Ill.: Dorsey Press, 1961), p. 169.

28. On the 1892 strike, see ADL 92/M/43.

29. Ardouin-Dumazet, *Voyage en France*, pp. 8–9.

30. On emergencies in Rive-de-Gier, see Audiganne, *Les populations ouvrières*, 1, 315. The length of time spent in the Richarme works is recorded in ADL 92/M/53.

31. M. Fournier, *Le roman d'un petit verrier* (Paris: Libraire Gedalge, 1925), p. 23. On the "dangers" of worker sociability in company-sponsored tenements, see M. Villermé, *Les cités ouvrières* (Paris: J. B. Ballière, 1850), p. 8.

32. When all the striking workers were expelled from the company tenements during the 1894 strike, only a minority of workers were affected; see *Le réveil des verriers*, Aug. 26, Sept. 7, 1894.

33. Based on manuscript census, Rive-de-Gier, 1891, ADL 49/M/314, an 11 percent individual sample of the population. Individual and family samples produce almost exactly the same geographic distribution by occupation. "Manoeuvres," who could be either glassworkers or metalworkers, were omitted.

Sectors were selected in order to create physically contiguous units of approximately the same population size. The street was the basic building block of the sector. Owing to the technique of the French census, it is not possible to divide the streets themselves, and this creates problems. For example, the rue de la Barrière was the historic center of the glassworkers' *quartier* in the eastern section, yet it was separated from the rest of the sector by the rue du Lyon; hence it is included in a different sector from the *quartier*. If it were possible to divide streets, the results would almost certainly show a greater concentration of glassworkers than the already large one indicated in our samples.

The map of Rive-de-Gier, for 1887, is from *Atlas des cartes cantonales du département de la Loire* (Saint-Etienne: Service vicinal, 1887). It was possible to establish the sites of the early nineteenth-century glassworks using the work of Pelletier, *Les verriers dans le Lyonnais*, and the plans for glassworks in ADL 40/M/141. The location of industry in 1894 was established using the fine map contained in the study by C. Chomienne, *Histoire de la ville de Rive-de-Gier, du canton, et de ses principales industries* (Saint-Etienne: no publisher, 1912).

34. Scott, *Glassworkers of Carmaux*, pp. 50–51.

35. Gras, *Histoire du commerce locale*, cites a study by M. Merlin on cabarets in the Stéphanois valley. On the need of glassworkers for alcohol, see Bontemps, *Guide du verrier*, p. 181.

36. Roquille, *Poèmes français*, pp. 253–56.

37. Fournier, *Le roman d'un petit verrier*, p. 88.

38. *Ibid.*, p. 71.

39. On M. Negrel, see ADL 10/M/79; on Pierre Blanc, see ADL 92/M/66.

40. On Ripagérien anarchism, see ADL 19/M/26 and ADL 19/M/19. The Ripagérien anarchists were a very mixed group, about one-third glassworkers, one-third metalworkers, one-third mixed miners, and one café owner. Several of the metalworkers were "manoeuvres." It is difficult to believe that this reflected the composition of most political milieus. First, the anarchists were not influential in Rive-de-Gier. Second, it is not clear that many of the "manoeuvres" were really unskilled workers. Anarchists in these years of repression were often harassed by the police and moved from one town to another picking up jobs as they went. All the unskilled workers listed as anarchists had only spent a brief time in Rive-de-Gier.

41. Both police reports are found in ADL 92/M/66.

42. *Le réveil des verriers*, Feb. 1, 1893. The newspaper was published in nearby Lyon and received a large part of its financial support from the Ripagérien local. Many articles written by Ripagérien glassworkers appear in the newspaper.

43. Scott, *Glassworkers of Carmaux*.

On the pace of technological change in the nineteenth and early twentieth centuries, there are two fine books: J. Shield Nicholson, *The Effects of Machinery on Wages* (London: Swan and Sonnenschein, 1878), and George E. Barnett, *Chapters on Machinery and Wages* (New York: Arcturus Press, 1926). On the effect of the different types of techniques on American worker productivity, see "Productivity of Labor in the Glass Industry," *Bulletin of the United States Bureau of Labor Statistics*, no. 441 (July, 1927), pp. 59–87.

44. On the Richarme works, see Seilhac, *Une enquête sociale*, pp. 29–31; on the old system, see Deffernez, *Des souffleurs de verre*, p. 14.

45. Eduard Didron and Clémandot, *Rapport sur les cristaux, la verrerie et les vitraux* (Paris: Imprimerie nationale, 1880), pp. 39–40; Louis Courtot and Eugene Rey, *Rapport des délégués ouvriers de la chambre syndicale des verriers réunis de Lyon* (Lyon: Association typographique, 1890), pp. 21–22.

46. Scott, *Glassworkers of Carmaux*, p. 204; ADL 92/M/53.

47. *Le temps*, Feb. 28, 1893.

48. *Le réveil des verriers*, Nov. 10, 1892.

The struggle of artisanal workers to regulate their trade is an old one which is just as important in artisanal trades today as yesterday. Caplow emphasizes the self-interest involved in job control, but Stinchcombe points out that craft control has its benefits for the whole industry and the public. See Theodore Caplow, *The Sociology of Work* (Minneapolis: University of Minnesota Press, 1954), pp. 166–68, and Arthur L. Stinchcombe, "Bureaucratic and Craft Administration: A Comparative Study," *Administrative Science Quarterly* 4 (Sept., 1959), 168–87.

49. *Le réveil des verriers*, Jan. 11, 1893.

50. On the behavior of Brunon and Richarme in the 1891 strike, see ADL 92/M/41. Louis Lepine, prefect of the Loire between 1890 and 1894, described his reliance on the advice of Montgolfier in his memoirs, *Mes souvenirs* (Paris: Pagot, 1929), p. 88.

51. ADL 92/M/66.

52. On the demands of the Ripagérien glassworkers, see Fédération des verriers de France, *Congrès national . . . 1891*, pp. 56–58, and Scott, *Glassworkers of Carmaux*, pp. 100–105.

53. On the attitude of glassworkers toward the *louers d'enfants*, see ADL 92/M/50. Fournier describes these children in *Le roman d'un petit verrier*, p. 82. This was a national problem; see Bonneff, *La vie tragique*, pp. 81–89, and *Fédération française des travailleurs du verre, Congrès national, Blancy-sur-Bresle, 8–11 septembre, 1904* (Paris: Delcleve Valenciennes, 1905). Rive-de-Gier was the only town in the Stéphanois valley with a sizable foreign population in the years before World War I, according to Jean-Charles Bonnet, "Les travailleurs étrangers dans la Loire sous la troisième république," *Cahiers d'histoire* 16, no. 1 (1971), 67–80.

54. On metalworkers' financial support, see ADL 93/M/66; on the negotiations, see ADL 10/M/101.

55. *Le stéphanois*, Jan. 20, 1893.

56. For a good summary history of the 1894 strike, see Office du travail, *Statistique des grèves, 1894*, pp. 236–45. Rich material on the strike can be found in ADL 92/M/52–60.

57. Reybaud, *Le fer et la houille*, pp. 144–47, is a rich source for information on mid-century Ripagérien metalworking. On the change in the organization of work in American heavy metalworking, see Katherine Stone, "The Origin of Job Structures in the Steel Industry," *Radical America* 7, no. 6 (1973), 19–61.

58. Roquille belongs to the category of worker-poets who flourished in the forties and fifties. For a discussion of this type, see Maurice Agulhon, *Une ville ouvrière au temps du socialisme utopique: Toulon 1815–1851* (Paris: Mouton, 1970), pp. 226–42. On Roquille, see M. Fournier, *Guillaume Roquille, poète ripagérien* (Saint-Etienne: Imprimerie de la Loire républicaine, n.d.).

59. Detailed histories of individual Ripagérien industries can be found in Chomienne, *Histoire de la ville de Rive-de-Gier*.

60. *Le temps*, Feb. 25, 1893.

61. Office du travail, *Statistique des grèves, 1893*.

62. Family sample, Rive-de-Gier, 1891.

63. The floor plan and a detailed description of the Marrel brothers' factories are contained in Marrel Frères, *Usines de Rive-de-Gier* (Paris: Le génie civil, 1893). On the effect of the layout of work on the formation of informal work group friendships, see Charles R. Walker and Robert H. Guest, *The Man on the Assembly Line* (Cambridge, Mass.: Harvard University Press, 1952).

64. Chomienne, *Histoire de la ville de Rive-de-Gier*, pp. 305–6; Urbain Le Verrier, *La métallurgie en France* (Paris: J. B. Ballière, 1894), p. 126; Reybaud, *Le fer et la houille* pp. 139–41.

65. Individual sample, Rive-de-Gier, 1891.

66. On the 1893 strike, see Office du travail, *Statistique des grèves, 1893*.

67 Information on these strikes can be found in ADL 92/M/142 and 92/M/168.

CHAPTER FIVE

Artisans and Industrial Workers in Saint-Chamond, 1871–1914

Saint-Chamond, that one imagines
To be a center for *rentiers*
Goes to bed to the noise of a factory
And wakes up to the song of the looms.[1]

From a song written by
a republican workingman

Strike actions in Saint-Chamond, the second city in the study, provide a clear contrast with those in Rive-de-Gier. In Saint-Chamond no important coalitions were formed between artisanal and industrial workers, and the industrial working class was relatively quiescent. Although the working class of Saint-Chamond was composed overwhelmingly of industrial workers, they did not play a correspondingly important role in strike actions. In 1895 an appeal made by local metal unionists to their workmates, most of whom were industrial workers, indicates the lack of worker militancy:

> . . . it is to our comrades that we launch this appeal, to those who, unconscious or frightened, back away, ceaselessly, before the plots of the reactionaries, bowing their heads with shameful apathy, heads which should radiate energy and indomitable hope.
>
> It is time to react, it is time to show ourselves worthy.
>
> Why should we stay inactive? Our capitalist adversaries, far from making concessions, are, on the contrary, more rapacious than ever, they menace the tranquility of our family by their depredations on our wages. Why do we not unite when the cohesion of the impoverished would be so profitable to all the oppressed?[2]

The Dilemma of Working-Class Quiescence

Trade unionism was weak among Saint-Chamonnais industrial workers. After the defeat of a coalition of dyers and braiders in

1878, no trade union was ever re-established among the unskilled workers making braided fabrics, who in 1891 composed 48.1 percent of the total workforce. The situation was only a little better in metalworking, where union membership fluctuated but seldom exceeded a small fraction of the 36.3 percent of the workforce in metal.[3] In 1911 a leader of the Saint-Chamonnais metal union lamented: "It is painful to admit that in an industrial city such as ours, trade union organization is so feeble in relation to such a large number of workers. Is it indifference or fear? Is it produced by brutalization due to gambling and alcohol? It is really an enigma for those who are conscious of their rights and duties."[4] Why was Saint-Chamond's labor movement so weak between 1880 and World War I?

The increased militancy of Saint-Chamonnais construction workers during the years between 1905 and 1914 highlighted the inactivity of Saint-Chamonnais industrial workers. In 1891 over 90 percent of the city's workforce could be classified as industrial workers, yet the 3.6 percent of the workforce in the construction trade made a major contribution to its strike activity (see Tables 17-19).[5] In the years between 1905 and 1914 strikes in the construction trades tended to last longer and involve more worker-days lost than in either of the two major industries, textiles and metalworking, which employed most of the workforce. In fact, the contrast in strike behavior between the artisanal construction trades and large industry is even clearer than it appears in the tables. In the thirty-five years between 1880 and 1914 only one strike, a moulders' strike in 1882, occurred in the large Compagnie des aciéries de la marine, which employed over 95 percent of the city's metalworkers. The remaining four strikes took place among blacksmiths and workers in a small tool plant. Similarly, the largest strike in textiles in the period 1900–1905 occurred among skilled dyers, a rapidly disappearing artisanal craft, and not among the braiders, who constituted 90 percent of the textile workforce.[6]

Rive-de-Gier illustrated the influence which a large artisanal working class, threatened by technological change, was able to exert on a large industrial workforce. The Saint-Chamonnais situation—a numerically large industrial working class and a small artisanal working class which was not threatened by technological change—produced a very different outcome. There were several

Table 17

Number of Strikers (Metalworking, Textiles, and Construction) in
Saint-Chamond, 1880–1914

	1880–84	1885–89	1890–94	1895–99	1900–1904	1905–9	1910–14
Metal	50	0	0	11	0	75	112
Textiles	0	0	740	0	85	508	45
Construction	0	0	200	0	0	180	481

Table 18

Duration of Strikes (in Days) in Saint-Chamond, 1880–1914

	1880–84	1885–89	1890–94	1895–99	1900–1904	1905–9	1910–14
Metal	20	0	0	6	0	2	44
Textiles	0	0	21	0	2	8	4
Construction	0	0	6	0	0	99	190

Table 19

Worker-Days Lost in Strikes in Saint-Chamond, 1880–1914

	1880–84	1885–89	1890–94	1895–99	1900–1904	1905–9	1910–14
Metal	1,000	0	0	66	0	150	770
Textiles	0	0	7,287	0	170	2,032	180
Construction	0	0	1,200	0	0	10,656	10,578

reasons for industrial worker quiescence in Saint-Chamond. First
was the structure of industrial work. The new industrial system in
metal and textiles did not encourage formation of the on-the-job
friendships which promoted worker solidarity, and skilled workers
lost some important controls over the work process which they
once possessed. Under the pressure of mechanization, patterns of
labor recruitment changed; textiles became an unskilled trade with
a young, migrant, female workforce which had little long-term
commitment to the trade. Second, the upstart industrial work
system created new social problems which industrial workers were
unable to solve by themselves. The new system destroyed the
domestic and craft structures which had provided the individual
worker with many social welfare benefits. In some cases employers
sought to create their own welfare system and so create a new type
of dependence among industrial workers. Many industrial workers
looked to the state to protect them, but even here industrial workers

did not act independently. The decline of politically experienced artisanal clubs laid the basis for the rise of a new socialist party led by middle-class intellectuals.

Work Structure and Strike Militancy: The Metalworkers

Of the three cities in our study, Saint-Chamond had most completely broken with its artisanal past. At the beginning of the nineteenth century Saint-Chamond was a center of artisanal metalworking. The transition from artisanal to industrial metalworking was gradual and involved several stages. Prior to 1850 Saint-Chamonnais metalworking was dispersed throughout the countryside. On the edges of the city lived the artisanal nailmakers, metalworking peasants who worked in their own home workshops. Inside the city skilled workers, foundrymen and forgers, worked in the few small nail plate factories.[7] In the years between 1850 and 1880 Saint-Chamonnais metalworking was centralized into one large plant (see Figure 10), but artisans continued to play an important role in production. Gun tubes were a specialty of Saint-Chammonais metallurgy, and they required large amounts of wrought iron.[8] The puddlers and foundrymen necessary to the production of wrought iron were extremely skilled workers who practiced a trade which drew on the skills of the artisanal metalworker. Using long metal rods, called *ringards*, the puddler and his several assistants "worked" the molten iron while it was in the oven. Years of training enabled the puddler to determine when the metal had "come to nature" and the pig iron was transformed into wrought iron. Puddling was a physically strenuous occupation which demanded experience and judgment.[9]

In the early stages of the evolution of the metal work structure skilled workers had considerable control over their work. The nail merchant was only an intermediary between the real producers and their customers. Even the puddlers and foundrymen possessed a far greater mastery of their craft than any of their employers or engineers. These were the type of metalworkers Le Play described so eloquently in 1848:

> . . .particularly in metallurgy there remain . . . a thousand phenomena of which scholars are ignorant but which have been reproduced

Figure 10. General view of the Compagnie des aciéries de la marine, c. 1910.

daily for thirty centuries in the workshop . . . the workers who re-
produce these phenomena at will, with so much precision are
the true repositories of experience accumulated since the beginning
of civilization . . . [the theoretician] is accustomed to see an obstacle
in what constitutes the principal strength of industry, the intelligent
intervention of men . . . I owe, nearly exclusively, to my relations
with workers the most exact knowledge. On every occasion where
it has been permitted me to appreciate the whole or parts of their
works, I have shown admiration for their address and intelligence. It
is a circumstance well worth remarking, to see men, in appearance
foreign to all intellectual education, appreciate with an exquisite tact,
the smallest nuances of phenomena which, up to now, science has
never suspected the existence. . . .[10]

Le Play's description of the self-reliant metalworker would have
seemed strange to a visitor to the Compagnie des aciéries de la
marine in the 1890s. Between 1870 and 1890 a new work system
was introduced into Saint-Chamonnais metals. The new system
was based on the increased role of supervisory personnel in the

workshop, the mechanization of artisanal skills, and employer control over the admission and training of the newly emerging class of highly specialized semiskilled workers.

Highly skilled work that the artisanal metalworkers had once performed was taken over by the engineer who now made his appearance on the shop floor. The school-trained engineer usurped drawing and designing responsibilities that had belonged to the skilled worker. In 1874 Reybaud noted the new restriction on worker autonomy: "The engineer will decide what [exactly is to be done with the steel plate] . . . he is the master of his work; whatever he will order, the forger can do nothing but conform. On the rigid steel plates he [the engineer] will have to trace the curves that resemble the model; for the rough steel artisan this was nearly a work of art. . . ."[11]

The growing role of engineers and supervisors usually coincided with the appearance of new machines. Mechanization standardized work, made it increasingly easy to supervise, and at the same time undermined the workers' monopoly of skills and thus their ability to resist supervision. The machine destroyed the community of experience and skill which was the foundation of artisanal worker solidarity. The Compagnie des aciéries de la marine played a pioneering role in the mechanization of French metalworking. It was the first company in France to use steam hammers and so mechanize forging.[12]

The puddler was more difficult to replace. All over the nineteenth-century industrial world, huge sums of money were spent to mechanize wrought iron production and do away with the skilled puddler. The puddler was the keystone of the artisanal structure in Saint-Chamond, where in 1874 Louis Reybaud found sixty-two puddling ovens in use. The mechanization of puddling proved impossible; instead, high-quality steel began to take the place of wrought iron. The number of puddling ovens in large-scale metalwork dropped dramatically while the number of Siemens-Martin open hearth ovens, which produced steel, increased. Tuiebault-Sisson noted that in Saint-Chamond "the transformation of cast iron into steel takes place in special ovens, the Siemens-Martin ovens, where the metal is not hand worked and whose doors stay closed during the entire process of metal production. This

work involves relatively little effort and simple unskilled workers
are able to perform it. . . ."[13]

The shift from wrought iron production to steel production also
brought a shift in the spatial distribution of the workforce that
weakened the cohesion of the work group and increased the role of
the supervisor. Furthermore, the disappearance of the artisanal
work team removed an important nucleus of worker resistance from
the shop floor. The puddler and his crew were centered around the
oven where they worked the iron. The Siemens-Martin process
broke up the physical proximity of the work group. The oven itself
was closed and no longer a focus of work organization. Workers
were scattered throughout the factory as crane operators, feeding
the pig iron into the oven, and as casters, pouring the liquid metal
into moulds. Supervisors coordinated the process while unskilled
workers carried equipment from one part of the shop floor to the
other. Communications, which had formerly passed directly from
worker to worker, were now relayed through the supervisor.[14]

The new work system also reached into the assembly and fitting
plants, which employed the largest single group of workers in the
Saint-Chamond complex. By 1901 the assembly plant was the
most closely supervised of all the workshops, requiring one engineer, eight subengineers, sixteen foremen, and sixteen *chefs d'équipe*.
When the Saint-Chamond plant was first opened, adjusters and
mounters had worked with their own tools and a few primitive
cutting machines. By the late nineteenth century machine tools
dominated the assembly plant:

> The puddlers aside, what are the workers of these factories? The
> moulders who, as their name indicates, make the moulds are well
> paid; a small number of adjusters [are also well paid], those [ad-
> justers] who do not do unskilled work. But these special workers
> aside, it is difficult not to describe the others as unskilled. When
> one goes through the assembly plant and the turners' workshop at
> Saint-Chamond, when one sees the machine tools, planing machines,
> drills, mortisers, etc., all working with a marvelous regularity while
> the workers who watch [the machines] . . . have nothing to do but
> start them and check their functioning from time to time, then one
> understands why today's workers are paid less than yesterday's.[15]

Wages in Saint-Chamonnais metalworking were roughly similar

to those in Le Chambon and Rive-de-Gier. The industrial worker received lower wages than the artisanal metalworker and was less able to support the trade unions and political clubs which facilitated the organization of strike actions. Metal wages in Saint-Chamond reveal the existence of a new group of more or less semiskilled workers composed of old artisanal groups, like the forgers, whose skills had been largely eroded by mechanization, and new groups, like the machinists, who worked on these machines. The wages of the semiskilled worker were closer to those of the unskilled worker than to those of the artisan. As in the other towns, metalworking was an adult male occupation; in 1894, 91.7 percent of all metalworkers were adult men.[16] In 1901 highly skilled foundrymen received 8.5 francs a day, semiskilled forgers and adjusters received between 5.0 and 5.5 francs, and unskilled workers received 3.5. In that same year the percentage of workers in unskilled occupations was 27.6 percent; the percentage of semiskilled workers was 37.8 percent or perhaps somewhat higher. Unfortunately, there are no figures which permit a clear distinction between highly skilled workers and supervisory personnel in Saint-Chamonnais metalwork.[17]

Most of these skill categories should be regarded as permanent occupations rather than as stages in a worker's apprenticeship. On the day they were hired, workers were enrolled as skilled or unskilled. If designated "skilled," they were sent to the requisite workshop for training; if "unskilled," they were sent directly to work. Each of the semiskilled work groups in metal was isolated from the others. Different skill levels were not hierarchically bound together by an apprenticeship system as they were in the artisanal trades. The larger machine tools used by semiskilled workers, such as the large-face plate lathe shown in Figure 11, were extremely specialized, and workers were not encouraged to acquire different skills. Charles Benoist carefully observed skill groups in Saint-Chamond and concluded that "the unskilled worker in metalworking does not resemble the pit boy, for example, or the mine hauler, who with age will pass successively to assistant and then full coalminer; [in metal] he enters as an unskilled worker and he remains an unskilled worker . . . it is seldom that once he is attached to a workshop he ever moves [to another work-

Figure 11. A large-face plate lathe at the Compagnie des aciéries de la marine, c. 1910.

shop]. . . ."[18] The same occupational stability characterized the semiskilled categories. Adjusters, planers, and machinists received substantially less money than the turners, but they were recruited from similar age groups (see Table 20).[19]

In heavy metal the company, not the worker, controlled apprenticeship and thus admission to the trade. Company control

Table 20

Age Distribution of Semiskilled Metalworkers at the Compagnie des aciéries de la marine, 1901

Years of Age	Adjusters	Turners	Planers	Machinists	Unskilled
18–27	31.4%	36.1%	22.3%	18.3%	16.7%
28–37	29.7	34.4	41.1	35.7	31.6
38–47	22.3	17.6	27.7	29.9	19.0
48–57	10.0	7.9	6.3	8.5	17.7
58 and above	6.6	4.0	2.7	7.6	15.0
N	229	227	224	224	700

Figure 12. Workshop for apprentices at the Compagnie des aciéries de la marine, c. 1910.

of apprenticeship was a serious blow to the worker's ability to resist company demands. The worker knew that he could be easily replaced, and this weakened his ability to resist. By 1872 the company had already offered some free apprenticeships to young men.[20] Figure 12 shows a company workshop in which supervisory personnel trained young apprentices. In 1883, when the moulders struck against the imposition of piece work, the company refused to negotiate. According to a government observer, "[the company] worked to form moulders from young men of intelligence and good will that it found in other occupations. By this method, today, it disposes of 25 moulders: it needs 15 more and it counts on soon recruiting these. . . ."[21] Although a craft union of moulders was again formed in 1890 and remained in existence for the rest of the period, it mostly provided mutual benefits for its members; it never again caused the company any serious trouble.

The close contact between workers in the same shop, disrupted by the introduction of the supervisor and the machine, was not renewed within the working-class neighborhood. Industrial work did not create the off-the-job friendships among workmates which was an important element of artisanal life. Semiskilled workers in the same trade were scattered all over Saint-Chamond (see Table 21). For instance, almost all turners worked in the same assembly shop in the metalworks, yet they lived in every section of Saint-Chamond.[22] In fact, turners, who were the most skilled and highest paid of all semiskilled workers, were even more dispersed than the adjusters, who were among the lowest paid and the least skilled. The index of dissimilarity for Saint-Chamonnais turners, 13.9, shows that this distribution was more similar to that of the general population than that of the adjusters, 16.9.

Occupation had no more influence than skill group in determining where workers lived. If turners showed little predisposition to live next to other turners, metalworkers showed no more predisposition to live next to other metalworkers. In 1891, 25.2 percent of all the households in town had a metalworker head.[23] In that year every section of town had an important concentration of metalworkers, although the south and southwest sections, the areas adjacent to the steelworks, had a particularly large proportion of metalworkers (see Table 22). But every section had a majority of

Table 21

Residential Patterns of Turners and Adjusters
in Saint-Chamond, 1891

Saint-Chamond	Turners		Adjusters	
	Number	Percent	Number	Percent
Western Section	11	10.9	12	11.1
North-Central Section	16	15.8	14	13.0
Northern Section	7	6.9	3	2.8
East-Central Section	10	9.9	13	12.0
Eastern Section	9	8.9	7	6.5
South-Central Section	12	11.9	12	11.1
Southern Section	20	19.8	22	20.4
Southwestern Section	16	15.8	25	23.1
N	101		108	

Index of Dissimilarity: Turners = 13.9; Adjusters = 19.3.

Table 22

Residential Patterns in Saint-Chamond, 1891: Family Sample of Metalworkers

Saint-Chamond	Metalworker Head of Household		Total Population Head of Household	
	Number	Percent	Number	Percent
Western Section	13	10.9	60	13.0
North-Central Section	11	9.2	65	14.1
Northern Section	18	15.1	64	13.9
East-Central Section	6	5.0	65	14.1
Eastern Section	11	9.2	45	9.7
South-Central Section	14	11.8	47	10.2
Southern Section	23	19.3	62	13.4
Southwestern Section	23	19.3	54	11.7
N	119		462	

Index of Dissimilarity = 16.3

nonmetalworker heads of households, and small shopkeepers and nonmetalworkers lived side by side with metalworkers.

A look at the changing climate of the working-class café is one way to understand the effect of the new work system on workers' leisure time. Leroy-Beaulieu's characterization of French workers in 1868 seems to apply equally well in the Stéphanois valley for the remainder of the century: "[for the worker] . . . the cabaret is becoming a place of meeting and a place of rest . . . the cabaret . . . holds for the working classes in present day society the sane place as the church in past times. . . ."[24]

Armand Audiganne traveled to Saint-Etienne, Rive-de-Gier, and Saint-Chamond and observed sadly: "Drunkenness is more common among the workers of the Loire than among the Lyonnais weavers; it forms the principal vice of the metalworkers and coalminers who know no other recreation than the cabaret. It is there that one sees the spirit of happiness swell up in them; the soul sparkles an instant through their animated eyes, only to perish just as suddenly in excess which extinguishes their last glimmer of moral activity."[25] These early nineteenth-century cafés were important centers of worker solidarity; in the café workers debated politics and organized trade unions.

Although the cafés remained central to male working-class life

during the whole period between 1880 and 1914, the political role
of the café changed as the work structure changed. As late as the
1880s the café still played a central role in Saint-Chamonnais
working-class political life. The early nineteenth-century working-
class café was formed by members of the same skill group drawn
together by their similar job interests and work experience. These
cafés were a natural center for the discussion of work conditions and the coordination of strike actions. Militant strike activity
led to radical politics and these cafés were often hotbeds of political activity.

As work mechanized, the neighborhood café replaced the old
artisanal establishment. The neighborhood café had a working-
class clientele which lived in the same area but did not work together and shared little common ground for collective action. As
a result the neighborhood café was much less likely to be involved
in politics than its artisanal predecessor.[26]

The depoliticization of café life had a dramatic effect on
working-class political organization. The early political clubs had
been highly informal organizations, deeply rooted in café society,
while the later political clubs tended to be more formalized and less
directly connected to café life. The early political clubs were
composed of artisanal workers who possessed some political
experience and were profoundly influenced by the spirit of
ouvrièrisme, the doctrine, widely held but rarely written down, that
workers rather than middle-class intellectuals should lead the
workers' movement. The later political clubs were composed of
industrial workers who had little political experience and often
looked to middle-class radicals and socialists for leadership.

The Saint-Chamonnais anarchist clubs of the eighties and
nineties provide an example of artisanal political clubs. These
anarchists' clubs were the most important political clubs in
Saint-Chamond, where the political environment produced the
town's most famous native son, Ravachol. In 1882 a police spy
described an anarchist club:

> There exists in Saint-Chamond, Place Notre-Dame, a little café kept
> by a man named Benavent, a not very talkative man . . . who is
> supposedly affiliated to the anarchist party . . . it is there (on the
> second floor of this café) that they (the anarchists) gather clandes-

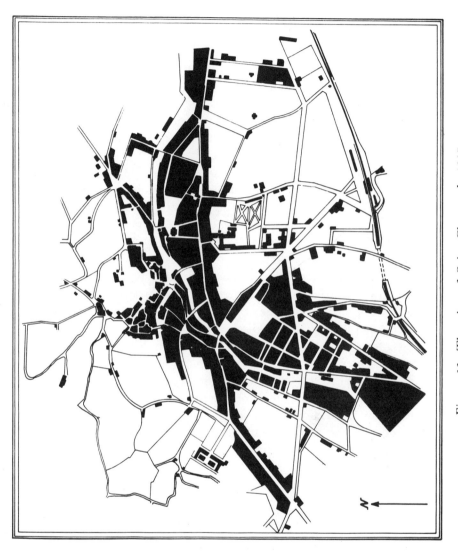

Figure 13. The city of Saint-Chamond, 1887.

tinely to form a little committee and to have themselves served
drinks while some, the orators called to make speeches in public
meeting, study rhetoric under the tutelage of the anarchist Payre.
  It is to this place of rendezvous that they give the sonorous title
"circle" and it is there that nine or ten of them met last Sunday.[27]

Although files exist on only a tiny number of anarchist militants,
the predominance of artisans is clear, and there is some indication of a change in the occupational composition of the Saint-
Chamonnais anarchist party which coincided with the change in
metal work structure: artisanal metalworkers were replaced by
construction workers. In 1882, of eight anarchists closely watched
by the police, five were highly skilled or artisanal metalworkers:
two moulders, one modeler, one coppersmith, and one knifemaker;
the remaining three were textile workers: two tailors and one
foreman in a braid factory.[28] By 1894, of eight anarchist leaders,
only three were metalworkers: one adjuster, one moulder, and one
forger; there were two textile workers, both dyers, and three
construction workers: two masons and one painter.[29]

  The political demands of the clubs were strongly influenced by
the working-class character of the cafés from which they emerged.
These Saint-Chamonnais radicals were somewhat unorthodox anarchists, for they urged the workers to vote. Indeed, the local Saint-
Chamonnais revolutionaries were not so much anarchists as
they were politicized workers distrustful of middle-class reformers.
In 1880 Payre had pleaded for the nomination of a working-class
candidate in the coming elections, and in 1882 at a public meeting
attended by the revolutionary leader Louise Michel, Payre urged
workers "always to vote for working-class candidates, even when
some of them like Tolain and Martin Nadaud become defectors."[30]

  This "anarchist" group was also involved in union politics. In
1880 Payre, a tailor by profession, was a member of a commis-
sion of metalworkers who tried, unsuccessfully, to form a metal
union.[31] Saint-Chamonnais anarchists were dealt a serious blow by
the harsh repression which followed the assassination of Carnot in
1893, and they entered a period of rapid decline.

  As late as 1894 café politics were still important in the formation
of socialist political clubs. In that year the socialist party, whose
chief leaders were metalworkers, established its own circle, called
the Cercle d'études sociales. This club was destined to become the

dominant working-class political rendezvous in Saint-Chamond in the years before World War I. This new industrial workers' club developed in a very different direction from its artisanal predecessors. The circle had its center in the café Roucharge, located in the southern section of Saint-Chamond where many metalworkers lived.[32] It began as an informal association but soon evolved very formal rules of procedure, with an elected committee to chair discussions and the power to expel dissident members. As it became a formal organization, its headquarters became less a private club and more a public meeting place. The masons' union and the leftist republicans also held meetings there.[33]

Interestingly, as the Cercle d'études sociales became more formal, it also became more open to middle-class influence. It was difficult for middle-class politicians to enter the metalworking café, where so much of the conversation focused on occupationally related questions. It was much easier for them to enter the public debating societies and lecture halls, which demanded skills that politicians possessed. While an autonomous working-class culture may have survived in the neighborhood café, it became increasingly divorced from political organization; political leadership passed from informally organized groups of artisanal workers to formally organized groups led by middle-class activists. The two best known leaders of the party were a pharmacist and a small property owner.[34] They became so identified with the socialist party that a republican mayor, in order to avoid forming an electoral coalition with the socialists, announced that he would accept socialists on his ballot only if they were truly members of the working class. Saint-Chamonnais socialists were indignant. According to an outraged article in *L'Unité socialiste-organe hebdomadaire de la fédération de la Loire:*

> In order to mask his schemes, the shameful committee . . . of this politician . . . has let it be understood that it would accept six socialists—no more—in the composition of the [electoral] list but only on the rigorous condition that these socialists would be purely workers, that is to say, the slaves of the factory or the workshop, each dressed in his collar of misery, bridled, held on a leash, muzzled at will, ready to return to the rolling mill . . . and suffer the worst punishments at the least sign of independence.
> But the tradesman and the property owner who have . . . come

over to our side . . . will not lessen their enthusiasm due to threats
. . . [the workers are] sheep that one would have reduced to docility,
not to speak of domesticity, and the most complete silence. . . .[35]

The rhetoric of Saint-Chamonnais socialism in 1901 would have
scandalized the anarchists of 1880. The differences were only
partly doctrinal. Saint-Chamonnais anarchism reflected the politics of the artisanal café, the independence of well-organized and
politicized artisanal workers. Saint-Chamonnais socialism reflected
the politics of the less well-organized, inexperienced, industrial
working class, the less politicized climate which also nurtured the
neighborhood café. The growing mass of industrial workers were
politically inexperienced and difficult to organize.

Work Structure and Strike Militancy:
The Textileworkers

While the metal work structure in Saint-Chamond changed rapidly in the course of the nineteenth century, the change in the
textile work structure was even more dramatic. In textiles, as in
metalworking, workers' control of the work process was completely
shattered; machines replaced skilled workers, and the work team
was broken up by removing the workers from the home and
scattering them along the shop floor. Moreover, the triumph of the
machine was even more complete in textiles. Textile production
demanded no skill and little physical effort. New patterns of labor
recruitment also made worker solidarity difficult. Textile work
ceased being a lifetime occupation of families and became a brief
stage in the life cycle of individual female family members. As a
result, workers no longer had a long-term interest or commitment
to conditions in the textile trade.

Artisanal ribbonmaking, which had been very important in
Saint-Chamond in the early nineteenth century, had a long local
history: Saint-Chamond had been involved in silk production and
manufacture even before Lyon. In 1600 Henri IV had allowed
Saint-Chamonnais silkthrowers to form a corporation, and their
confrérie still existed in 1800. In the eighteenth century Saint-
Chamond shared primacy in silk production with Saint-Étienne.
Even more than in metalworking, Saint-Chamonnais textiles were

the nucleus of a large network of rural industry. Saint-Chamonnais merchants employed commissioned agents and horsemen laden with raw silk to make regular rounds, from one small Stéphanois valley town or farming settlement to another. While the majority of silkweavers maintained family workshops in the countryside, some lived in Saint-Chamond, where many other highly skilled textile artisans, silkthrowers and dyers, were also concentrated.[36]

Whereas in metalworking the rise of an industrial work structure created a new category of semiskilled workers, in extiles the rise of an industrial work structure multiplied the number of unskilled workers. A refractory textileworker could be even more easily replaced than a metalworker. In the early nineteenth century ribbon-weaving began to abandon Saint-Chamond and concentrate in Saint-Etienne, while a new braidmaking industry developed to replace it. From its introduction in 1807, braidmaking was already mechanized. The braidworker was a machine tender who routinely performed two main tasks: replacing used bobbins and rethreading machines when the silk fibers broke.[37]

Between 1860 and 1870 mechanical braidmaking passed from the home workshop to the large factory where workers were closely supervised and the work load increased. There were three major reasons for the consolidation of braidmaking into factories. First, the employer wanted to ensure work quality. As Jules Simon complained, "[the employer] insists on the necessity of supervising the worker so that the whole plan will be well executed, the woof tight, and the weaving done neatly."[38] Second, in factories single workers could tend a larger number of looms. In 1900 Beauquis estimated that individual workers in braid plants tended between twenty and thirty looms simultaneously.[39] Finally, braidmaking became an increasingly integrated technical process; machines were invented for preparing the raw silk and finishing the braids, and there were soon machines for throwing, mangling, reeling, and sheering silk. By 1870 the homeworker had become a bottleneck in the production process.

In contrast to metalworking, where the breakdown of family industry created a nearly all-male workforce, the transformation of the textile industry created a nearly all-female workforce. In 1891 textiles was the largest single employer in Saint-Chamond: in that

year textiles employed 48.1 percent of the working-class population, and 96.4 percent of these workers were women.[40] As the
braid industry developed in Saint-Chamond, it spawned subsid-
iary industries, all of which were thoroughly mechanized and all
of which overwhelmingly employed women workers: in 1894
braidmaking employed 73.1 percent of the textile workforce; silk-
throwing, 15.9 percent; and elastic fibers, 11.0 percent. The only
skilled workers in Saint-Chamonnais textiles were the skilled male
dyers who worked in small independent shops or workshops an-
nexed to the larger braid factories.[41]

Wages in textiles were low and, without outside help, it would
have been impossible for women textileworkers to support a
sustained strike. In 1894 women workers were paid beween 1.0
and 1.9 francs a day, compared to 3.5 francs for unskilled male
workers.[42]

But the wages of individual textileworkers can only be evaluated
in the context of a family economy. In 1891, with the important
exceptions of workers living in company-owned dormitories and
of widows, there were almost no single women heads of household
in Saint-Chamond. Indeed, the family economies of metalworkers
and textileworkers were closely related. Many textileworkers were
the daughters of metalworkers and lived with their families. In
1891, 24.6 percent of the families with a metalworking head of
household had members working in the textile trades.[43]

Mechanization of the textile trade severely disrupted the family
economy of Saint-Chamonnais workers. The creation of a female
workforce and, more important, the concentration of the trade into
large factories excluded most mothers and all young male children
from the textile workforce and thus reduced family income. These
lowered family incomes weakened the ability of Saint-Chamonnais
workers to support trade union organizations and strike actions. In
the first half of the nineteenth century many Saint-Chamonnais
workers had their own home workshops. In 1874 Louis Reybaud
noted the existence of a mixed family economy of metalworking
and textiles:

> It often happened [that I found in the Stéphanois valley] in the
> same household, the husband, for example, was a forger, the wife
> was in the ribbon trade, the children prepared spools; there was no

one without something to do. When these conditions are met, affluence reached its highest degree, the standard of living is that of the solid middle class. . . . It is chiefly in Saint-Chamond that this combination is possible. . . . Iron remains the principal occupation, silk is additional, the work of women and non-earning family members. . . . Children have an option, and when it is time, the father leads the strongest to work at the foundry and the rolling mill; the others continue to make braid or silk with the young girls and the mother.[44]

By the time he visited Saint-Chamond, this family economy was in decline, the wages of the skilled metalworkers were falling, and the family workshop was losing ground; the family economy had completely disappeared by the end of the decade.

The family work unit was replaced by the individual woman textileworker who spent only a few years in the workforce and left it to become a mother. These women workers had little long-term commitment to the industry because they had no expectation of remaining at work for more than five or six years; they had little interest in building solid trade union organizations. In 1899 L.-J. Gras estimated that nine-tenths of all women textileworkers were between sixteen and twenty-one years of age.[45]

In order to find young workers, the textile mills had to recruit workers in every section of Saint-Chamond. This dispersion of the workforce made informal social contact difficult; perhaps even more inhibiting was the family role, for girls who returned from work just in time to help their mothers prepare dinner had little time for extra-familial activities. In fact, women textileworkers participated in the whole range of family activities and were effectively cut off from close relations with their fellow workers. Textileworkers and metalworkers lived side by side in all sections of Saint-Chamond; indeed, as has been shown, they often lived in the same household. Table 23 illustrates the distribution of textileworker heads of household; these were usually widows and their families or male skilled workers. Table 24 gives a more accurate picture of textile residential patterns; it shows the distribution of textileworkers who were members of families.[46] The index of dissimilarity for textileworker heads of household (17.3) is higher than that for metalworker heads of household (16.3), while the index of

Table 23

Residential Patterns in Saint-Chamond, 1891: Family Sample of
Textileworker Heads of Household

Saint-Chamond	Textileworker Head of Household		Total Population Head of Household	
	Number	Percent	Number	Percent
Western Section	7	10.9	60	13.0
North-Central Section	16	25.0	65	14.1
Northern Section	10	15.6	64	13.9
East-Central Section	12	18.8	65	14.1
Eastern Section	4	6.3	45	9.7
South-Central Section	6	9.4	47	10.2
Southern Section	7	10.9	62	13.4
Southwestern Section	2	3.1	54	11.7
N	64		462	

Index of Dissimilarity = 17.3

Table 24

Residential Patterns in Saint-Chamond, 1891: Family Sample of
Textileworker Members of Household

Saint-Chamond	Textileworker Member of Household		Total Population Member of Household	
	Number	Percent	Number	Percent
Western Section	20	10.0	194	12.7
North-Central Section	39	19.4	189	12.3
Northern Section	44	22.0	224	14.6
East-Central Section	27	13.4	205	13.4
Eastern Section	17	8.5	184	12.0
South-Central Section	15	7.5	138	9.0
Southern Section	26	12.9	211	13.8
Southwestern Section	13	6.5	188	12.3
N	201		1,533	

Chi-square = 30.0 p < .011
Index of Dissimilarity = 14.5

dissimilarity for textile members of families (14.5) is very close to
that of metalworker members of families (14.3). Table 25 shows the
distribution of braiding workshops; no obvious relation obtains between the sectors where plants were located and worker residence.

When the supply of local women workers became insufficient,

Table 25

Geographic Distribution of Textile Plants in Saint-Chamond, 1894

Saint-Chamond	Number of Plants	Workers Employed in Plants	
		Number	Percent
Western Section	3	290	11.1
North-Central Section	8	437	16.7
Northern Section	4	66	2.5
East-Central Section	2	62	2.4
Eastern Section	3	790	30.3
South-Central Section	1	102	3.9
Southern Section	0	0	0
Southwestern Section	5	864	33.1
N	26	2,611	

the companies reached into the countryside to recruit workers. By 1891 young migrants who lived in dormitories built and maintained by the company were an important component of the textile workforce in Saint-Chamond. In that year 25.1 percent of those employed in textiles, all women, lived in these dormitories. Although they did not live with their families, many of these women also belonged to family economies, since they worked to save and send money to their families in the countryside. Most of these women came from poor rural areas in the department of the Loire, but some came from nearby mountainous regions: Auvergne, Vivarais, and the Dauphinais.[47]

The company-owned dormitory was a characteristic feature of labor recruitment in the Lyonnais and Stéphanois regions. The company provided sleeping room and kitchen facilities; the worker was expected to bring her own food and prepare it as well as to provide her own clean linen, furniture, and household articles. The condition of these company-owned dormitories was a frequent source of scandal. In 1888 the best words that the factory inspector could find to say about them was that "they were kept more cleanly than in the past."[48] Beauquis reported on the Lyonnais dormitories:

The kitchens . . . generally possess . . . low ceilings, they are poorly lighted, badly aired, and often very humid. . . .

In the same building as the kitchens, generally under the same roof, are found the sleeping rooms, in which beds are piled up according to need, without any care to proportion their number to the vacant places, or, more important, the volume of necessary air. Each bed is constituted simply by a metal or wooden frame and a mattress filled with corn straw or regular straw. In order to avoid a too great waste of bed linen, sometimes furnished by the companies but more usually by the workers themselves . . . formerly, two and up to three workers were expected to sleep in the same bed.[49]

Under different circumstances the company-owned dormitory might have been a source of worker sociability and comradeship, but actually they seem to have been more important in helping preserve the workers' social ties to the countryside and in isolating them from their urban fellow workers, thus retarding worker solidarity and organization. Victor Jury, the head of the textile employers' union, explained that the work hours of textileworkers were arranged to facilitate weekly visits to the countryside.[50] For most dormitory workers in the Lyonnais and Stéphanois regions, weekly visits to the countryside were an economic necessity. According to Abel Chatelain, most of the food that Stéphanois and Lyonnais textileworkers prepared in the company dormitories came from their parents' farms. Homemade rye bread and home-produced potatoes, cabbage, and bacon enabled textileworkers to save or send home a little surplus from their meager wages.[51]

Company-supervised dormitories put severe restrictions on the social life of women textileworkers; single women workers could not readily enter the politicized café society to which single male workers belonged. The youth and sex of textileworkers provided the justification for employer supervision. The women who stayed in these dormitories were young; in 1891 the average age in the larger dormitories was between eighteen and twenty-one, and there were many workers of fourteen, fifteen, and sixteen years of age. Victor Jury assured farm families that their daughters would be "seriously supervised."[52] Textileworkers occasionally rebelled against excessively strict or prying supervisors. In 1912 a four-day strike of forty-five workers broke out against two foul-mouthed and "spying" supervisors.[53] But while they resented individual supervisors, Saint-Chamonnais textileworkers never demanded the end of supervision. The social and economic consequences of illegitimacy were too serious. Around 1900 a certain song became popular in Saint-Chamond, written by a railway clerk for a working-class singing society and entitled "L'Ouvrière Saint-Chamonnaise":

> She is the popular elite
> Who suffers and struggles with dignity
> Whose courage is exemplary
> And her conduct the same,
> If her language and her manners
> Are a little free sometimes,
> She has morals much more strict,
> Than many bourgeois girls.[54]

Work Structure and Strike Militancy: The Construction Workers

In Saint-Chamond construction workers were a much smaller group than metalworkers or textileworkers and attracted much less attention. In contrast to metalworkers and textileworkers, construction workers possessed the work group cohesion and high wages which enabled them to construct a solid trade union organization. Except for the unskilled ditchdiggers, construction workers such as cement-mixers, masons, plasterers, and joiners were skilled workers who labored together in teams. Several of these trades, such as the masons and joiners, possessed formally organized apprenticeship structures. Wages of construction workers were either comparable to or exceeded those of the most skilled sections of the industrial working class: in 1911 cement-mixers made 7.0 francs a day, masons 6.5, and plasterers 5.5.[55] In the case of the more highly skilled construction workers, strong work group ties seem to have affected residential patterns. The index of dissimilarity for the more highly paid masons, 34.1, is much higher than that for the less well paid plasterers, 17.3 (see Table 26). Thus residential patterns reinforced worker solidarity and aided trade union organization.

While in Rive-de-Gier glassworkers' trade union organization and strike activity were responses to the fear of technological change, in Saint-Chamond construction worker union organization and strike activity were responses to the wave of inflation which, as was seen in Chapter Three, began around 1907 and reached

Table 26

Residential Patterns of Masons and Plasterers in Saint-Chamond, 1891

Saint-Chamond	Masons		Plasterers	
	Number	Percent	Number	Percent
Western Section	5	5.7	8	15.1
North-Central Section	11	12.6	9	17.0
Northern Section	9	10.3	5	9.4
East-Central Section	2	2.3	11	20.8
Eastern Section	0	0	3	5.7
South-Central Section	21	24.1	3	5.7
Southern Section	17	19.5	6	11.3
Southwestern Section	22	25.3	8	15.1
N	87		53	

Index of Dissimilarity: Masons = 34.10; Plasterers = 17.30.

its peak in 1910–11. Of all the working-class groups in Saint-Chamond, only the construction workers were able to respond to inflation by trade union action. There were five strikes by construction workers between 1910 and 1911; they all had exclusively wage demands, and most of them won significant wage increases. Between 1906 and 1914 the wages of construction workers advanced much more rapidly than did those of metalworkers.[56]

Inflation, Unemployment, and Worker Protest

Between 1910 and 1914 Saint-Chamonnais workers did not refer to price indexes, but they had no doubt of the reality of inflation. Although local workers did not strike, they did protest. In September, 1911, a CGT call for demonstrations against rising prices met with an unexpectedly favorable response in Saint-Chamond. The demands of the protesters recall those of the French food riots of the eighteenth and early nineteenth centuries. *L'Eclaireur de Saint-Chamond* reported:

> About 3,000 workers, meeting in the Conference Hall on September 15, demanded the absolute suppression of markets in courtyards, alleys, and sheds, etc., declaring that there ought to be only one place of sale, the public square, and they demanded rigorous controls and more efficacious sanitary inspection.

They blamed the inhumane tradesmen who prefer to throw their merchandise away rather than lowering prices, they asked the municipality to have the prices of all tradesmen posted publicly.[57]

Later in 1911 the trade union movement in Saint-Chamond tried to take advantage of popular sentiment and organize more of these demonstrations, but the later meetings were much less successful than the earlier ones.[58]

The new work system had its greatest impact on the worker at the shop level, but many of the forces which transformed the shop floor also affected other aspects of worker life. The mechanization of work and its concentration into large factories demanded large amounts of capital, and in order to compete successfully, employers had to enlarge their market. The industrial work system which transformed the workshop in metalworking and textiles also transformed the character of the market for Saint-Chamonnais products; as a result, new elements of instability were introduced into industrial worker life. The new Saint-Chamonnais industries were particularly concentrated in sectors of the economy where demand fluctuated wildly, and unemployment became the bane of the Saint-Chamonnais industrial worker. Changes in fashion or foreign tariffs could make or break the braid industry. Between 1891 and 1894, as world tariffs rose, the value of the braids produced in Saint-Chamond declined somewhere between 20 and 30 percent.[59] This same "boom or bust" economy occurred in metal construction, where the Compagnie des aciéries de la marine competed on the international armaments market with Krupp and Skoda. An order from the Spanish navy could set the workshops buzzing, while a lost bid brought the huge machines to a standstill.

Unemployment was a particular problem for industrial workers. Craft unions responded to unemployment by limiting production and restricting entry to the trade, but industrial workers had lost control of production and apprenticeship, and could do little to help their members. Powerlessness in the face of economic crisis seriously weakened the appeal of industrial unionism in Saint-Chamond.

Economic crisis affected more than the minority of unemployed workers; in one way or another it affected almost every worker in Saint-Chamond. Economic crisis meant not only selective unemployment but also the general reduction of the length of the workday and the work week with a consequent general loss of income. For example, even in the course of a "mediocre" year like 1894, a large number of industrial workers and their families might feel the economic pinch. The year 1894 opened with a crisis in the dyeing and braid industry. As a result of a crisis in Stéphanois ribbons, the work week in dyeing was reduced from six to five days, and workers were discharged in the Oriol works, the largest braid factory in town. By June, 1894, the economic crisis had reached the metalworks, and 250 workers were discharged from the Compagnie des aciéries de la marine. In August the second-largest braid plant in Saint-Chamond, the Société industrielle, let go two-thirds of its workforce. The police commissioner reported: "No industry is prosperous, far from it, all the industrial establishments, metalworking, braidmaking, etc. . . . are discharging personnel and reducing the length of the workday, stocks are accumulating and there are no orders. . . ."[60] This situation was still substantially unchanged in December, 1894, and it was not until 1895 that unemployment actually began to decrease.[61] For more than a year the income of Saint-Chamonnais workers had fluctuated wildly.

Economic crisis had a paradoxical effect on the metal industrial union in Saint-Chamond: crisis swelled union ranks but diminished its ability to carry out strike actions; the net result was to discredit the metal union. The same unemployment which caused worker discontent reduced the resources available to workers to support strikes and strengthened the ability of the company to resist work stoppages. The paradoxical nature of unemployment was well illustrated during the economic crisis of 1901–2, when trade union membership reached its peak. In 1901 the Compagnie des aciéries de la marine began to lay off workers: eighteen adjusters were discharged in the assembly plant and thirty-eight in the boiler plant. In response, workers claimed that the discharges were made arbitrarily, according to the whims of the foreman. Instead of layoffs, the workers demanded the reduction of the workday for each shift, so that more workers could be employed to do the available work; thus, while all workers would receive a pay cut, no one would be discharged. The company flatly refused this demand.

As discharges continued, union membership and attendance at union meetings began to climb, from 200 union members to 400 and then 600 (see Graph 9). In 1902 a trade union delegate from Saint-Chamond boasted of the union's organizing success to a national convention of metalworkers.[62]

Although union membership in 1902 reached as high as one-half of the metal workforce, it was not to last; as the crisis worsened, the basis for all trade union action was undercut. Union leaders hesitated to strike because they were unsure whether the non-union metalworkers would follow them. According to the police, "the leaders [of the potential strike] are unionized, and they are asking themselves with considerable anxiety, if they will be followed by their comrades who do not belong to the union."[63] Such concern was well-advised because there was little prospect that a strike in 1901 could have been successful. During the economic crisis the company was not afraid to shut down one of its works, and it was actually looking for an opportunity to fire workers. In addition, there were unemployed workers in the streets who could easily be recruited to take the place of striking workers. Under these circumstances a strike could not fail to end in catastrophe. Union leaders could only explain these realities to their new membership and ask them to be patient. In July, 1901, a turning point was reached:

> .. . . the meeting was well attended this evening . . . [around 1,500 workers attended], the idea of an immediate strike was discarded.
>
> Several speakers succeeded one another in the podium. The majority of the speakers were influential members of the metal union, and they revealed that, given the actual state of affairs, a strike would lead to the collapse of the union which has lately become so powerful.
>
> The truth of these statements was completely admitted by everyone concerned, and it was decided that a subscription would be taken to aid all the unemployed who were members of the union.[64]

Unfortunately, by the time the crisis had subsided, so had the union membership.

Unemployment not only inhibited worker action, it also increased the power of the employer. The company was not slow to take advantage of the industrial workers' fear of unemployment. As

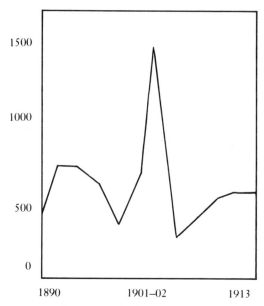

Source: *Annuaire des Syndicats 1890–1914.*

Graph 9. Total Trade Union Membership in Saint-Chamond, 1890–1913.

early as 1875 a rather too enthusiastic police inspector had informed the prefect of his detection of a secret plan to carry out a strike and the company's immediate response:

> The Directors [of the company] were completely ignorant of this fact [the planned strike] and have been very surprised to find out about it. As my information was very precise . . . the directors decided to upset the workers' plans, and, this evening, the Director posted a sign announcing that, starting next Saturday, the night shift would be discontinued, which would throw 150 workers out of their jobs, but in spite of this very prudent measure . . . the workers well know that the company has received an order for 1,800 cannons. . . .[65]

The increasing concentration of French industry reinforced the ability of the steel company to use the threat of unemployment against labor discontent. By 1900 the Compagnie des aciéries de la marine controlled a network of steel plants across France: the company owned works in Assaily, Givors, Homecourt, Hauto-mont, and Boucou, in addition to Rive-de-Gier and Saint-Chamond. If worker militancy was found intolerable in one plant, production might be shifted to another plant. In 1903 a metal-worker leader claimed that one of the reasons for the collapse of Saint-Chamonnais unionism was the spread of company-inspired rumors that union militancy was prolonging unemployment.[66]

The Foundations of Paternalism

The increased size of Saint-Chamonnais industry and the de-cline of worker control of production strengthened the position of the employer and created the basis for the emergence of a re-vitalized doctrine of employer paternalism. Formerly, artisanal societies had played an important role in determining seniority, protecting aged workers, and contributing to sick or disabled workers. Industrial unions were generally too weak to assume these responsibilities, and the nineteenth-century state refused these fresh obligations. Most of the burden fell on the working-class family, but in some cases the employer stepped in and took control of yet another aspect of working-class life. In so doing, the employer created a new spirit of dependence which reinforced his control over the worker.

Victor Jury, the head of the textile employers' union, eloquently explained employer intentions: "The Directors of the shops (and this is the characteristic spirit of Saint-Chamonnais employers) are generally paternal; the great majority of employers consider themselves as moral replacements for the father of the family and treat their workingmen and workingwomen with justice. . . ."[67] The most tangible products of employer paternalism in textiles were company-provided pension benefits and accident insurance. The hope of a company pension must certainly have acted to prevent older workers from opposing the company. Pension benefits were only important for the small core of women, usually single women or widows, who made braidmaking a lifetime occupation. Given the low wages in braidmaking, employer pensions were probably an important component of these workers' plans for a secure old age. But employers' pensions could not be taken for granted, for the pensions were given in a completely arbitrary fashion. The company recognized no routine obligation to give any particular worker a pension, and each pension was the subject of an individual decision.[68]

Paternalism in metalworking rested on the personal authority of the local company director, Adrien de Montgolfier. Montgolfier was a shrewd administrator who cultivated a reputation for generosity and disinterest which proved invaluable in combatting the workers' movement. The sincerity or extent of paternalism in metalworking is difficult to evaluate. Professionally cynical police commissioners often doubted Montgolfier's intentions. In 1882 a police commissioner reported:

> A dinner for 300 was given today by M. de Montgolfier for the principal employees of the large forge and steel factory in Saint-Chamond.
>
> The ostensible motive for this invitation was to thank the employees for their attendance at the marriage of Miss Montgolfier which took place a little while ago.
>
> But the secret motive was to ensure that the workers would not respond to a strike call . . . none of the leaders who are traveling around the workers' centers have yet come here to preach the strike. As for the workers, it is difficult to know how they will respond. . . .[69]

Montgolfier claimed to protect his "old" and "loyal" workers, although on several occasions workers in his plant accused him of arbitrary dismissals and the systematic removal of older workers.[70]

Paternalism could sometimes be used by workers to force concessions from employers, but ultimately such victories only reinforced employer power. In 1911 a workshop of "old and experienced" workers addressed a letter to Montgolfier requesting a wage raise but leaving the actual amount to Montgolfier's discretion. This was a difficult appeal for Montgolfier to ignore, especially since he privately recognized that inflation was lowering workers' wages, and he did grant a moderate wage raise.[71] Almost immediately this increase had to be extended to workers in other workshops, and it became a general wage increase. But while workers' appeals to paternal authority could sometimes win gains, such victories only resulted in confirming and strengthening the influence of a doctrine which inhibited worker organization. The workers' letter of appeal had ended: "If we have asked you for a wage raise, it is in the spirit of confidence in the success of our demands. There is no question of a strike, of a rebellion, nor of any conflict which might stop production in the steelworks."[72]

The decline of the well-organized, fiercely-political artisanal club also made itself felt in local politics. Between 1901 and 1919 Aristide Briand was able to perform the remarkable feat of harmonizing the interests of republicans, radical socialists, and independent socialists in Saint-Chamond, everyone, in fact, but the Saint-Chamonnais reactionaries.

Aristide Briand was always something of an anomaly among Saint-Chamonnais socialists. Saint-Chamonnais socialists did not play any role in the selection of Briand as the socialist candidate in 1901, and it was only after his election that he acquired a substantial constituency in Saint-Chamond. His candidacy was imposed on local socialists, much against their will, by Stéphanois socialists.[73] The district in which Briand ran included all of Saint-Chamond as well as a portion of Saint-Etienne and several other valley towns. In the 1901 election, which he won on the first ballot, Briand ran well ahead of his conservative republican opponent in Saint-Etienne but trailed behind in Saint-Chamond.[74]

Briand's appeal in Saint-Chamond was based on personal magnetism. Almost immediately after his election Briand joined the government as *ministre des cultes*, and later as president of the *conseil*. Everyone in Saint-Chamond hoped to benefit from his proximity to power. His rapid move in a conservative direction conciliated moderate radical socialists and conservative republicans in Saint-Chamond; yet he was also able to build a constituency among Saint-Chamonnais workers. In 1902 Briand successfully fought for a bill to reduce unemployment in the armament industry by lowering the legal age at which armaments workers could receive pensions, and in 1904 he submitted his own bill for the same purpose.[75] Petrus Faure suggests that Briand used his governmental authority to ensure that government contracts would be delivered to the Compagnie des aciéries de la marine.[76] But Briand's personal intervention was largely unnecessary in the wave of prosperity which swept Saint-Chamonnais metalworking as France began to rearm after 1902.

By 1906 many Saint-Chamonnais workers who had initially been skeptical of Briand were completely won over. Each year Briand moved further to the right, but local socialists loyally stood by him. In 1906 an attempt by left-wing trade unionists to organize a metal strike failed when moderate trade unionists countered with a proposal to send their grievances to Briand in place of striking.[77] Even after Briand crushed the postalworkers' strike in 1910, the majority of socialists and trade union leaders still refused to denounce him. According to the police commissioner, moderate socialists and trade unionists replied to their left-wing critics that they were only waiting for the fall of his government to censure him, yet when his government did fall they remained silent.[78] Not until the great postwar upsurge of 1919 was Briand forced to abandon his Saint-Chamonnais district.

The refusal of Saint-Chamonnais socialists and trade unionists to publicly denounce Briand, although they privately deplored his actions, reflected their own organizational weakness. Basically Saint-Chamonnais workers reaped few rewards for their support. A local conservative concluded:

> . . . the arrival of Briand in our peaceful valley, for a moment, caused a wave of enthusiasm and, for a while, galvanized local spirits and opened the perspective of great hopes. . . . For a long time everyone forgot the nauseating smell of the Gier, the horror of the murderous slums, the unlighted streets which enclosed every youth in their narrow walls, the unpaved streets filled with refuse, a hospital which filled with dread every sick person who entered . . . no one noticed the need for communal action until the departure of the tribune who found here his political cradle. . . .[79]

While the trade unionists and socialists who rallied to Briand had little choice, their support for Briand further weakened their own organizations. Workers placed their faith in Briand's direct intervention, and during this period of national labor upsurge, with the sole exception of the construction workers, local labor organizations atrophied. During these same years the local socialist party gradually merged into the radical socialist party. The merger was a crippling blow to Saint-Chamonnais socialism, and it never fully recovered. The branch of the Section française de l'internationale ouvrière (SFIO) which later re-emerged never measured up to its predecessor.

In the years between 1878 and 1914 the Saint-Chamonnais industrial working class played little role in strike activity. Saint-Chamonnais metalworkers and textileworkers were considerably less involved in strike actions than Ripagérien artisanal glassworkers and industrial metalworkers. The reason for Saint-Chamonnais worker quiescence can be found in the very nature of the work which they performed. Saint-Chamonnais industrial workers lacked the group cohesion and financial resources of artisans, and, unlike Ripagérien industrial workers, they could not find allies who possessed such vital resources. The only militant section of the Saint-Chamonnais working class was the small group of construction workers, and they lacked both incentive and resources to provide significant aid to the mass of Saint-Chamonnais workers. The very weakness of the Saint-Chamonnais workers' movement provided ground for the rise of opportunist socialists like Aristide Briand, whose growing influence further weakened the local movement in the years after 1901.

If the example of Rive-de-Gier shows the substantial protest which coalitions of artisanal and industrial workers could generate, the example of Saint-Chamond shows the almost overwhelming obstacles to participation in sustained protest which confronted industrial workers. But some important questions still remain about the role of artisans in strike coalitions. Glassworking, with its elite of glassblowers who dominated an elaborate skill hierarchy and received high wages, presents only one aspect of artisanal worker life. Most French skill hierarchies were less sharply defined and not so well paid. Also, the glassblowers, looking down from the apex of a steep craft pyramid, could not fail to be aware of the need to advocate a broad political philosophy capable of drawing in different types of workers, both other glassworkers and metalworkers. But were the large masses of less well-paid artisans capable of a similar consciousness? In order to better understand the political capacities of artisanal workers, it is necessary to observe them in their own environment, and the next chapter looks at our predominantly artisanal town.

NOTES

1. J. Vacher, *Poésies et chansons de Jacque Vacher* (Saint-Etienne: Société de l'imprimerie de "La Loire republicaine," 1898), pp. 111–112.

2. *Le peuple de la Loire*, May 21, 1895.
3. Industrial census, 1891, ADL 54/M/8.
4. *L'Action ouvrière et paysanne*, Feb. 11, 1911.
5. Industrial census, Saint-Chamond, 1891.
6. Information on Saint-Chamonnais strikes comes from Office du travail, *Statistique des grèves*, 1890–1914, and ADL 92/M—Grèves.
7. Detailed information on the history of artisanal metalworking in Saint-Chamond can be found in: Gras, *Essai sur l'histoire de la quincaillerie*; Perrin, *Saint-Etienne et sa région économique*; Condamin, *Histoire de Saint-Chamond*; and Thiollier, *La chambre de commerce de Saint-Etienne*.
8. On the centralization of Saint-Chamonnais industry, see Reybaud, *Le fer et la houille*, on Saint-Chamonnais gun tubes, see J. S. Jean, *Steel: Its History, Manufacture, Properties and Uses* (London: Span, 1880), pp. 226–28.
9. On the history of French puddling, see Jean Vial, *L'Industrialisation de la sidérurgie française 1814–1864*, 2 vols. (Paris: Mouton, 1967). For a description of the actual process of puddling, see Jean-Paul Courtheaux, "Privilèges et misères d'un métier sidérurgique au XIXe siècle: Le puddleur," *Revue d'histoire économique et sociale* 37 (1959), 161–84, and G. D'Avenel, "L'industrie du fer," in *Le mécanisme dans la vie moderne* 1 (Paris: Armand Colin, 1896), 110–54.
10. F. Le Play, "Description des procédés métallurgiques employés dans le pays de Gaulles," *Annales des mines* 13 (1848), 16.
11. Reybaud, *Le fer et la houille*, pp. 136–8. On the rise of shop floor supervision in England, see Sidney Pollard, *The Genesis of Modern Management* (London: Edward Arnold, 1959).
12. Chomienne, *Histoire de la ville de Rive-de-Gier*.
13. *Le temps*, Feb. 25, 1893.
14. An illustrated album depicting the organization of work in Saint-Chamond was produced by the Compagnie des aciéries de la marine, *Usines de Saint-Chamond*, 3 vol. (Paris: E. Mesière, 1900–1914). For a description of the work process in open hearth steelmaking, see H. M. Vernon, *Fatigue and Efficiency in the Iron and Steel Industry*, no. 5 (London: Industrial Fatigue Research Board, 1920), and David Brody, *Steelworking in America: The Nonunion Era* (Cambridge, Mass.: Harvard University Press, 1960).
15. *Le temps*, Feb., 1893. Information on Saint-Chamonnais supervision in the Compagnie des aciéries de la marine appears in Benoist, "Le travail dans la grande industrie," pt. 1, pp. 610–11.
   On the evolution of machine tools in nineteenth-century Europe, see D. F. Galloway, "Machine Tools," in *A History of Technology*, ed. Charles Singer *et al.*, 5 (Oxford: Clarendon Press, 1958), 636–57, and K. R. Gilbert, "Machine Tools," in *ibid.*, 4, 417–41.
   Keith Burgess describes the response of British skilled workers to the mechanization of machine tools, in "Technological Change and the 1853 Lock-Out in the British Engineering Industry," *International Review of Social History* 14 (1969), 215–36.
   The mechanization and division of labor, already far advanced in Saint-Chamond by 1900, disarmed Saint-Chamonnais workers and facilitated the introduction of even more brutal methods of shop-floor control, such as Taylorization; Saint-Chamonnais workers responded apathetically to a CGT rally against Taylorization (ADL 93/M/11). On Taylorization in France during this

period, see Patrick Friedenson, *Histoire des usines Renault*, 1 (Paris: Editions du Seuil, 1972), 70–78; Andre Heron, "Le taylorisme, hier et demain," *Les temps modernes* (Aug.-Sept., 1975), pp. 220–78; and Aimée Moutet,"Les origines du système de Taylor en France," *Le mouvement social* 58 (1967), 3–39.

16. ADL 10/M/102.

17. Wage estimates for 1901 come from Benoist, "Le travail dans la grande industrie," pt. 2. Benoist is probably reliable for the daily wages which were posted by the company but probably unreliable for the daily wages of workers on piece rates. More consistent with other estimates of Stéphanois workers' wages are the calculations made in the Office du travail's *Bordereaux des salaires . . . 1901* for Saint-Chamond, pp. 127–71. Benoist seems to have depended more heavily on information provided by the company than by the police commissioners, who report a substantially lower income for many categories of workers; police figures for workers on piece rates are much more comparable to those of similar categories of workers in neighboring towns.

18. Benoist, "Le travail dans la grande industrie," pt. 2, pp. 643–44.

19. *Ibid.*

20. "Enquête de 1871–1875," *Chambre consultative*, AN C3022.

21. "Rapport de l'ingénieur ordinaire des mines," Sept. 19, 1883, ADL 92/M/21.

For a description of the work of the moulder, see A. Tisson, *L'Art du mouleur* (Paris: Bouelry, 1897). Christian Gras looks at the effect of mechanization on the national union of moulders between 1900 and 1909, in "L'Ouvrier mouleur à travers le journal de sa fédération," pp. 51–68.

22. Manuscript census, Saint-Chamond, 1891, ADL 49/M/315.

For a description of the work of the turner, see Samuel Smiles, *Industrial Biography: Iron Workers and Tool-Makers* (Boston: Ticknor and Fields, 1864), pp. 256–63.

For a comprehensive discussion of work techniques and residential patterns in a modern steel town, see Charles R. Walker, *Steeltown, an Industrial Case History* (New York: Harper Brothers, 1964).

23. Based on a 10 percent sample of all the families in Saint-Chamond drawn from the 1891 manuscript census.

24. Paul Leroy-Beaulieu, *De l'état moral et intellectuel des populations ouvrières* (Paris: Libraire Guillaumin, 1868), pp. 73–74.

On French working-class drinking habits in the nineteenth century, see Marrus, "Social Drinking in the Belle Epoque," pp. 115–41. An interesting interpretation of the changes in British alcohol consumption in the nineteenth century which might well apply to France is Dingle, "Drink and Working-Class Living Standards in Great Britain 1870–1914," pp. 608–22.

25. Audiganne, *Les populations ouvrières*, 1, 32.

26. Much of this theorizing about cafés comes from Gareth Stedman Jones, "The Remaking of the English Working Class," *Journal of Social History* 7 (Summer, 1974), 460–508.

There is considerable continuity across time and space in the organization of the artisanal café, centered around occupation. John Money describes the eighteenth-century ancestors of Jones's working-class pubs, in "Taverns, Coffeehouses and Clubs: Local Politics and Popular Articulacy in the Birmingham Area in the Age of the American Revolution," *Historical Journal* 14 (1971), 15–47.

The nineteenth-century artisanal taverns and clubs of American workers, described in a series of fine articles by Daniel J. Walkowitz, John T. Cumbler, Michael Feldberg, and Paul Faler in *Labor History*, vol. 3 (Summer, 1974), have substantial continuity with one patronized by modern American construction workers, according to E. E. LeMasters, *Blue Collar Aristocrats* (Madison: University of Wisconsin Press, 1975).

27. Dec. 1, 1882, ADL 10/M/79.

28. ADL 10/M/79.

29. ADL 19/M/11–12.

30. July 16, 1882, ADL 10/M/79.

31. Sept. 11, 1880, ADL 93/M/11.

32. Mar., 1894, ADL 10/M/102.

33. On rules, see the description of the meeting of May 2, 1897, ADL 10/M/90. On a meeting of masons in May, 1908, see ADL 10/M/139; of leftist republicans in Dec., 1900, see *L'Eclaireur de Saint-Chamond*, Dec. 8, 1900.

34. *L'Unité socialiste*, Apr. 13, 1900.

35. *Ibid.*, Apr. 29, 1900. A fine study of the changing politics of industrial workers over an extended period of of time is Jeanne Gaillard, "Les usines Cail et les ouvriers métallurgistes de Grenelle," *Le mouvement social* 33–34 (Oct., 1960–Mar., 1961), 35–53.

36. It is possible to reconstruct the organization of work in Saint-Chamonnais and Lyonnais artisanal silkmaking in considerable detail. Some relevant studies of the silk trade are: Condamin, *Histoire de Saint-Chamond*, pp. 625–46; Jules Simon, *L'Ouvrière* (Paris: Hachette, 1871); Reybaud, *Études sur le régime des manufactures*, pp. 219–20; P. Donot, *Études historiques sur les origines de la fabrication des rubans . . .* (Lyon: H. George, 1889); Natalie Rondot, *Les soies*, vol. 1 (Paris: Imprimerie nationale, 1887); and Justin Godart, *L'Ouvrier en soie* (Lyon: Bernoux and Cumin, 1899).

37. For an early description of mechanization in silk, see Audiganne, *Les populations ouvrières*, 2, 82–83, 91.

For a description of the Perricault loom, which mechanized Saint-Chamonnais braiding, see Gras, *Histoire de la rubanerie*, pp. 679–700. More technical descriptions of the actual process of braiding are contained in A. Beauquis, *Histoire économique de la soie* (Paris: Donot and Pinot, 1900), p. 199, and H. Baret, *Manuel de rubanerie, passementerie, et lacets* (Paris: Ballière, 1924), pp. 258–65.

For an elaborate study of the skill demanded in silk weaving, which was very similar to braiding, see P. M. Elton, *An Analysis of the Individual Differences in the Output of Silk Weavers*, no. 5 (London: Industrial Fatigue Research Board, 1920). For some detailed pictures of braiding machines, see W. A. Douglas, *Braiding and Braiding Machinery* (Eindhoven: Centrex, 1964).

38. Simon, *L'Ouvrière*, p. 72.

39. Beauquis, *Histoire économique de la soie*, p. 199; see also Gras, *Histoire de la rubanerie*.

40. Industrial census, Saint-Chamond, 1891. A contemporary analysis of the role of women in factory work in the mid-nineteenth century is Paul Leroy-Beaulieu, "Les ouvrières de fabrique autrefois et aujourd'hui," *Revue des deux mondes*, 97 (Feb. 1, 1872), 630–57.

41. ADL 10/M/102. See also Balas Frères, *L'Industrie française des tresses et lacets* (Lyon: Association typographique, 1890).

42. On wages in 1894, see ADL 10/M/102; wages had only risen to 2.0 francs by 1906, according to ADL 92/M/142.

43. Manuscript census, Saint-Chamond, 1891.

44. Reybaud, *Le fer et la houille*, pp. 152–53.

Margaret Hewitt makes the important point that the transition from domestic to factory production was traumatic for married women, in *Wives and Mothers in Victorian Industry* (London: Rockliff, 1958). The family division of labor between metalworking and textiles effectively prevented the continuation of the domestic work unit into the factory, as was the case in some areas of the Nord (William Reddy, "Family and Factory: French Linen Weavers in the Belle Epoque," *Journal of Social History* 8 [1975], 102–12) and in many areas of England (Neil J. Smelser, *Social Change in the Industrial Revolution* [Chicago: University of Chicago Press, 1959]).

Esther Boserup provides an international context for the discussion of women's work in preindustrial societies, in *Woman's Role in Economic Development* (New York: St. Martins Press, 1970).

45. Gras, *Histoire de la rubanerie*, p. 738. Nationally, French women textile-workers played a far smaller role in trade unions and strikes than their proportion in the industry would warrant; see Guilbert, *Les femmes et l'organisation syndicale avant 1914*.

46. Manuscript census, Saint-Chamond, 1891.

47. The recruitment of labor from these areas was part of a century-old tradition; see Olwen Hufton, *The Poor of Eighteenth Century France, 1750–1789* (Oxford: Clarendon Press, 1974), and "Women and the Family Economy in Eighteenth-Century France," *French Historical Studies* 9 (Spring, 1975), 1–22.

48. ADL 88/M/18.

49. Beauquis, *Histoire économique de la soie*, pp. 101–2.

50. Victor Jury in *Association française pour l'avancement des sciences*, 26th sess. (Aug., 1897), 2 (Saint-Etienne: Théolier, 1897), 125–26.

51. Abel Chatelain, "Les usines-internats et les migrations féminines dans la région lyonnaise," *Revue d'histoire économique et sociale* 48 (1970), 373–94.

52. Jury in *Association française*, pp. 125–26. Information on dormitories comes from the manuscript census, Saint-Chamond, 1891.

53. ADL 92/M/204.

54. Gonon, *Histoire de la chanson Stéphanoise et forézienne*, p. 202.

This interpretation of illegitimacy conflicts with that outlined by Edward Shorter in *The Making of the Modern Family* (New York: Basic Books, 1975). An important reply to Shorter is that of Louise Tilly, Joan Scott, and Miriam Cohen, "Women's Work and European Fertility Patterns," *Journal of Interdisciplinary History* 6 (Winter, 1976), 447–76.

55. On the wages of construction workers, see the information on strike demands in ADL 92/M/190.

Some descriptions of the organization of work in carpentry in late nineteenth-century Paris are: Joseph Barbaret, *Le travail en France: Monographies professionelles*, "Charpentiers et scieurs de long," 3 (Paris: Berger-Levrault, 1887), 272–382; Pierre Du Maroussem, *Charpentiers de Paris*, vol. 1 (Paris: Arthur Rousseau, 1891); and F. Le Play, *Les ouvriers européens*, vol. 5 (Paris: Tours, A. Mame, 1877–79). The work process in Paris was probably similar to that in Saint-Chamond, but there is no evidence of any Saint-Chamonnais equivalent to Parisian workers' elaborate *compagnonnage* organizations.

56. Material on construction workers' wages can be found in files on strikes, ADL 92/M/90 and 93/M/84.

57. *L'Eclaireur de Saint-Chamond*, Sept. 25, 1911.

58. On other Saint-Chamonnais demonstrations, see AN F/713605. A fine study of the nationwide anti-inflation movement, which describes in passing the demonstrations in the Stéphanois valley, is Jean-Marie Flonneau, "Crise de vie chère et mouvement syndicale, 1910–1914," *Le mouvement social* 72 (July–Sept., 1970), 49–81.

59. Gras, *Histoire de la rubanerie*, p. 736.

On the participation of the Compagnie des aciéries de la marine in the international armaments market, see M. C. Curey, *L'Artillerie de Saint-Chamond à l'exposition universelle de 1900* (Paris: Berger-Levrault, 1901).

60. ADL 10/M/103.

61. The whole series of reports is found in ADL 10/M/102–3.

62. Reports on the rise of metal unionism in Saint-Chamond are found in ADL 92/M/107. Reports on union meetings are in ADL 93/M/11.

For the Saint-Chamonnais delegates' report to the national convention, see Union fédérale des ouvriers métallurgistes de la France, *Compte rendu des travaux, 20–22 Septembre 1901* (Paris: Imprimerie économique, 1901), pp. 43–44.

63. ADL 92/M/107.

64. *Ibid.*

65. June 2, 1875, ADL 92/M/14.

66. Union fédérale des ouvriers métallurgistes de la France, *Compte rendu des travaux, 16–20 Septembre 1903* (Paris: Association ouvrière, 1903), pp. 230–31.

67. Jury in *Association française*, pp. 127–28.

68. *Ibid.*, p. 127. A formally organized aid society which had existed in the eighties preserved the right of the employers to decide how all money would be allocated; see ADL 93/M/6.

69. Apr. 16, 1882, ADL 10/M/79.

70. Demands of the workers in 1901 are in ADL 92/M/107, in 1906 in ADL 92/M/140.

71. ADL 93/M/11.

72. *L'Eclaireur de Saint-Chamond*, Apr. 15, 1911.

73. AN F/7 12499.

74. ADL 3/M/35.

75. Archives de la chambre de commerce de Saint-Etienne, carton 105, dossier 16.

76. Faure, *Histoire du mouvement ouvrier*, p. 455.

77. ADL 92/M/140.

78. ADL 93/M/67.

79. M. Fournier, *L'Essor d'une ville ouvrière, l'oeuvre sociale de municipalité de Saint-Chamond* (Saint-Etienne: Imprimerie de la Loire républicaine, 1934), pp. 22–23.

CHAPTER SIX

Artisans and Industrial Workers in Le Chambon-Feugerolles, 1871–1914

The psychology of workers is such that they only appear animated . . . in groups. They mistrust individuals; secretaries are placed in close dependence on the union which appoints them and revokes them *ad nutum*. It is the idea of the General Strike which most formidably expresses the massive power of this action by groups.[1]

Between 1888 and 1914 Le Chambon-Feugerolles emerged as a center of militant trade unionism; the whole valley of the Ondaine became known as the "red valley."[2] Although at the beginning of the twentieth century local strike activity reached extraordinary levels, overall, Chambonnaire strikes shared several important characteristics of national strike actions. First, as in the nation as a whole, the size of Chambonnaire strikes increased dramatically between 1890 and 1914 (see Tables 27–29). Second, participation in strikes changed; while artisans continued to be involved in mass strikes, industrial workers began to play a predominant role.

The contrasts between each of the three large waves of mass strikes that occurred in the prewar years will illustrate the changes in local strike patterns. In the earliest period of Chambonnaire strike militancy, during the years between 1889 and 1890, industrial workers played only a minor part in strike actions. In the next wave of strikes, in 1906, industrial workers were more active but artisanal workers continued pre-eminent. In that year a strike broke out over an employer's attempt to punish his workers for observing May Day. Initially, metalworkers, boltworkers, and fileworkers went out on strike together, but only the artisanal fileworkers were able to sustain the struggle for any length of time.[3]

The third and largest outbreak of strike activity in Le Chambon resulted from concerted actions of artisanal and industrial workers; two large strikes, the first in 1910 and the next in 1911, attracted

Table 27

Number of Strikers (Metal Trades) in Le Chambon-Feugerolles,
1885–1914

	1885–89	1890–94	1895–99	1900–1904	1905–9	1910–14
Metalworkers	0	0	26	46	938	210
Boltworkers	0	470	600	120	936	2,035
Fileworkers	1,345	37	130	420	1,215	1,800

Table 28

Duration of Strikes (in Days) in Le Chambon-Feugerolles,
1885—1914

	1885–89	1890–94	1895–99	1900–1904	1905–9	1910–14
Metalworkers	0	7	10	113	24	42
Boltworkers	0	23	1	145	54	281
Fileworkers	25	17.5	2	154	57	42

Table 29

Worker-Days Lost in Strikes in Le Chambon-Feugerolles, 1885–1914

	1885–89	1890–94	1895–99	1900–1904	1905–9	1910–14
Metalworkers	0	0	260	1,142	7,270	11,148
Boltworkers	0	4,660	600	13,780	10,747	128,210
Fileworkers	23,189	647.5	260	6,520	54,180	75,600

attention because of their size and duration. Industrial workers were the most important participants in these strikes, although they received substantial aid from artisanal workers.[4]

The mass strike actions which took place in Le Chambon in the years immediately before World War I occurred in a very different political atmosphere from the mass strikes in Rive-de-Gier in the nineties. While French socialism had continued to expand, it did not achieve the reforms which had seemed imminent in the nineties. The formation of a social reform alliance had encouraged the rapid growth of mass socialist parties and strikes, but increased worker militancy frightened away the radical socialists who were members of this coalition.[5] By now Clemenceau, a man whom Marx had hoped to win over to the socialist cause, had become the "first cop of France," president of a government whose cardinal principle was repression of the labor movement. Opportunist socialist politicians like Briand and Millerand, who had staked out a left-wing position in anticipation of the formation of a socialist–radical socialist governmental coalition, began to move in an increasingly conservative direction as prospects dimmed. Socialism continued to make progress in France in the years between 1906 and 1914 despite the growing conservatism of the opportunist socialists, which embittered some local militants and made them wary of all political parties.

In an effort to better understand the dynamics of mass strike actions, the analysis which follows will concentrate on the development of the two mass strikes which marked the highpoint of strike activity in the predominantly artisanal town. Several important aspects of these strikes which will be discussed are: the influence of mass-membership, industry-wide unionism on worker solidarity; the contribution of work structure to union participation; and the stimulus to artisanal militancy provided by technological change and the spread of revolutionary syndicalist doctrines.

The General Strike, 1910–11

The climax of Chambonnaire strike activity in the prewar period undoubtedly occurred in 1910 and 1911. These two strikes were closely related; in the first, the power of local unionism reached unparalleled heights; in the second, union influence was checked by resurgent employers. A look at the 1910 strike shows the maximum mobilization capabilities of the Chambonnaire working class. The attempt of a boltmaker, M. Besson, to fire a militant worker provoked the initial strike of industrial workers. But more important than this single incident, Besson was an old opponent of the union; in 1901 a strike at his plant had lasted 137 days, and in 1910 he still refused to acknowledge the presence of the union. The metal union demanded that the employer rehire the discharged worker and protested against his arbitrary action by asking that he formally recognize the union. Besson refused, and on December 22, 1909, his workers struck. The local metal union, whose membership included both artisanal fileworkers and industrial boltworkers and metal fabrication workers, gave the strike complete support and opened its strike fund to the boltworkers.[6] All the bolt manufacturers were opposed to official recognition of the union; to demonstrate their resolve, they agreed not to hire any of the striking workers and pledged to fill Besson's orders. When the boltworkers learned of this agreement, they retaliated on February 16, 1910, fifty-six days after the commencement of the original factory strike, with a general strike of all boltworkers.[7]

The declaration of the general strike of boltworkers revealed weaknesses in the industrial workers' union organization that worsened the striking workers' position. While most boltworkers obeyed the strike call, some did not; almost daily skirmishes ensued between striking boltworkers and nonstrikers, and a demonstration marched to the outskirts of town where it sacked and set afire a rural café owned by a nonstriking worker. Nonstrikers formed a small, "independent," "yellow" union to oppose the strike. The bolt manufacturers remained obdurate, rejecting the mediation of a *juge de paix* proposed by the union.[3]

Suddenly, the struggle dramatically escalated. On February 23, in an act of solidarity, all the fileworkers and some metalworkers joined the striking boltworkers; at least 1,900 artisanal fileworkers and several hundred metalworkers followed the 900 industrial boltworkers already on strike. Most of the town's workers were now participating in the strike. As a result of this new pressure, negotiations began but brought no sign of settlement. Meanwhile, the situation of the Besson workers became desperate. The expansion of the strike to include an ever-larger number of workers had exhausted union funds, and only outside contributions maintained the union strike kitchens, the *soupes communistes*, to which whole families flocked. As the conflict lengthened, violence spread; several nonstriking workers were fired upon, employers' homes were attacked, beatings occurred, and dynamite was used against several factories.[9]

The support of the local Chambonnaire community for the strike was considerable, and at its peak the town was almost in a state of insurrection. The arrest of a major strike leader on March 15 brought the struggle to a climax. Early that morning the authorities asked Jean-Marie Tyr, an anarchist leader of the union, to come to the city hall; he was not suspicious of this invitation because since the strike had begun he had often conferred there. But upon entering the city hall, he was arrested, charged with "complicity" in arson, robbery, and housebreaking, and quickly whisked away in an automobile to Saint-Etienne. After waiting several hours for his return, some strikers found out about his arrest, and word quickly spread.

The highhanded behavior of the authorities outraged local sentiment. At an afternoon meeting the cry "To Saint-Etienne" arose, and a march started out to that city. A journalist described the march: "Drums and bugles preceded the quickly marching column. . . . Above the crowds' heads were seen cudgels and pieces of wood, some carried a broom with an inscription on it, someone else waved a little red banner. Women cut branches of wood and used them as canes. One gallant old woman, in her seventies at least, wrinkled, infirm, haltingly followed the column. She was singing the *Carmagnole* at the top of her lungs."[10] While this march was in progress, the *procurer général* in Saint-Etienne received a telephone call from the prefect. "He [the prefect] announced that . . . a column of 1,500 strikers was marching on Saint-Etienne to demand the freeing of Tyr. The prefect told me that it was his opinion that the arrest of Tyr was a provocation and that the evening would see 'gunshots and bloodshed' in the streets of Le Chambon. He asked me not to oppose the freeing of Tyr."[11]

Tyr's release was a symbolic act; the morale of the united Chambonnaire working-class community rose while that of the discredited employers fell. Soon after, both sides returned to the conference table and this time worked out a compromise. On April 5, 104 days after the strike began at the Besson factory and 41 days after the solidarity strike of fileworkers and metalworkers, a contract was signed establishing factory committees composed of union appointees and elected representatives from each factory who were empowered to represent the feelings of the workers to their employers.[12]

Although anticlimactic, the last act of the 1910 strike was yet to come. A couple of weeks after the strike, on April 24, the eve of the mayoral elections, a group of workers, incensed at the conduct of the mayor during the strike, attacked the city hall and burned it down. While the leaders of the attack were only loosely associated with the workers' movement, their act had important repercussions for all local workers because it ensured the defeat of the socialist candidate for deputy, whose victory had appeared likely. Many workers and nearby farmers who supported militant actions during the strike were repelled by senseless incendiarism, and socialist defeat weakened the political position of local unionism; the uncertain issue of the approaching election in part explained the solicitude of the prefect in releasing the union leader Tyr.[13] Moreover, the fire also gave the prefect an excuse to issue a decree prohibiting public demonstrations in Le Chambon.[14] The enforcement of this decree was an important factor in the defeat of the boltworkers in the 1911 strike.

The 1911 strike was the last of the great prewar struggles. In this bitterly contested strike-lockout the union lost the measure of recognition won in the earlier strike. The odds were heavily against the boltworkers from the beginning. The recently formed employers' organizations gained strength after the light metal trades merged into a unified organization, replacing the old separate trade organizations. Also, the economic situation in 1911 did not favor strike activity. The screw and bolt industry, prosperous in 1910, declined in 1911, and employers laid workers off. The intransigent employer who provoked the 1911 strike owned a larger bolt factory in Saint-Etienne and, for lack of orders, had been considering temporarily closing his factory in Le Chambon.[15] Perhaps most important of all, the market for files also declined; thus the artisanal fileworkers were not able to support the industrial boltworkers on the massive scale of the preceding strike. Sensing new opportunities, the "yellow" union formed in 1910 had remained in existence.

The 1911 strike focused on the issue of union recognition. A bolt employer, M. Mermier, accepted union proposals for a compromise wage cut but refused to allow the union to initial the new agreement. In response, the workers went out on strike on May 12. On May 28 the bolt employers announced a general lockout to support Mermier; the union retaliated by calling a general strike of all workers in the bolt trade.[16] The violent acts of the 1910 strike were repeated on an even wider scale. Two bolt factories, one of them Mermier's, were almost completely burned down. Menacing leaflets were received by employers from an anonymous "Organisation révolutionnaire du combat." The boltmakers turned to the Comité des forges for aid.[17]

The lockout ended on July 20, 1911, yet few workers returned to work. The return to work happened only slowly, and not until August 23 did the bolt factories resume normal production. While the union remained in existence, every effort was made to root out union militants and many of the leaders of the bolt strike were forced to leave Le Chambon.[18]

Despite their ultimate defeat, the 1911 strike represented a valiant effort of industrial workers to defend their position against a more powerful opponent. During this strike Chambonnaire industrial workers were able to carry out a sustained struggle of a kind which, time and again, Saint-Chamonnais workers had proved themselves incapable of. This difference is mainly explained by the presence of artisanal workers in Le Chambon. Although Chambonnaire industrial workers were the major participants in both the 1910 and 1911 strikes, their ability to make a substantial effort depended on artisanal support; indeed, in the 1910 artisanal strike solidarity had turned likely defeat into victory. In this strike artisanal fileworkers supported industrial boltworkers without raising any of their own independent demands. A student of the strike, Léon de Seilhac, explained the decision of the fileworkers to declare their solidarity strike: "They thought that the boltworkers were too newly unionized and too small (only 5% of the union and 10% of the boltworkforce) to confront a strike without being surrounded by the fileworkers, experienced trade unionists and 90% unionized. . . ."[19]

But solidarity strikes were only one of the means used by fileworkers to stimulate the development of an industrial workers' movement. The most enduring contribution of the fileworkers was probably an organizational one. Although numerous attempts were made to form boltworkers' and metalworkers' unions, the fileworkers was the only group which remained continually in existence between 1888 and 1901; in 1901 the fileworkers fused their union with the embryonic organizations of the bolt- and metalworkers to form a general union of the metal trades, the Chambre syndicale des ouvriers métallurgistes du Chambon-Feugerolles et ses extensions. Within this organization the fileworkers continued to exert influence. Petrus Faure claims that "the fileworkers, the most numerous [union members], among whom the spirit of struggle was most developed, played the leading role," adding that while the fileworkers were the most important, "the strikes which took place were chiefly those of boltworkers."[20]

Finally, the fileworkers exerted influence on the industrial workers' movement in a variety of ways, both formal and informal, between 1888 and 1914. In the early years of Chambonnaire strike activity, fileworkers carried out the most militant and successful strikes and served as an example to other groups. More than this, they consciously tried to spread unionism to other segments of the working class; on several occasions they sponsored speakers on the need for a separate union for boltworkers and metalworkers.[21] Although the fileworkers did not carry out a solidarity strike in 1911, they did financially and politically support the striking boltworkers. In his thesis Jean-Paul Martin best summarizes the fileworkers' spirit:

> The fileworker militants were at the bottom of all the attempts made at Le Chambon to spread the movement to other groups; there is an excellent probability that without them and their always active solidarity the level of worker organization among the boltworkers or toolmakers would be much lower or even nonexistent. . . .
>
> After the fusion [1901] the fileworkers still played a leading role; organizing aid to strikers . . . the fileworkers put the elasticity of their own schedule [at the boltworkers' disposal] in order to join them in their daily demonstrations whenever they occurred, the file-workers continually had an influential effect [*effet d'entrainment*] on the other trades. . . .[22]

Trade Union Organization

In Le Chambon-Feugerolles, as in Rive-de-Gier, the presence of a strong trade union helps explain artisanal solidarity with industrial workers. The most important formally organized work-ing-class group in Le Chambon was the trade union. Unions contributed to worker mobilization in two ways. First, the forms of trade union organization helped define the groups which the union sought to mobilize. In the late nineteenth century English and American craft unions generally confined themselves to one particular skill or high-wage group. The early formation of an industry-wide union in Le Chambon-Feugerolles had important

consequences for worker solidarity: industry-wide unionism promoted cooperation between artisanal and industrial workers. Second, the union acquired control over collective resources which
were made available to striking workers. Strike funds, union
halls, and experienced leaders all helped to lower the costs of
strike activity for individual workers. The artisanal filecutters were
the group best equipped to form trade unions, and unionization in
turn increased their cohesion and collective resources. It was
chiefly through trade union organization that artisans exerted
influence on industrial workers' strike activity.

While many of the leaders of Chambonnaire strike actions were
anarchists, they did not neglect organization. In fact, as the incident of the "exodus of the infants" demonstrates, local workers
were exceptionally well organized. During the prolonged strike of
1910 strikers' families sent their children to be taken care of by
trade unionists in other cities. This aided the strike in two ways.
First, outside unionists relieved the financial stress on strikers by
assuming responsibility for feeding and taking care of strikers'
children. Second, the sending away of the children made head-
lines all over France and won public sympathy for the strikers
by advertising their desperate plight. The methodical and precise organization exhibited during the carefully staged and well-
publicized "exodus of the infants" calls to mind a syndicalist Busby
Berkely working with a hammer and sickle motif:

> At eight o'clock in the morning the cortege forms itself at the
> Vernicherie.
> Preceded by drums and bugles, accompanied by the Union
> Harmony [the union band], the long train of demonstrators, about
> 3,000, winds itself along the streets of Le Chambon.
> Women and girls are numerous. They have placed red cockades in
> their hair or their bosom. Some have been charged with collecting
> money on the sidewalks and these gracious strikers collect a good
> deal of money.
> The infants, numbering around 60, are put into two large vehicles.
> Some stewards selected from among the members of the strike
> committee watch over them and make sure that they are warmly
> covered.
> The union banner and four or five red flags, as well as some
> inscribed placards, dominate the cortege.

At the city limits of Le Chambon, some mothers address warm goodbyes to their children who, with the insouciance of their age, are singing in chorus, while their mothers are left behind.

Two hundred and fifty boltworkers are off work in La Ricamerie . . . they come to join the cortege which enters into this working city at around nine o'clock, to the strains of the "International" played by the Union Harmony.

The city hall is decorated with faisceau of red flags.

On the square, a large stand has been set up, also ornamented with red flags. . . .

The cortege masses itself in the square while the collectors circulate in the street, receiving handsome contributions. . . .[23]

The well-coordinated mass actions carried out by the Chambonnaire union were made possible by its industry-wide form of organization. From its inception, local organization adopted an all-inclusive form which incorporated both skilled and unskilled workers. Several important studies have been carried out of trade union organization in the English filemaking trades, and some points of comparison can be established. The late start of French trade unions, compared with British unions, encouraged industry-wide unionism at a time when craft unions and a tradition of factionalism and bitterness reigned in the British file trades. In the first half of the nineteenth century the Sheffield file trades had been organized along industry-wide lines, but in the wake of the mechanization of file forging, which culminated in a mass strike in 1866, the more skilled crafts set up their own union. The formation of craft unions had a logic of its own, and there were soon separate unions for hardeners, grinders, cutters, hand forgers, and machine forgers.[24]

When the Chambonnaire fileworkers' union was organized in 1888, four years after the legalization of trade unions in 1884, no heritage of organizational factionalism existed. File forgers, the majority of whom worked machines, were admitted into the union with all the other workers at the factory level. Not only were forgers an important component of the small-shop workforce, but feelings of artisanal superiority were muted because in 1888 forgers received higher salaries than cutters or hardeners.

Industry-wide unionism in Le Chambon was not established

on a solid foundation until the rise of a mass membership union between 1900 and 1901. Before 1901, in the case of the bolt- and
toolworkers, the establishment of a union was the prelude to a
strike; once the strike was over, the union dissolved.[25] Although a
union existed continuously in the file trades between 1888 and
1901, this same erratic trend can be seen in the membership of the
fileworkers' union (see Graph 10). After the militant strikes of 1888
and 1889 fileworker union membership approached 20 percent of
the workers employed in factories, but membership declined
precipitously between 1895 and 1900, when most grievances were
settled by union committees and employers.[26]

Fileworkers provided the mass constituency for Chambonaire
unionism, and this remained true for the whole period. Only in
1900, when a series of strikes occurred over mechanization in the
file industry, did the majority of factory workers in the file trades
join the union, and these organized fileworkers formed the core of
the all-inclusive union established in 1901 (see Graph 11). In 1910
fileworkers were still the vast majority of union members; in that
year de Seilhac estimated that 90 percent of the factory-based
fileworkers were unionized while only 20 percent of the boltworkers belonged to the union.[27]

The different forms of trade union organization powerfully
influenced worker mobilization. Although English artisans did
participate in solidarity strikes, there were serious obstacles in their
way. The leaders of English filecutter unionism, who had
abandoned the forgers after the unsuccessful 1866 strike, could not
induce other craft unions in the file trade to unite with them to
protest against the mechanization of cutting. The formation of
separate craft unions created competing hierarchies of full-time
paid officials who were not disposed to risk their union organization
and their paid office for solidarity with other unions. In 1866 in
Sheffield the general strike against machine forging lasted sixteen
weeks; at the end of the century the spread of machine cutting met
no such determined resistance.

The influence of Chambonnaire industry-wide unionism was
broad-ranging. The all-inclusive union of fileworkers was only a
transitional stage on the way to the formation of an industry-wide
union of the metal trades. All-inclusive unionism did not create

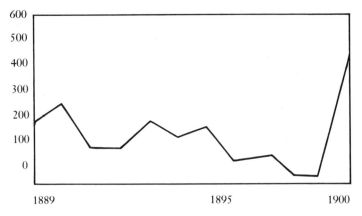

Graph 10. Fileworkers' Union Membership, 1889–1900.

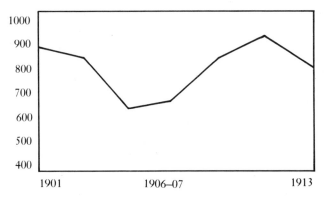

Graph 11. Metalworkers' Union Membership, 1901–13.

artisanal-industrial solidarity but was a product of it; mass-membership unionism only strengthened this artisanal-industrial worker coalition and placed it on a permanent basis. Thus, although the Chambonnaire union was only incompletely incorporated into the national labor movement, it had a broad local base.[28]

In order to fully understand the role of artisanal workers in promoting industrial worker strike activity, it is necessary to analyze the contributions of mass-membership unionism to strike actions. The metal union in Le Chambon possessed considerable resources, including the ability to raise large sums of money; through the metal union, fileworkers in large part financed industrial worker strikes.

This picture of Chambonnaire trade union resources does not fit with the common view of French unions as financially weak, for the poverty of pre–World War I French unions is probably exaggerated. French national unions were dramatically less wealthy than their English counterparts, but individual locals possessed a good deal of money. As Charles Rist observed in 1911, "very many French trade union locals are richer than the federation of which they are a part."[29]

Moreover, union treasuries or union dues are poor indications of the financial resources routinely available for strike actions. A single-minded preoccupation with the accumulation of retirement and insurance funds gave English unions some strength and stability, yet the existence of these large funds probably discouraged union members from risking their savings in mass strikes. While English workers expected to receive substantial benefits from their unions, French workers did not. Although some French unions provided modest benefit services, more frequently, as in Le Chambon, French unions depended on levying *ad hoc* assessments for burial expenses, hospital costs, or contributions for widows. At the height of the Sheffield trade union revival between 1891 and 1893, the members of the craft organization of Sheffield filecutters contributed five times the dues paid by members of the industry-wide metal union in Le Chambon, but Sheffield craft workers were paying mostly for welfare benefits, not strike funds or union business.[30]

Dues were not the only source of income for the Chambonnaire metal union; during strikes, important contributions were made by local merchants and regional trade union organizations. A very large proportion of union income was raised through special subscriptions and fund-raising activities, the major sources of the 23,000 francs raised for the building of a union hall in the wake of the 1910 strike.[31] Unfortunately the secondary literature on the Sheffield file trades does not provide sufficient information to compare the voluntary contributions received by English and French workers.

An examination of union financial commitments even further narrows the differences between the resources routinely available to striking Chambonnaire and Sheffield workers. The entire Chambonnaire metalworkers' treasury was a strike fund, and the

Chambonnaire union may have on occasion provided more strike pay for its members than the Sheffield filecutters' union. Because of its welfare obligations, the Sheffield union limited itself to paying about 30 percent of regular pay during strikes. To be sure, English workers on strike received voluntary outside contributions, but the practice of business unionism would hardly seem likely to inspire public generosity.[32]

The Chambonnaire union did not make a fixed commitment to strike pay, and its performance varied considerably because the union gave whatever it had in its treasury. The strike fund, which received most of its contributions from filecutters, was freely distributed to all workers. While detailed financial records for the union do not exist, existing information indicates that the largest portion of strike aid was given to boltworkers. During the 137-day boltworkers' strike of 1901 the union raised 63.9 percent of normal pay for strike benefits; for an 88-day toolworkers' strike in 1904 it raised 37.9 percent of normal pay; and for a 22-day boltworkers' strike in 1905 it raised 14.7 percent. Neither union's strike fund was designed to finance a long general strike, but even in the case of the general strikes of 1910 and 1911 the financial contribution of local and national French union organizations was not negligible; the union raised 6 percent of normal pay for strikers in 1910 and 7.1 percent in 1911.[33]

Financial aid was not the only contribution the union made to striking workers. The union executive, composed of three members from each of the principal trades, played an important role in coordinating strike action among the trades, and the union strike kitchen was important in the strikes of 1901, 1906, 1909–10 and 1911. The unions' *soupes communistes* (see Figure 14) enabled the union to use its financial resources more efficiently than the same amount of money distributed to individual workers.[34] Finally, the union constructed a large hall to promote "fraternity" among its members. But the hall was not finished until early 1911, when prewar strike activity was entering its final phase.

Work Structure and Strike Militancy:
The Fileworkers

In Le Chambon-Feugerolles industry-wide unionism served as a conduit for the flow of financial contributions, political support,

Figure 14. A strike kitchen *(soupe communiste)* in 1910.

and organizational experience from artisanal to industrial workers. If a strong local industrial workers' movement was to be built, this kind of unequal exchange had to occur, because valuable resources were disproportionately concentrated in the hands of artisanal workers. And resources were necessary to carry out strikes and construct trade union organizations. In Le Chambon-Feugerolles, as in Rive-de-Gier and Saint-Chamond, the structure of work helps explain the resources at the disposal of different working-class groups. In many ways the mass of artisanal fileworkers of Le Chambon bears little resemblance to the glassworker aristocrats of Rive-de-Gier; yet if we look at their common artisanal work structure and its effect on family economy and group cohesion, there are surprising parallels. In both Le Chambon-Feugerolles and Rive-de-Gier the higher wages and tighter cohesion of artisanal workers enabled them to build trade union movements strong enough to aid industrial workers.

Filemaking in Le Chambon required many different metalworking skills, but the heart of filemaking was filecutting. Of 1,900 filemakers in 1906, an estimated 11 percent were forgers or strikers, 3 percent were hardeners, 65 percent were filecutters, 18 percent were apprentices, and 2 percent were unskilled workers.[35] Almost all the apprentices must have been cutters, since the forgers did not require any apprenticeship.

In some skilled trades employers were able to play off the workers who labored in the workshop against those involved in domestic production; this could not be done in Le Chambon because domestic fileworkers had close personal ties with shopworkers. Most of the forging, hardening, and grinding was done in the small workshops. Every factory had a certain number of filecutters, usually men working at the shop, but factories also "put out" a good deal of the cutting. In home workshops men, women, and teenaged children cut files. The number of workers involved in domestic cutting fluctuated greatly because many family members became cutters during boom periods and then quietly dropped out when the market declined.

For technical reasons it was not practical for employers to "put out" filecutting far into the countryside. Filecutting was only one step in filemaking.[36] Files were forged and then annealed (*le recruit*), irregularities were corrected by hand (*le dressage*), and the files were soaked in a chemical bath before the cutting (*le taillage*). After the files were cut, it was necessary to heat them once again, let them harden in another series of chemical baths (*le décapage*), and then soak them in oil (*le graissage*). Because the fear of rust hung over this entire process, homeworkers were expected to pick up uncut files from the workshop every day and return the cut files the same day or the next morning.[37]

The small shop was the pivotal point of fileworker organization, for it was there that resistance to the employer usually began, and spread back to the homeworker. Much of this opposition depended on a cohesive work group bound together by personal ties. The layout of work in these shops, which employed between fifteen and thirty-five people, seems to have favored worker contact, which in turn encouraged the formation of close on-the-job friendships. Filecutters usually sat together facing a window, often the street window; shops were invariably poorly lighted and cutters depended heavily on natural light.[38] Since workers often needed to sharpen their chisels and it was difficult to maintain the body continuously in the filecutting position, filecutting involved frequent breaks. Similarly, the pace of filecutting could vary tremendously and the most rapid pace could not be maintained for long. Thus it was doubly necessary for workers to take breaks, and a long break could be made up by an intense effort.[39]

The filecutter's ability to resist his employer was strengthened by the worker's ownership of the tools of his craft and the family control of apprenticeship. A discharged fileworker simply returned home, made his own files, and sold them to "subcontractors"; his income was reduced but not destroyed. Even in the shop, workers were expected to furnish their own set of hammers whose handles were invariably well worn to fit the hand of their owners, and many filecutting families possessed their own workshops consisting of an anvil and some chemicals. Children were trained in the trade at home, and women and female children often became skilled filecutters.[40] In the mid-nineties Ardouin-Dumazet visited the town and noted:

> In this row of industrial cities aligned from the Rhone to the Loire, Le Chambon-Feugerolles strikes one chiefly by the familial character of its industry. . . . In the whole city, and in the old sections particularly, one hears the incessant noise of the hammer tapping on steel with little blows that are sharp and repeated. If one approaches the shops, located at crossroads and the ground-level floors of old dwelling places fronting on alleys, one can see through the windows, men, women, young girls, and infants striking with hammer blows on a chisel . . . it is not unusual to meet, standing in the same shop, an old septuagenarian and a little ten year old girl, accomplishing the same noisy task.[41]

Regardless of whether their jobs were in the city or the countryside, shared artisanal skills drew fileworkers together inside the city (see Figure 15). Eighteen major filemaking plants were scattered over the town of Le Chambon and there were several plants on the outskirts of town, yet a breakdown of the 1901 census shows that in this semirural commune where half of the population lived in the countryside, 73.5 percent of the fileworkers lived in the city of Le Chambon. Even the majority of workers in the Trablaine file plant, several kilometers from Le Chambon, lived inside the built-up city area.[42]

Filemaking paid wages that enabled workers to support a union

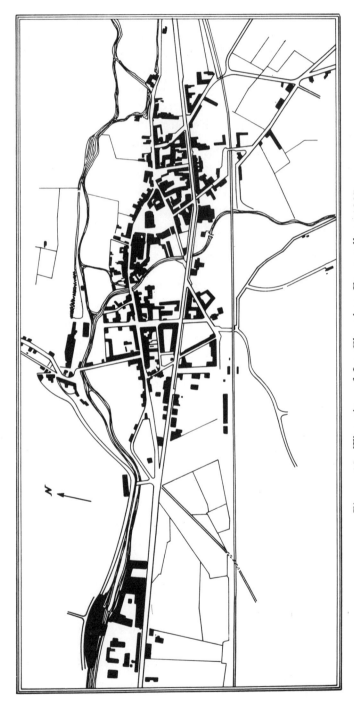

Figure 15. The city of Le Chambon-Feugerolles, 1887.

organization and to acquire the personal savings necessary to maintain a long strike. Filecutting did not pay high individual wages, but it did pay a high family income. Male filecutters received lower wages than many other skilled workers but, unlike many other skilled workers, they could bring their wives and daughters into the trade. In 1906 an adult male forger, a semiskilled industrial worker, received 5.5 francs a day while a male filecutter received about 5.0 francs, but the family income of a young filemaking couple was about 8.0 while that of the forger remained 5.5.[43] Filecutting offered several advantages to working-class women. Women fileworkers could perform skilled labor in a town where there was almost no other employment for adult women, and women fileworkers could work at home while minding their children; all other employment involved factory work, which meant leaving children at home alone or with neighbors.

Along with the small shop, which encouraged on-the-job friendships and centralized urban residential patterns of fileworkers, the working-class café contributed to the maintenance of relations with workmates outside the job. Like Ripagérien glassworkers, Chambonnaire fileworkers spent a great deal of their time in cafés, and when workmates were near, the café conversations of fileworkers often turned to occupational interests. The fileworkers' union was founded during a series of secret meetings in a local café. One of the most important syndicalist leaders was a café owner; his wife tended bar while he worked as a filecutter. Anarchist, syndicalist, and socialist workers all had their own particular cafés, and fileworkers were active in every variety of radical politics.[44]

It is difficult to count employer organization or the lack of it as a worker resource, but the organization of work helped determine whether a militant worker confronted a large number of small employers or a small number of very large employers. In the case of the fileworkers, the near impossibility of employer organization facilitated worker organization. A very heterogeneous group of twenty-five to thirty-five major file employers employed between 1,900 and 2,500 workers;[45] four or five large workshops employed between 180 and 90 workers, but model shop size was 30. A great deal of factionalism existed among the file employers. The Chambre syndicale des fabricants de limes, founded in 1885, never included anything like a majority of file employers. It was in constant decline after 1889 and was replaced in 1901 by the scarcely more successful Chambre syndicale des fabricants de limes du département de la Loire et de la Haute Loire.[46] As Léon de Seilhac noted,

> File production includes the most diverse and dissimilar establishments. There are worker-employers working with three workers, there are large employers and even tradesmen, chiefly barbers, who exercise as a sideline the profession of file manufacturer. . . . One will easily understand how workers scattered in small and unimportant workshops in twos or threes or tens, enjoy a near absolute freedom and treat their employer as an equal. These workers are easily recruited by the trade union and no forceful employer opposes himself to their affiliation and one will even find a number of small file employers singing the praises of the workers' trade union organization.[47]

After 1906, and with great difficulty, file employers' organizations did make progress, but only with the aid of other metal employers.

The Formation of a Working-Class Coalition: Le Réveil Chambonnaire

An inspection of the work structure in artisanal filemaking reveals the group solidarity and financial ability which gave these workers enormous potential for collective action; but no analysis of mobilization capacity can explain fileworkers' willingness to use their power on behalf of industrial workers. What did fileworkers have to gain from joint action with industrial workers? Once again, in Le Chambon as in Rive-de-Gier, technological change acted to radicalize and politicize artisanal workers. For reasons of family solidarity, craft interest, and union solidarity artisanal fileworkers were drawn to support boltworkers.

The nature of technological change in the file industry helps explain fileworker solidarity with industrial workers. Technological change was an environmental factor in Le Chambon between 1866 and 1899. Handcutters knew that machines for filecutting existed and were spreading in the United States and England; the existence of machinery foreclosed any filecutter hopes of becoming an "aristocracy of labor."[48] The crisis in the local file industry came between 1899 and 1901. In 1899 a mechanized file factory was opened in Le Chambon, and the protest movement against this factory led to the mobilization of fileworkers. One consequence of this struggle was the strengthening of the coalition between fileworkers and industrial workers.

In order to put fileworker mobilization into perspective, the halting progress of technical change must be examined. The mechanization of filecutting was a gradual process, a slow piling up of inventions before a workable filecutting machine appeared. At first glance, filecutting looks like the kind of monotonous, repetitive task which could be easily mechanized. Many men applied themselves to the task. A sketch exists of a filecutting machine made by Leonardo Da Vinci in 1500, and the *Encyclopédie* of 1765 describes both the process of handcutting and a filecutting machine. Prior to 1865 none of these machines proved practical; except for the mechanization of forging, there was really no difference between Chambonnaire filemaking in 1888 and the methods used by an eighteenth-century filemaker like Peter Stubbs of Warrington.[49] The eighteenth century English "Filehewers Lamentation" was echoed in a Stéphanois song composed in the last part of the nineteenth century: "Tap, tap. It is in order to amuse myself that my hammer cuts the files . . . for a few centimes, seated from dawn, I cut and recut the file without a single wrinkle forming on my brow. Each artisan begins his work to the gay refrain of my hammer while the steel takes on its snakey scales. . . ."[50]

The first practical filecutting machines made their appearance in 1865, yet throughout the whole of the prewar period the competitive advantage of machines was seriously diminished by technical problems. Filecutting machines developed in the United States around 1865, were introduced into England in 1872, but did not establish themselves in Sheffield until the nineties. In 1899 factories with cutting machines were opened in Cosne in the Nièvre and at Trablaine near Le Chambon-Feugerolles. Handcutting did not completely disappear anywhere in the pre–World War I period, although the ravages of mechanization advanced further in those countries which had the highest-paid filecutters, the United States and England.[51]

The major technical difficulty of machine cutting had little to do with the actual cutting apparatus; later inventors had only modified Leonardo's basic design. Behind the seemingly simple filecutting machine lurked the far larger problem of alloy steel. Until steelmakers were able to produce a uniformly high-quality alloy steel, many machine-cut files were ruined. Eric N. Simons noted:

> . . . the special skill of the worker [filecutter] lies not only in the steadiness and evenness of his chisel blows, but in the sensitiveness of touch that enables him to detect the minutest bulges of the metal under his finger so that he knows precisely where to strike the next blow to ensure even spacing. Moreover, he can vary the force of his blows to suit the hardness of the steel, which may be variable. In this way he produces a uniform depth of cut.[52]

Only after World War II were the difficulties of alloy steelmaking really solved. A further complication was that in the years before World War I no satisfactory machines for testing the quality of the file existed, and this introduced another degree of uncertainty into machine cutting.

An equally important problem was the lack of standardization of French filemakers, for there was no common agreement on file measurement and each filemaker had his own conventions and his own different array of files. This made it difficult for customers to change their supplier, but it also made mechanization less feasible. The lack of standardization was reinforced by the naturally wide variety of file sizes. Even today of all common tools the file is undoubtedly the one available in the greatest variety. Files come in different lengths, shapes, and cuts: an almost infinite number of combinations is possible.[53] Usually one of the great advantages of mechanization is the production of large numbers of an identical product. The use of a machine in filecutting did not produce such a solid advantage because only limited numbers of any one type of file were needed.

A couple of minor problems, although not insurmountable, also slowed down the introduction of machine-cut files. For one, early machine-cut files were not designed for the worker, since the file cuts were too regularly spaced and ill-adapted to broad surface filing; workers accustomed to the handcut file needed to be retrained to use machine-cut files. In addition, file users depended on a trusted supplier. Customers were suspicious that cheap files were "rejects" which had been improperly tempered. The difference between a regular file and a reject was invisible to the eye but immediately apparent when used by an experienced mechanic.[54]

But technical difficulties only partly explain the slow progress of mechanization; labor costs must also be considered. Filemaking was labor-intensive. Before deciding to purchase machines, the employer had to consider the cost of labor balanced against the cost of the machines. Filecutting machines were not particularly expensive, but a factory needed many different machines, while highly skilled filecutters received relatively low wages. Chambonnaire filecutters may have received as much as 25 percent less than Sheffield filecutters, although it is very difficult to make a precise comparison.[55] The slow progress of mechanization suggests that machines were not dramatically more profitable than handcutting.

Despite all these problems, the fileworkers regarded machine cutting as a real threat. In July, 1899, an article in *L'Eclaireur de Saint-Chamond* reported:

> The working class of Le Chambon is at present boiling over. This boiling over is provoked by an economic phenomenon which is at the same time very grave and very simple: the invasion of machinery into file production.
>
> A company has been established at Trablaine for the mechanical manufacture of files and this has resulted in a great anger among the workers. According to them, the number of workers is going to be reduced, they will be deprived of their skill and reduced to misery.[56]

At first glance the Trablaine factory does not seem to justify this anger. The factory employed only about 170 workers in the production of both tools and files; it possessed devices for machine cutting but the majority of cutters were handcutters. Although highly capitalized, the factory was not controlled by large investors; it was jointly owned by five small Chambonnaire filemakers. At Trablaine the fileworkers confronted more the specter of mechanization than its reality. The introduction of the filecutting machine forced filecutters to recognize that the basic process of cutting could be mechanized and raised the possibility that a machine which was initially built to produce a few basic file sizes might be adapted to a wider range.[57]

Its symbolic nature makes this struggle no less significant. Between 1899 and 1901 the fileworkers, partially supported by the smaller filemakers, waged a last-ditch effort to prevent the new factory from finding a workforce. The workers of the five factories being consolidated into the new mechanical factory refused to work there and appealed to all metalworkers to support their struggle. In 1899 the union declared that its members would refuse to work in a factory which employed anyone who had ever worked at Trablaine.[58]

The union's short-term failure set the conditions for its ultimate success. Although the boycott was initially successful, workers, attracted by higher wages, did go to Trablaine; despite frequent strikes, Chambonnaire employers did hire ex-Trablaine workers. Workers who were excluded from the local metal union formed a new, independent machine cutters' union at Trablaine. But after observing the mechanical file factory in existence for three years, the union abandoned its opposition and in 1901 admitted the machine cutters into the general metal union. The blunt fact was that between 1899 and 1901 the example set by the Trablaine factory was not followed, nor did another mechanical file machine enter Le Chambon until 1907.[59] Two reasons for this are likely, and their relative importance is hard to estimate. First, the wages of Chambonnaire filecutters were too low to justify mechanization. Second, the union's boycott forced the Trablaine factory to offer exceptionally high wages and this put it at an even greater disadvantage.

In order to break the boycott, the Trablaine factory offered higher wages than those of other Chambonnaire plants. Forgers who received 5.5 francs in other filemaking plants received 6.0 francs at Trablaine. This was a short-sighted policy. As the manager of the Trablaine factory explained in 1904, "[our wage scale] was elaborated . . . chiefly in order to put an end to the conflict which appeared at the moment of the introduction of machine cutting."[60] The company at Trablaine repeatedly tried to revise its wage scale downward, but the workers, supported by the metal union, resisted these attempts.

After 1906 machine cutting began to revive and the tempo of mechanization slowly accelerated. Despite the Chambonnaire filecutters' advantage of being located close to the chief center of French high-quality steel, they began to meet stiff international competition. The Chambonnaire filemakers' share of the national market was declining, although local demand was still very high because these were the years when the automotive industry developed in Saint-Etienne, creating a large demand for files.[61] In 1906 filecutters won a pay increase which damaged their competitive position; as a result, in 1907 two more file factories introduced cutting machines. That same year the Union des fabricants de limes de France was established and at once set to work standardizing French files.[62] Already in 1910 the local Chambre syndicale de la fabrique de quincaillerie reported that "the small [file] workshops tend to disappear, because of the competition of the better tooled large establishments."[63] By 1912 Chambonnaire workers were preparing to adjust themselves to the change. The Chambre syndicale complained, ". . . [the decline of apprenticeship is continuing. . . .] In order to fill the gap . . . the manufacturers are orienting themselves towards mechanized production. They are favored by the local production of machines [filecutting machines] which until recently were imported from outside the country. . . ."[64] Nevertheless, only after World War I did handcutting finally gave way to machine cutting.

Whatever its relative importance in slowing down the spread of mechanization, the struggle against the Trablaine factory was significant in shaping fileworkers' consciousness. In order to maintain their boycott, fileworkers needed the solidarity of other metalworkers. The three-year ordeal led to a growing cooperation between the fileworkers' union and the newly formed bolt- and toolworkers' unions. When their skills were threatened, Chambonnaire fileworkers naturally became more concerned about the general level of wages in Chambonnaire metalworking. Adult male wages in metalworking were generally higher than the average male fileworker's wage, and this tended to improve the competitive position of fileworkers. The long struggle between 1889 and 1901 which brought fileworkers together with other metal trades played an important role in the formation of the general metal union in January, 1901.[65]

The distribution of occupations within the family also helps explain the alacrity with which fileworkers merged their organization into a metalworkers' industrial union. The development of mechanization in the file industry placed limits on the opportunities for fileworker economic development, and members of artisanal families moved or married into other aspects of the local metal industry. Many families contained both artisanal filecutters and skilled industrial workers, and so these artisanal workers had a stake in the development of a strong industrial workers' movement. Furthermore, many members of artisanal filemaking families moved into the skilled industrial branches of the file industry, generally as forgers, stampers, and grinders; women filecutters married these skilled industrial workers. In 1901, 19 percent of the artisanal filecutters in Le Chambon lived in the same household with a skilled industrial worker employed in the file trade. Three percent of artisanal fileworkers lived in the same household as skilled industrial workers in the bolt trade, and another 4.9 percent lived in the same household as unskilled boltworkers.[66] Thus many members of artisanal families had a direct interest in the outcome of the boltworkers' strikes.

While only 7.9 percent of fileworkers lived in the same households with boltworkers, a substantially larger number of the small town's fileworkers were related to boltworkers. In 1910 and 1911, when the boltworkers went out on extended strikes, the pressure on fileworkers to go beyond contributions grew. In both strikes the boltworkers had a strike kitchen in their union hall, and week after week whole families trudged down the city's streets to get daily meals. The sight of sons and daughters, sisters and brothers, nephews and cousins on their way to the strike kitchen (see Figure 16) must have been a powerful incentive to fileworkers' solidarity. Pressure grew as the strikes became more militant. In the course of both strikes relatives were involved in skirmishes with nonstrikers and were arrested by the police. In 1910 the fileworkers actually went out on a solidarity strike for three weeks with the boltworkers, and their strike helped to bring that strike to a successful conclusion. In 1911 many fileworkers wanted to go out on strike again in solidarity with the boltworkers, but fileworkers' union leaders argued that poor business conditions in their trade would doom the solidarity strike to failure.[67]

Figure 16. Whole families go to the strike kitchen.

Finally, fileworkers supported the boltworkers' strike for political reasons. Chambonnaire fileworkers believed that the bolt-workers' strikes were only the opening shots in a campaign against Chambonnaire unionism, and they had good reason for their suspicions. The 1910 and 1911 strikes were both fought over the question of union recognition. If the metal union could be successfully challenged in the bolt industry, sooner or later it would be challenged in the file industry.[68]

Even more disturbing to fileworkers was the unaccustomed solidarity of employers in both strikes and the growing power of employer organization. The strikes revealed the existence of a newly united and aggressive *patronat*. In 1906 Chambonnaire bolt and file employers, who had always been organized separately, merged to form the Chambre syndicale de la petite métallurgie et quincaillerie. This organization began to establish relations between the local metal employers and the national metal employers' organization, the Comité des forges. The growing menace of employer organization posed a threat to all Chambonnaire metal workers.[69]

Revolutionary Syndicalism

In the early twentieth century in France the rise of industry-wide forms of union organization, the increased sensitivity of artisans to shop-floor issues, the growing working-class suspicion of political parties, and the formation of coalitions of artisanal and industrial workers all created a favorable terrain for the spread of anarcho-syndicalist ideas. In turn, the spread of revolutionary syndicalism, which emphasized strike militancy, shop-floor issues, and the importance of the "active minority," further reinforced the tendency toward cooperation between artisanal and industrial workers.

In the years after 1906 revolutionary syndicalist ideas spread to the leaders of the trade union movement in Le Chambon; syndicalist books and newspapers circulated among union militants. Between 1907 and 1914 the local metal union was visited frequently by national leaders of the CGT, who cited it enthusiastically as an example of syndicalist success.[70]

There was much in the syndicalist philosophy that attracted the local activists, who nearly all came from artisanal fileworker backgrounds. The syndicalists criticized the parliamentary maneuvers and rhetoric of the socialists. To a "sterile parliamentarianism" they counterposed their own concern with shop-floor issues. Hubert Lagardelle, a Parisian intellectual whose friend, Ernest Lafont, was the socialist mayor of nearby Firminy, and who contributed to *La bataille syndicaliste*, a journal read by local militants, best summarized these sentiments: "If working class life is exercised and nourished in the shop and factory, then the trade union movement is the expression of it. The intimate preoccupation of the worker, provoked by the conditions of work which are established at the employer's shop, and whose hard effects are felt in the home, find their tribune and their echo in the union."[71]

Typically, syndicalism preached solidarity and cooperation between artisanal and industrial workers. Syndicalist leaders boasted of their success in initiating and winning mass strikes.

They stressed the need for militancy without being very specific about tactics or goals. And, occasionally, syndicalists pandered to artisanal prejudices. In 1911 Lagardelle contrasted "democracy" unfavorably with "workers' democracy":

> "Workers' democracy" supports itself essentially on the organized proletariat. This is its political principle. The conception of an abstract equality gives place here to the notion of real differentiation. . . . All are not on the same level, because all do not have the same aptitudes. . . . The world of work is a world apart. The work of production is different and not able to be carried out by the methods of governmental politics. It [the world of work] presumes a certain level of competence and thus renders a strong hierarchy necessary. The hierarchy is formed naturally according to *the law of elites* in the organization of the working class, and it is the creation of this hierarchy by selection which gives to it [the workers' democracy] a profoundly "democratic" base.[72]

The importance of the "active minority," stressed by syndicalist theoreticians, appealed to threatened artisans, who were often the leaven of the trade union movement.

The spread of revolutionary syndicalist ideas in Le Chambon occurred during a period when feelings of artisanal-industrial worker solidarity were already very strong. Syndicalism postdated the formation of the industry-wide union of metalworkers and the solidarity strikes of 1901 and 1906. Its appeal was greatest to trade union militants, and it succeeded in convincing a handful of dedicated and intelligent activists to devote their full time to trade union affairs. But it is difficult to evaluate the influence of syndicalism outside the cadre of the trade union movement. Certainly, the majority of Chambonnaire trade union members did not have the same scorn for politics as did local syndicalists; with even-handed deliberation local workers elected syndicalists to trade union office and SFIO socialists to political office.

Syndicalism did affect the relationship between the local socialist party and trade unions, although the two remained closely associated. The success of syndicalism in the city's trade union movement meant that strikes would not be used to promote political coalitions as they had in Rive-de-Gier in the nineties. Still, socialists and syndicalists worked together in strike situations,

and successful mass strikes were associated with the spread of socialism. In Le Chambon syndicalism symbolized and accelerated
a tendency toward working-class unity within the trade union
movement which already had deep roots in the evolution of the
Chambonnaire working class.

Work Structure and Strike Militancy:
The Boltworkers

In contrast, the work structure, residential patterns, and leisure
life of boltworkers and metalworkers all acted to undermine rather
than facilitate union organization. Boltmaking in particular provides a contrast to filemaking. Unlike filecutters, boltworkers and
metalworkers were mostly industrial workers; they neither earned
fileworker wages nor had the opportunity to form close on-the-job
friendships. The technical transformation of boltmaking in the
Stéphanois region was already complete in 1876 when Zola's
L'Assommoir, which described the decline of artisanal boltmaking in
Paris, appeared.[73] A majority of boltworkers were young women
and children; one-third of the bolt workforce was composed of
skilled industrial workers receiving 5.00 francs a day, another third
were completely unskilled young men earning 2.25 francs, and the
remaining third were women and girls earning 1.75 francs.[74]

In contrast to the camaraderie of the small filemaking workshop,
bolt manufacture discouraged the formation of informal work
groups by tying the individual worker to a large noisy machine,
thus hindering the formation of on-the-job friendships and
weakening group cohesion. As soon as the steel was cut, young
boys heated the metal until it turned a "lively red" then, using large
tongs, they carried the red-hot steel to the stamping machine
where, with the aid of the "heater," the stamper fitted the hot metal
into the machine which stamped it into a screw and bolt shape. The
next step was "threading," in which young women inserted the
screws and bolts into cutting machines that cut four screws
simultaneously and demanded constant feeding; the threader who
allowed herself to be distracted from her work by casual
conversation risked serious accident. Also, women "oilers" made

sure that the equipment and the metal parts were protected from rust. Male fitters worked in a separate machine shop and adjusted the metal parts to fit industrial specifications.[75]

The location of workers' residences in the bolt trade discouraged workers from maintaining friendships outside the factory. The majority of leaders of the Chambonnaire boltworkers' strike were drawn from the group of adult male semiskilled workers who resided in the city; no women were prominent in the strike and only a couple of young unskilled workers. Although all eight bolt factories were located in the center of Le Chambon, a large part of the workforce was recruited from outside the city. Almost all the skilled fitters and maintenance men lived in Le Chambon, while many unskilled young women and children had to walk three or four kilometers to work every morning. Both Petrus Faure and the Bonneffs, men familiar with the bolt trade, claimed that the majority of young boltworkers were recruited from the sons and daughters of miners in neighboring La Ricamerie or surrounding coal settlements. Miners were less well paid than metalworkers and their families more in need of supplementary incomes.[76]

When workers seldom saw one another outside the job, strike actions were difficult to carry out. Young working women living with their families were often forbidden to enter the cafés that were centers of male trade unionism; women often lacked the leisure time necessary for participation in union activities, for when they returned home from work, they had chores to do. In addition, many of the younger workers expected to work in the bolt industry for only a brief period, a few years before marriage or descending into the mines, and consequently had no long-term interest in the trade. Most young male workers had no expectation of permanent employment in the bolt trade. According to the Bonneffs, young teenage boys worked as "heaters" until they were old enough to join their fathers in the mines. Assuming that the official estimates of the bolt workforce are correct, there may have been as many as 280 of these children working in Le Chambon, composing 35.2 percent of the total workforce.[77] The well-known communist leader Benôit Frachon provides a good example of the typical young boltworker. The son of a miner, Frachon at twelve became a heater at a local boltworks. During the 1910 boltworkers' strike, when he was seventeen, he first became actively involved in the workers' movement.[78]

Unlike the permanently weak employer organizations in the file trade, the bolt employers gradually united to take common action to prevent strikes. Serious employer organization only occurred after 1909 in the bolt trades, and it developed in response to worker militancy. The eight bolt manufacturers, employing an average of 100 to 120 workers each, were members of the Chambre syndicale des fabricants de boulonnerie de la Loire, but the bolt industry was highly competitive and individual employers often ignored their organization and the opinions of their fellow employers by being either more conciliatory or more provocative toward the trade union. After 1906, and rapidly accelerating after 1910, bolt employers began to unite more closely and to organize across industrial lines. The small number and uniform size of the bolt employers made group coordination more feasible than among the file employers.[79]

Work Structure and Strike Militancy: The Metalworkers

As the organization of work in the bolt trades represents one important nineteenth-century alternative to domestic industry, the organization of work in metal construction represents another alternative. Boltmaking was unskilled, low-paying, and employed large numbers of young women and children. As in our two other cities, heavy metalworking, although predominantly unskilled, contained a small number of highly skilled industrial workers, was relatively high-paying, and employed almost exclusively adult men (see Table 30). While metalworkers received wages superior to those of fileworkers, they possessed little group cohesion and they faced a much stronger employer. The pay scale in metalworking was more finely graduated than in the other Chambonnaire metal trades and there were more substantial wage differentials. In the Claudinon and Limouzin plants, which employed 90 percent of workers in metalworking, the top 10 percent of skilled workers, puddlers and foundrymen, were highly paid, earning 8.0 francs a

Table 30

Sex and Age Distribution of Metal Trades in Le
Chambon-Feugerolles, 1906

	Percent Men	Percent Women	Percent Children	N
Fileworkers	57.9	23.7	18.4	1,900
Boltworkers	49.4	32.9	17.7	790
Metalworkers	92.5	0.3	7.0	1,058

day. Another 10 percent, fitters and moulders, received well above average pay for skilled adult males, earning between 6.0 and 6.5 francs. The forgers, the majority of the workers, constituting 50 percent of the workforce, received 5.5 francs a day, while a substantial number of unskilled workers (23 percent) received 3.0 francs. (The remaining 5 percent of the workers were apprentices, the only nonadults in the plant.)[80]

The Claudinon plant, which employed 80 percent of the workers in metalworking, gives some idea of the variety of work structures found in one large-scale industrial organization. In different shops within this factory there were skilled industrial workers working in strong informal work groups and semiskilled workers working in almost total isolation. In the puddling mill there was a foreman, a master puddler, several assistant puddlers, a roller or "third assistant," and hammerers and machinists, and all of these men were skilled workers. In the several forging shops the work hierarchy was simpler and less skilled. The foreman served as "chief forger" and directed unskilled workers carrying large pieces of metal toward the different forging machines and their operators.[81]

The job of the forger hardly encouraged informal conversation or brought workers into close contact because the forger was much more a machine operator than a member of a work group. The Claudinon plant produced tools and metal parts which all required forging and was equipped with power hammers of eight and twenty-five tons as well as a rolling press. In 1901 a French sociologist, Charles Benoist, made a detailed study of the organization of work in metalworking in Firminy, Saint-Etienne, and

Saint-Chamond. His description of the large forging shop in the Verdier works in Firminy gives some sense of the noise and isolation of the forger:

> . . . the forging shop is the kingdom of mastadons, gigantic power hammers and scarcely less impressive rolling presses rule, perhaps more powerful still are the hammers of 30, 60 and 100 tons. . . . Domesticated and subjected to men whom they could crush with a single blow these monstrous machines are obedient almost to their finger tips and it seems that a child could operate them. The piece to be forged is placed on the base which serves as an anvil. The forger arranges the edges or the surface of a piece in a position where the hammer will strike it. The blow falls, a fist of 60,000 or 100,000 kilos strikes from above, so hard that the earth trembles and a painful moan escapes from it. . . .[82]

Unlike the homes of fileworkers, the homes of metalworkers were scattered all over the countryside. Because metal plants required large amounts of space, Chambonnaire metal plants were situated on the edge of town. The Claudinon plant itself was located a couple of kilometers west of Le Chambon, making it as convenient for many rural workers to work at the plant as for most urban workers. Table 31 shows the residential patterns of a metalworker in the Claudinon plant compared with those of a medium-sized file plant, Rolland-Peyron. In 1901, 56.9 percent of all metalworkers lived in the countryside. Although workers in metal construction were more dispersed than in the other metal trades, the same tendency for skilled workers to reside in the city which was found among fileworkers and boltworkers can be found among metalworkers. In 1901, 60.0 percent of all puddlers and foundrymen lived in the built-up area of Le Chambon, 52.3 percent of all forgers and turners, and 43.7 percent of all unskilled workers. This pattern would probably be even clearer if the occupations of the large number of workers who identified themselves simply as "metalworkers" were known. These workers were most likely less skilled workers who did not identify themselves with any particular skill group; only 18.8 percent of these workers lived in Le Chambon.[83]

The great majority of semiskilled or unskilled metalworkers had little in common once they left the plant. Because it was necessary

Table 31

Worker Residential Patterns in Le Chambon-Feugerolles, 1901: A File Factory and a Metal Plant

	Rolland-Peyron Percent Fileworkers	Claudinon Percent Metalworkers	Percent Total Population
Urban Areas			
Main Street-North	32.8	15.5	19.8
Central Area	14.8	19.3	17.8
Eastern Area	36.9	8.2	12.8
Total Urban	84.5	43.0	50.4
Rural Areas			
West of Le Chambon	0.8	30.9	13.5
East of Le Chambon	6.6	7.6	21.2
South of Le Chambon	8.2	18.4	14.9
Total Rural	15.6	57.0	49.6
N	122	825	11,079
D = 46			

for metal employers to reach far into the countryside in order to find a sufficient supply of adult men, workers in the same shop might well live on opposite sides of the commune. While 30.9 percent of Claudinon workers lived on the west side of Le Chambon where the plant was located, 18.4 percent lived in the area south of the city, and 7.6 percent lived on the east side of the city four or five kilometers from their workplace.[84] Friendships formed on the job could not be reinforced when workers returned to an agrarian world or a close-knit coal community.

Metalworking in Le Chambon was dominated by the large Claudinon et cie, ruled imperially by its founder, Jacques Claudinon, and later by his successor, Georges Claudinon. The Claudinons's position in metalworking was incomparably stronger than that of the file or bolt employers. The paternalism of the Claudinon brought benefits for the loyal worker and a means of chastising the disloyal and unruly. At the moment when he founded the company in 1851 Jacques Claudinon established a retirement and health fund. Workers were obliged to contribute 2 percent of their salary to this fund, and Claudinon contributed an equal amount. Benefits were available only so long as the worker was employed at the Claudinon plant and were not refunded if the worker was discharged. Later he constructed the Cité Claudinon, a company-owned housing development for metalworkers.

Both Georges and Jacques Claudinon were important figures in local political and industrial life, for they had a near monopoly of skilled worker employment in metalworking, and few workers could afford to offend them. Jacques Claudinon built a large house on the edge of town, the Château Claudinon, and maintained a personal presence in the city. He was mayor between 1858 and 1860 and again from 1870 to 1875. His successor as head of the company was also his political successor; Georges Claudinon was mayor of Le Chambon from 1898 to 1919 and deputy from the Loire between 1898 and 1906.[85] In contrast to the fileworkers, who were often able to impose settlements on divided small employers, metalworkers faced a single large employer who controlled all metalworking employment, was an important landlord, and dominated the local political scene.

The case of Le Chambon-Feugerolles concludes the survey of Stéphanois valley strike militancy. Le Chambon provides a dramatic example of industrial worker militancy and artisanal solidarity. In Le Chambon mass strikes were tied to the militancy of local artisanal workers who were threatened by technological change. Chambonnaire artisanal fileworkers possessed the group solidarity and financial loyalty which enabled them to build a strong trade union organization. While technological change gave artisanal fileworkers a concern with the conditions of local industrial workers, both craft and family interests led the fileworkers to share the resources of their trade union organization with industrial workers.

The key role played by artisanal workers in the strike of 1910 becomes even clearer in the perspective of the two other towns in this study. Metalworkers in Saint-Chamond were not greatly different from the boltworkers of Le Chambon, and, despite repeated provocations, they never went out on strike. Unlike the other two cities, the artisanal working class in Saint-Chamond was very small and remained unaffected by technological change. Strike actions in Le Chambon had a great deal in common with those of Rive-de-Gier. In both cities industrial workers' strike actions occurred during periods of crisis for artisanal workers. Although Ripagérien artisans did not go out on strike in solidarity with metalworkers as did Chambonnaire artisans in 1910, still, the metalworkers' strike of 1893 in Rive-de-Gier was in many ways a joint enterprise. In both cities threatened artisanal workers powerfully shaped the participation of industrial workers in strike conflicts.

NOTES

1. Maxime Leroy, *Les techniques nouvelles du syndicalisme* (Paris: Garnier Frères, 1921), p. 181.
2. See Faure, *Le Chambon rouge.*
3. On strikes in Le Chambon-Feugerolles, see ADL/92/M.
4. Daily coverage of the 1910 and 1911 strikes can be found in *La tribune,* a Stéphanois newspaper, and there are detailed police reports in the departmental archives, ADL 92/M/171–78 and ADL 92/M/180–86. Some secondary literature which discusses one or another aspect of these strikes: de Seilhac, *Les grèves du Chambon;* Faure, *Le Chambon rouge;* Martin, "Le syndicalisme révolutionnaire chez les métallurgistes de l'Ondaine 1906–1914"; and Janet Jacobs, "A Community of French Workers, Social Life and Labour Conflicts in the Stéphanois Region 1890–1914" (Dissertation, St. Anthony's College, Oxford, c. 1973). In 1910 the *commissaire de police* estimated that there were 1,050 boltworkers (27.2 percent of the workforce in the metal trades), 1,171 workers in heavy metalwork (30.3 percent), and 1,644 fileworkers (42.5 percent); see ADL 92/M/174. The only other substantial groups of workers in the commune were miners, but the manuscript census of 1901 shows that 83.8 percent of the miners lived on the outskirts of town. These mining settlements were only the fringes of much larger communities centered in the neighboring towns of La Ricamerie and Firminy; miners' unions, clubs, and political activity were located in these towns, and miners played little role in Le Chambon.
5. See Loubère, "French Left-Wing Radicals," and "Left-Wing Radicals, Strikes and the Military."
6. On the 1901 Besson strike, see ADL 92/M/107 and *Le stéphanois,* Feb. 20–Mar. 19, 1901. The official version of this strike is given in the report of May 7, 1901, ADL 93/M/107.
7. Dec. 28, 1909, January 15, 17, and 20, 1910, ADL 92/M/171.
8. For a detailed description of the sacking of the café de la Marine, see Faure, *Le Chambon rouge,* pp. 54–55. On negotiations, see *La tribune,* Feb. 15, 1910.
9. On violence, see *La tribune,* Mar. 11 and 14, 1910; Mar. 12, 13, and 31, 1910, ADL 92/M/175. Violence closed the Claudinon plant for one day, but it resumed work the next day; see report of Feb. 22, 1910, ADL 92/M/173.
10. *La tribune,* Mar. 16, 1910.
11. AN BB/18 2432 (II).
12. May 7, 1910, ADL 92/M/171.

13. Certainly the socialists were confident of victory (*La lutte sociale*, Apr. 30, 1910), and the prefect's solicitude was exceptional (*Le mémorial de la Loire*, Mar. 1, 1910). Court records listed the names but not the occupations of those accused and condemned for the incident; see Cours d'appel de Lyon, July 13, 1910, AN BB/18 1432 (II). De Seilhac presents a report of the trial in the appendix to his *Les grèves du Chambon*, pp. 99–104.

14. "Interdictions des attroupements sur la voie publique," Apr. 25, 1910, ADL 10/M/143.

15. Even the *commissaire de police* thought Mermier's behavior "equivocal"; see Mar. 3, 1911, ADL 92/M/180.

16. Oct. 2, 1911, ADL 92/M/189.

17. Mar. 19, 1911, ADL 92/M/180; July 1 and 14, 1911, ADL 92/M/184; Aug. 3 and 26, 1911, ADL 92/M/186. *La tribune* of May 16, 1911, describes the fire at Mermier's factory.

Chambonnaire strike violence might be attributed to the bitter feelings produced by the long strike. H. M. Gittelman shows that lockouts and broken strikes often led American workers to turn to violence; see "Perspectives on American Industrial Violence," *Business History Review* 47, no. 1 (Spring, 1973), 1–23. This approach has appeal, and it does seem to explain some Chambonnaire violence. But my inclination is to put the 1911 strike in the context of the successful 1909–10 action. As William Gamson suggests in *The Strategy of Social Protest* (Homewood, Ill.: Dorsey Press, 1975), violence can also represent a rational strategy chosen by actors to accomplish their goals. Violence had proved effective in bringing about negotiations in 1910. There is also some evidence that the union leadership, which formally condemned violence, informally supported it. Laurent Moulin, a leader of the trade union in 1911, claimed that Tyr was involved in illegal activities; see Martin, "Le syndicalisme révolutionnaire," p. 165.

18. To fix the date on which work resumed is difficult. There are three figures: the employers' figures, the union's, and the police's. The police reported that the employers' claims were "inexact" (Aug. 7, 1911, ADL 92/M/186), and their figures are closer to the union's. On employer repression, see Sept. 17 and Oct. 1, 1911, ADL 19/M/26.

19. De Seilhac, *Les grèves du Chambon*, p. 33.

20. Faure, *Le Chambon rouge*, p. 37. Born in 1891 in the Stéphanois valley, Petrus Faure spent his childhood and young manhood in Le Chambon. He was active in the metal union and speaks from personal experience. In 1919 he succeeded Georges Claudinon to become mayor of Le Chambon. In 1932 he was elected deputy from the Loire and helped draft the French social security law.

21. June 3 and July 12, 1889, ADL 92/M/26; Feb. 10, 1889, ADL 93/M/14.

22. Martin, "Le syndicalisme révolutionnaire," p. 40.

23. *La tribune*, Feb. 28, 1910.

24. Two fine studies of the Sheffield cutlery trades which devote a good deal of space to filemaking are: G. I. H. Lloyd, *The Cutlery Trades: An Historical Essay in the Economics of Small-Scale Production* (London: Frank Cass, 1913), and Sidney Pollard, *A History of Labour in Sheffield* (Liverpool: Liverpool University Press, 1959).

25. In 1889 the *inspecteur spécial* reported: "Some boltworkers have recently taken the initiative of forming a trade union. . . . The promoters of this movement do not conceal that as soon as their number of members permits them to struggle victoriously against their employers they will put themselves on strike . . ." (June 2, 1889, ADL 92/M/26). And that is exactly what happened.

26. The early fileworkers' union was considerably better organized than any of the early boltworker or metalworker ventures into trade unionism. The police reported that the trade union had 300 active members, only half of whom were up to date on their dues in 1894. The Office du travail's *Annuaire des syndicats* for 1894 lists the dues-paying members, 161, not the "active" members. In that year the union had 2,200 francs in its treasury and had just finished donating 100 francs to the striking forgers of Rive-de-Gier and 250 francs to striking workers in the Tarn; Jan. 1 and 11, 1894, see ADL 92/M/14.

27. De Seilhac, *Les grèves du Chambon*, p. 33.

28. Pollard gives an overview of fileworker activity in the last quarter of the nineteenth century, in *History of Labour in Sheffield*, pp. 127–28, 138–41.

Craft unionists attempted to organize unskilled workers even before the "New Unionism" of the 1890s in Great Britain. The difficulties involved show the problems of a craft union approach to mass organizing. See M. P. Howard, "The Strikes and Lockouts in the Iron Industry and the Formation of the Ironworkers Union 1862–1869," *International Review of Social History* 18 (1973), pt. 3, 396–427, and a two-part article by Keith Burgess, "Trade Union Policy and the 1852 Lock-Out in the British Engineering Industry," and "Technological Change and the 1852 Lock-Out in the British Engineering Industry," *International Review of Social History* 14 (1969), 215–36, and 17 (1972), 645.

29. Charles Rist, "La situation financière des syndicats ouvriers français," *Revue économique internationale* 1 (Jan., 1911), 34–67. A French sociologist, Jennine Verdes, has argued that many aspects of pre–World War I French unionism can be explained by its numerical weakness, in "Le syndicalisme révolutionnaire et le mouvement ouvrier français avant 1914," *Cahiers internationaux de sociologie* 36 (Jan.-June, 1964), 117–36.

30. Pollard, *History of Labour in Sheffield*, p. 342.

31. The only account of the 23,000 francs raised to build the *maison syndicale* appeared in the *Voix du peuple* of Nov. 14, 1909: "They had demanded nothing of the public powers, not even of their municipality. It is by supplementary dues, by numerous lists of subscriptions distributed in all the local workshops that they have amassed a capital of 15,000 francs." The *Voix du peuple* was found in AN F/7 13605. Pollard has an important section on "The Friendly Society Functions of the Trade Societies," which deals with this question, in *History of Labour in Sheffield*, pp. 148–52.

32. Pollard, *History of Labour in Sheffield*, p. 342.

33. Faure, *Le Chambon rouge*, pp. 36–42; May 7, 1910, ADL 92/M/171; Oct. 2, 1911, ADL 92/M/182.

34. Food and pocket money were distributed at the *soupes communistes;* see *Le stéphanois*, May 8, 1901.

35. June 25, 1906, ADL 92/M/140.

36. Pagé describes filemaking technique in vol. 3 of *La coutellerie*, "La Lime," pp. 474–79. The first volume of this work discusses the organization of cutlery in the sixteenth through eighteenth centuries. Le Chanbon had been involved in the cutlery trade since the late sixteenth century. On filemaking, see also Gras, *Essai sur l'histoire de la quincaillerie et petite métallurgie.*

37. Faure, *Histoire de la métallurgie*, pp. 57–74.

38. Conditions in filemaking shops have been studied by Léon and Maurice Bonneff, "La fabrication meurtrière des limes," in *La vie tragique*, pp. 182–98.

39. An interesting study of filecutting was made by a French time-study expert,

Charles Fremont, *Files and Filing*, trans. George Taylor (London: Sir Isaac Pitman and Sons, 1920). Fremont notes: "The number of hammer-strokes per minute was recorded—(1) For continuous working—i.e., without any stoppages, and consequently for a short period only; (2) for medium working—i.e., taking into account the workman's stoppages, the necessary result of the exigencies of working. It is certain that the average amount of work for a complete working day is considerably less than the preceding one, because it involves longer relaxations which have to be added to stoppages due to the exigencies of working . . ." (p. 106). According to Fremont, fileworkers could average as high as 105 strokes a minute with a three-pound hammer, but their "secondary work rates" fell to 67 taps a minute.

40. Chambonnaire filemaking is described by Faure, "La Lime," in *Histoire de la métallurgie*.

41. Ardouin-Dumazet, *Voyage· en France*, pp. 80–81.

42. In order to examine the relation between workplace and residence, I divided the commune of Le Chambon into six major regions, three urban and three rural. In 1901 the urban areas contained 50.4 percent of the population and the rural areas 49.6 percent. The metal trade's population from the 1901 census was divided along these regional lines. Fileworkers were more concentrated around factories than urban-rural differences indicate. Some file factories were located outside of town in rural areas. Most fileworkers lived in the section of town in which their factory was located or in a section adjacent to the factory.

43. For wages of fileworkers, see ADL 92/M/140. The employment of women in the Chambonnaire metal trades was not exceptional. In Birmingham in 1901, 25,000 women were employed in the metal trades and some were skilled workers: press operators, lathe workers, solderers, and polishers; see Edward Cadbury, Cecile Matheson, and George Shann, *Women's Work and Wages: A Phase of Life in the Industrial City* (Chicago: University of Chicago Press, 1906).

44. On café life, see Faure, *Le Chambon rouge;* Faure, *Un témoin raconte*, pp. 23–24; and "Interview with Laurent Moulin," in Martin, "Le syndicalisme révolutionnaire."

45. A 1900 estimate lists 2,500 workers in the file trades (July 3, ADL 92/M/98), and in 1906 an estimate of 1,900 (June 25, ADL 92/M/140). To say how much this reflects market changes and how much varying estimates is difficult. The 2,500 estimate is probably wide of the mark, since 1,245 people identified themselves as fileworkers in 1901.

46. The office du travail's *Annuaire des syndicats* contains information on patronal unions as well as worker unions.

47. De Seilhac, *Les grèves du Chambon*, pp. 12–13.

48. On the idea of a "labor artistocracy," see Eric J. Hobsbawm, "The Labour Aristocracy in Nineteenth Century Britain," *Labouring Men: Studies in the History of Labour* (Garden City, N.Y.: Anchor Books, 1967). Some interesting factual material is also found in R. Q. Gray, "Styles of Life, the 'Labour Aristocracy' and Class Relations in Late Nineteenth Century Edinburgh," *International Review of Social History* 18 (1973), pt. 3, 428–52.

49. A copy of Leonardo's sketch of a filecutting machine appears in Friedrich Klemm, *A History of Western Technology* (New York: Charles Scribner's Sons, 1959), p. 126, and in the *Encyclopédie ou dictionnaire raisonné des sciences, des arts et des métiers* (Neufchatel: Samuel Faulche, 1765); see the entry under "Lime," 9,

537–41. See also T. S. Ashton, *An Eighteenth-Century Industrialist, Peter Stubbs of Warrington, 1756–1806* (Manchester: Manchester University Press, 1939).

50. Jacques Vacher, "Le Tailleur de Limes," *Poésies et chansons de Jacques Vacher* (Saint-Etienne: Imprimerie de la Loire républicaine, 1898), pp. 63–64. Vacher was a volunteer for Garibaldi's expedition, a Stéphanois *ébéniste* and a member of the Alliance républicaine. Compare the lines from this song with the "Filehewers Lamentation" of William Mather (1737–1804) in Lloyd, *The Cutlery Trades*, p. 166:

> Of starving I am weary,
> From June to January.
> To nature its contrary;
> This, I presume, is fact.
> Although without a stammer
> Our Nell exclaims I clam her
> I weld my six pound hammer
> 'Till I am grown round backed.

51. For a bibliography of filecutting machines, see Sheffield City Libraries, "Select Bibliography on Filecutting Machines," *Research Bibliographies*, n.s., no. 49 (Apr., 1948). The most complete listing of the gradual change in filecutting machines is Otto Dick, *Die Feile und Ihre Entwicklungsgeschichte* (Berlin: Julius Springer, n.d.); see pt. 2, "Die Entwicklung den Feilenhamummaschinen," pp. 81–171. For the introduction of filecutting machines on the European continent, see G. Aubert, *Fabrique de limes et de rapes, usines à Cosne (Nièvre)* (Paris: Publications industrielles, 1900), and *Usines métallurgiques de Vallorbe, fabrique de limes et burins en tous genres* (Paris: Publications industrielles, 1900). On the spread of cutting machines in the United States and England, see Pollard, *History of Labour in Sheffield*, pp. 127–28, 204.

52. Eric N. Simons, *Steel Files, Their Manufacture and Application* (London: Sir Isaac Pitman and Sons, 1974), p. 31.

The great progress in nineteenth-century steel production was one of a substantial cost reduction for the lower grades of steel owing to mass production. No great innovation occurred in the production of quality steel; in 1925 an American steel manufacturer wrote: "It should be noted that while vast economies have been effected in the consumption of ore and fuel in latter processes, no improvement has been made in the quality of wrought iron and high carbon steel—the old blades of Damascus, Toledo and Bilbao have never been excelled" (*The ABC of Iron and Steel*, ed. A. O. Backert [Cleveland: Penton Publishing, 1925], p. 95).

Henry Diston noted: "It has been said that the early failure of many machine made files was caused by lack of care in the selection of the material used, not entirely by the lack of efficiency in the machine . . ." (*The File in History* [Philadelphia: Keystone Saw, Tool, Steel and File Works, 1920], p. 23).

53. W. T. Nicholson, *A Treatise on Files and Rasps* (Providence: Nicholson File Co., 1878), p. 3; Simons, *Steel Files*.

54. Nicholson, *Treatise on Files and Rasps*, pp. 55–56.

55. There is no really adequate study of fileworkers' wages. The best study is that of Sidney Pollard, "Wages and Earnings in the Sheffield Trades 1851–1914," *Yorkshire Bulletin of Economic and Social Research* 6, no. 1 (Feb., 1954), 49–64. Pollard's study is a good statement of some general problems and some general

solutions, but it still leaves some important questions unsolved. No study really consistently distinguishes between the average piece-rate wages of "inworkers" and "outworkers." The most likely assumption is that estimates are, unless otherwise stated, for inworkers, whose earnings were much more easily investigated. "Inworkers'" wages were higher than those of "outworkers" for at least two reasons. Inworkers did not have to pay for all chemicals and equipment, while outworkers were expected to pay for everything. Second, in Le Chambon, as in Sheffield, the smaller files were the province of women, who were mostly outworkers (interview with Petrus Faure, July 25, 1974). Smaller files were less remunerative, but women did make all file sizes when small files were not available. Using wage estimates for "women" fileworkers (June 14, 1904, ADL 92/M/129; July 13, 1900, ADL 92/M/98), I would suggest somewhere around 2.50 to 3.00 francs a day as outworking women's average wages when men were receiving 3.25 to 4.00 francs. This is very tentative.

A comparison of the wages of inworkers is on somewhat firmer ground. Faure *Le Chambon rouge*, p. 26, gives the average fileworker's wage in 1899 as 3.25 francs. Lloyd, *The Cutlery Trades*, p. 211, gives an average Sheffield filecutter's wage as 20.5 shillings, which would mean that Chambonnaire filecutters received 76 percent of the wages of Sheffield filecutters. These are only approximations. There is no discussion of how they were reached. Tariffs for piece rate for Chambonnaire filecutters do exist, but in themselves are not very helpful; see ADL 92/M/26.

56. *L'Eclaireur de Saint Chamond*, July 23, 1899.

57. Faure, "Les conflits de l'usine de Trablaine," in *Le chambon rouge*, pp. 31–32.

58. At least three strikes had as one of their principal complaints the firing of a worker who had worked at Trablaine. Two strikes occurred in 1900 and were successful, and the third strike occurred in Feb., 1901, and was a compromise. On the 1900 strikes, see June 24, ADL 92/M/98, and *Tribune républicaine*, June 24 and 26, Sept. 3 and 4. For the 1901 strike, see Feb. 23, ADL 92/M/107. This strike took place several weeks after the foundation of the general metal union. Within a month after this strike the machine cutters' union was dissolved into the general metal union.

59. Chambre syndicale de la fabrique de quincaillerie "Rapport sur les travaux de l'année 1908," pp. 11–12.

60. June 14, 1904, ADL 92/M/129.

61. In 1901 the industrial census listed the five departments which employed the most fileworkers and gave the percentage of fileworkers employed. Their results were: Loire, 27 percent; Seine, 11 percent; Nord, 8 percent; Côte d'Or, 8 percent; and Nièvre, 8 percent; see Bureau de la statistique générale, *Résultats statistiques du rencensement général de la population, 1901* (Paris: Imprimerie nationale, 1902). In 1906 the industrial census found: Loire, 20 percent; Côte d'Or, 12 percent; Nièvre, 12 percent; Nord, 12 percent; Meurthe-et-Moselle, 11 percent; and Seine, 9 percent; see *Résultats statistiques du rencensement général de la population, 1906* (Paris: Imprimerie nationale, 1906).

On competition, see Chambre syndicale de la fabrique de quincaillerie, "Situation industrielle—limes—1911," p. 26.

Unfortunately Fourastié's price series for files do not begin until 1909: Jean Fourastié, *Documents pour l'histoire et la théorie des prix*, 2 (Paris: Armand Colin, n.d.), 192–95, 226–27.

62. Chambre syndicale de la fabrique de quincaillerie, "Rapport sur les travaux de l'année 1908," pp. 11–12.

63. Chambre syndicale de la fabrique de quincaillerie, "Situation industrielle —limes—1910," pp. 25–26.

64. *Ibid.*, 1911, p. 26.

65. The only discussion of the formation of the general metal union is found in a series in *Le drapeau rouge, organe de la fédération de groupes de jeunesse socialiste-révolutionnaire* in their issues of Sept. and Oct., 1901, nos. 9 and 11. It notes, "Some successes obtained from time to time, notably the grinders' strike, the 'affair of Trablaine,' etc. . . . made [the fileworkers' union] again a beautiful and powerful organization." It stresses the quick victory for the ten-hour day as one source of worker unity and notes that in 1901 "the entente between the unions was so perfect that they all fused together, including the one at Trablaine."

66. In 1901, 38.2 percent of filecutters lived in a household with at least one other fileworker member. Twenty-four percent of the skilled industrial workers employed in the shops had family members who were fiilecutters, and 74 percent of these industrial workers were heads of households; see 1901 manuscript census, ADL 49/M/132.

67. Oct. 2, 1911, ADL 92/M/182.

An important discussion of the relationship between family strategies, economic structure, and female employment can be found in Joan Scott and Louise Tilly, "Women's Work and the Family in Nineteenth-Century Europe," *Comparative Studies in Society and History* 17 (1975), 36–64. Some very interesting theorizing about the conditions under which family ties form and dissolve is Michael Anderson, *Family Structure in Nineteen Century Lancashire* (Cambridge: Cambridge University Press, 1971).

68. On the 1901 Besson strike, see Faure, *Le Chambon rouge*, pp. 38–41.

69. The growth of the employers' organizations can be traced in the yearly reports of the Chambre syndicale de la fabrique de la quincaillerie.

70. Some prominent revolutionary syndicalist visitors to Le Chambon were Merrheim in 1907 (ADL 10/M/93); Jouhaux, Lefebvre, Pataud, and Pouget in 1910 (ADL 92/M/175–177; *L'Action*, Apr. 29, 1910); and Merrheim and Pericat in 1911 (ADL 92/M/184–186).

71. *La grève générale et le socialisme: Enquête internationale*, ed. Hubert Lagardelle (Paris: Marcel Rivière, 1905), p. 28.

72. Hubert Lagardelle, *Le socialisme ouvrier* (Paris: V. Giard and E. Brière, 1911), pp. 58–61.

73. On boltworkers' wages, see ADL 92/M/140. On boltworking, see Emile Zola, *L'Assommoir* (London: Penguin Books, 1970 [1876]), pp. 176–78.

A description of the technical changes in Chambonnaire boltmaking can be found in Faure, *Histoire de la métallurgie*, "La Boulonnerie," pp. 75–96.

74. June 25, 1906, ADL 92/M/140.

75. A detailed description of Chambonnaire boltmaking is found in Bonneff, *La vie tragique*, pp. 337–40.

76. *Ibid.*; Faure, *Un témoin raconte*, p. 22.

77. June 25, 1906, ADL 92/M/140.

78. See Benoît Frachon, "Souvenirs de Benoit Frachon—À l'appel d'octobre," *Institut Maurice Thorez—Cahiers* (Apr.–June, 1967), 63–72.

79. Office du travail, *Annuaire des syndicates*. See also the "Rapport sur les travaux de l'année," published yearly between 1907 and 1913 by the Chambre

syndicale de la fabrique de la quincaillerie et petite métallurgie; a section of the report was always devoted to boltworkers. Employer organization in the bolt trades fits the national pattern for employers' organizations during these years; see Stearns, "Against the Strike Threat," pp. 474–500.

80. *Commissaire de police*, ADL 92/M/140.

81. The best introduction to the organization of work in French metalworking is Vial, *L'Industrialisation de la sidérurgie française*. Vial notes: "Technically it seems that the freedom of action [freedom to protest] is much greater and much better exercised when the worker remains the more master of his technical activity and the more near he is to the finishing side of the job" (1, 350).

On puddling, see Courtheaux, "Privilèges et misères d'un métier sidérurgique." For a good technical description of the work of the puddler, see U.S. Steel, *The Making, Shaping and Treating of Steel* (Pittsburgh, Pa.: U.S. Steel, 1957), pp. 209–15.

The puddler gradually disappeared from the steel mills between 1910 and 1920, not so much because the process was technically obsolete but because new techniques of steel production were developed which did not need such skilled labor. In 1925 an American steelmaker commented: "Wrought iron has failed to keep its place in the race with soft steel, chiefly on account of the high labor cost. The work is most laborious and requires no little skill. Indeed, the skill of experience, of art, is superior to knowledge of theory. These conditions make it necessarily difficult to obtain men, since the intelligence necessary can obtain higher reward for less efforts in other pursuits, with the result that whole districts have abandoned puddling because the furnaces could not be manned" (James R. Roe in *The ABC of Iron and Steel*, ed. Backert). Even in a capital-intensive production process like iron- and steelmaking, labor costs could determine the choice of the means of production.

82. Benoist, "Le travail dans la grande industrie," pt. 1 p. 596; see also pt. 2, pp. 637–61. These essays are partly incorporated into his two-volume work, *La crise de l'état moderne* (Paris: Plon-Nourrit, 1905).

83. Manuscript census, ADL 49/M/132. The Chambonnaire manuscript census for 1901 is particularly interesting because local census enumerators listed the factory where each worker was employed as well as his profession.

84. *Ibid.*

85. On Claudinon and the Claudinon plant, see Faure, *Histoire de la métallurgie*, "La grosse métallurgie," pp. 25–56, and Thiollier, *La chambre de commerce de Saint-Etienne*.

CHAPTER SEVEN

Conclusion

In the years between 1871 and 1914 the structure of French industrial growth powerfully influenced the evolution of working-class protest. Industrial development in France did not break cleanly with the preindustrial past; rather, it built gradually on preindustrial foundations which encouraged its slow expansion along already settled lines. On the eve of the Industrial Revolution France possessed a highly skilled artisanal labor force, concentrated in luxury production; the protracted character of French industrial development meant that a large portion of this workforce survived into the late nineteenth century. Moreover, artisanal workers not only persisted but multiplied as France acquired an international reputation as a producer of quality goods. But even in France machines and the division of labor began to make inroads on artisanal production. Mechanization created a new urban proletariat of semiskilled workers at the same time as the fear of mechanization radicalized artisans. And economic growth occurred in an environment of dramatic political change; in 1871 the advent of the republic opened the way for the entry of the mass of workers into the political arena. The effects of economic growth and political enfranchisement on worker protest can be seen in the Stéphanois region, one of the more developed French industrial regions.

These three Stéphanois case studies have attempted to analyze the conditions under which artisanal workers became militant and the impact of artisanal militancy on the development of industrial worker protest. The kinds of questions asked in regard to each of the towns are: Did the industrial workers' movement begin anew on the ashes of artisanal protest, or did it grow out of the artisanal revolutionary tradition? To what degree were the mass worker struggles that developed in the late nineteenth century the direct product of the growth of an industrial proletariat? And to what extent was working-class militancy shaped by the interests of the preindustrial workforce that already existed in the urban and industrial background?

The results of the study suggest the importance of looking at nineteenth-century worker protest and solidarity in terms of coalitions of different working-class groups, each with its own specific demands and ability to protest. Following this line of argument, "craft interest" is defined as the collective interest of a particular skill group, and it is not necessarily counterposed to "class interest" defined as the common interests of different working-class groups. Such an interpretation may prove helpful in explaining the rapid growth of worker protest in the late nineteenth century, for it implies that militant artisans may have acted as catalysts to promote the growth of industrial worker protest. Where powerful groups of artisans existed and shared common interests with industrial workers, conditions were particularly favorable for worker solidarity and mass strike actions.

The foregoing arguments focus on the importance of the work process. Fortunately, rather detailed descriptions of the work processes in Stéphanois filemaking, boltmaking, glassmaking, and heavy metalworking exist, permitting a close analysis of the effects of skill in promoting worker solidarity. The initial assumption that shared artisanal skills created a cohesive group of workers who gathered together both on and off the job has been strongly supported by the evidence concerning worker residential patterns, leisure-time activities, and trade union organization. In all three cities artisanal workers were more urbanized and concentrated within the city than were industrial workers. Fragmentary evidence about leisure activities suggests that artisanal workers more often tended to gather in occupationally segregated cafés. In every case, artisanal workers were more thoroughly unionized than industrial workers, and their participation in trade union activity was less subject to fluctuation.

Considerable evidence supports the argument that artisanal mobilization resulted from fear of technological change that threatened to deprive artisans of skills, the source of their high wages and group solidarity. In both of the cities which possessed a large number of artisans, Rive-de-Gier and Le Chambon-Feugerolles, technological change played an important role in radicalizing artisanal workers. In both towns, moreover, technological change was not an irresistible, lightning-fast process, leaving embittered and obsolete workers in its wake; for glassworkers and fileworkers technological change was a constant threat which conditioned a large part of their lives and actions. In those industries where technological change was gradual, skilled workers could hope that by increased organization and militant struggle precious time could be gained during which younger workers could cast about for other positions. Ripagérien and Chambonnaire artisans did not protest against mechanization *per se*, but they did seek to prevent employers from using mechanization against artisanal workers.

Furthermore, the struggle of threatened artisans led them to form alliances with industrial workers. Technological change encouraged workers to organize and defend their rights. As mechanization eroded their skills, artisans became increasingly dependent on organization to enforce their position in the workshop, and their reliance on trade unionism made artisans very suspicious of any employer campaign against unionism in their town. Artisanal workers feared, often correctly, that any employer attack on the union organizations of industrial workers might be only a prelude to an attack on *their* unions. Additionally, in Le Chambon, owing to the stagnating position of the filecutters, the relatives of artisanal fileworkers began to seek individually high-paying jobs as semiskilled metalworkers, and this was another cause of artisanal solidarity with industrial workers. Finally, the growth of militant artisanal trade unions caused artisanal workers' organizations to become actively involved in socialist and radical politics, thus drawing them into alliances with other workers. In Rive-de-Gier artisans had their own political demands, but in both cities artisans sought to prevent the authorities from openly supporting the employers' side in strike conflicts.

A comparison of the industrial composition of the three towns and their strike militancy strengthens the argument that artisanal workers played a key role in involving industrial workers in strike conflicts; the contrast between Rive-de-Gier, the mixed artisanal-industrial town, and Saint-Chamond, the predominantly industrial town, is particularly telling. Although there was a difference in average plant size between the two cities, the number of industrial workers and the type of metalwork they performed were nearly identical. In Rive-de-Gier industrial metalworkers participated in a mass strike which attracted attention all over France, while in Saint-Chamond industrial metalworkers remained quiescent. As shown in Chapter Four, a large part of the reason for the metalworkers' participation in strike activity was the presence of threatened glassworkers in Rive-de-Gier, while Saint-Chamond lacked any appreciable number of artisans.

These local-level investigations tell a great deal about the dynamics of strike coordination in the Stéphanois region. Artisanal workers threatened by technological change strengthened the ability of industrial workers to participate in strike actions, and this sometimes led to simultaneous strike actions. In the case of Le Chambon-Feugerolles artisanal workers actually went on strike in solidarity with industrial workers. In the case of Rive-de-Gier artisanal and industrial strike activity was not quite so closely coordinated; the mass strike of metalworkers occurred in 1893 and the great strike of glassworkers at the beginning of 1894. Nevertheless, the same technological threat which led Ripagérien artisanal workers to support industrial workers' strike activity led them, a short time later, to go out on strike themselves. That strike actions by artisanal workers were closely related in time to those of industrial workers was no mere coincidence.

The example of the Stéphanois towns also offers some insights into French working-class politics. Chapter One emphasized the importance of universal manhood suffrage and the timing of its establishment in promoting worker solidarity. The political contribution to the formation of a working-class coalition in Rive-de-Gier drives this point home; the glassworkers were strongly prompted to support the metalworkers' strike in order to rally the metalworkers behind a socialist candidate committed to defend strikers against the hostile local administration. The formative influence of artisanal radicalism on the emerging French party system is equally evident; in both Le Chambon-Feugerolles and Rive-de-Gier socialist parties gained strength in the wake of massive artisanal struggles against technological change. To say what would have happened in France if the spread of manhood suffrage had not coincided with artisanal militancy is difficult, but the chances of coalitions forming between artisans and industrial workers would have been damaged if long tradition had firmly entrenched artisans in existing political parties or if industrial workers had been enfranchised later than artisans.

The tri-city study reveals more than just the local basis of trade union and socialist growth; it also shows the impact of national political events on provincial politics. In both cities where mass strikes occurred, the growth of a substantial radical and, later, socialist opposition at the national level helped to politicize and spur on local militants. The spread of socialism nationwide made it easier to become a socialist in small towns; by joining the socialist cause, local workers could not only hope to build a cooperative commonwealth in the future but to win reforms in the here and now. Concrete political events, such as the formation of a radical-socialist coalition in the 1890s and the reformist drive of socialism after 1906, also affected local worker coalitions.

In contrast to the enthusiasm provoked by the growth of a nationwide socialist party, specific socialist ideologies seem to have had little influence on Stéphanois politics. This may be accounted for partly by the absence of significant regional support for the more doctrinaire socialists, such as the Guesdists or the Blanquists. But it can also be explained by the relative indifference of most of the major political currents to local political events; differences between Allemanists, Broussists, or Guesdists were mainly relevant to national issues, such as whether to support a liberal government or to defend Dreyfus; no specifically Guesdist strike tactics or Broussist trade union policy existed. Only revolutionary syndicalism in Le Chambon-Feugerolles, by formally divorcing socialist from trade union affairs, affected local-level politics, and this formal separation concealed an informal liaison.

But, ultimately, of cardinal significance for an understanding of working-class politics was the transition occurring in the structure of work, as the artisan was replaced by the industrial worker. In some ways the case study approach, which illuminates the nature of mass strike coalitions with great clarity, obfuscates important features of emerging industrial worker political life. By its very nature the case study emphasizes the local and the communal at the expense of the national and the aggregate. As a result, in the case study informally disciplined, strongly organized artisanal mobilization appears vividly, but nationally organized, bureaucratically disciplined industrial worker mobilization appears only dimly.

The picture of industrial worker protest presented is less complete than that of the artisan because so much of the strength of industrial worker mobilization was based on national organization and coordination. On the city level, the world of industrial worker protest would never be as completely organized or totally united as that of the artisan. Viewed from the perspective of the local activist, the decline of artisanal work decreased the potential for working-class protest. In addition, a balanced view of the rise of industrial worker protest is difficult to capture because, in late nineteenth-century France, industrial worker organizations still remained in embryo; disciplined national organizations were only just beginning to appear and as yet exerted little influence on the local scene. Yet, already in the prewar period, the future outlines of industrial worker mobilization were vaguely discernible. By 1914 trade union and socialist organizations in all three cities were affiliated with national organizations, trade unions with the CGT, socialists with the SFIO. The less experienced and more weakly organized local industrial workers' organizations sought shelter under the banners of large and disciplined national organizations, and while the size of the workforce increased slowly after the turn of the century, membership in trade unions and socialist parties increased dramatically.

At the same time as membership in national organizations was growing, their internal discipline and control over their membership were increasing. After 1906 a disciplined socialist party, the SFIO, was founded and, despite great opposition, gained Stéphanois adherents. For the first time in France a mass working-class party was formed which attempted to enforce some minimum conditions for membership; the most well known of these conditions was the refusal to participate in "bourgeois" governments. Even in the "anarchist" trade union movement organizational discipline became tighter after 1902. Slowly, mass working-class organizations capable of coordinating mass strike actions across the country and launching political campaigns around nationwide political programs were growing. Within twenty years disciplined socialist and communist parties and trade unions had won the allegiance of the great majority of working-class activists.

Although worker protest in the Stéphanois in the years between 1871 and 1914 only indistinctly prefigured the rise of nationally coordinated industrial worker organizations, still, the mass upheavals which shook the area had a significant effect in stimulating industrial workers' protest. First, militant artisans organized industrial workers and promoted the growth of industry-wide unions which served to institutionalize worker solidarity within the trade union movement; the early and continued presence of industrial unions in France promoted worker coalitions and discouraged the formation of separate and potentially quarrelsome craft unions. Also, artisanal militancy helped to win segments of the working class to reformist and revolutionary doctrines which led to the establishment of a socialist party. Once founded, socialist parties and trade unions had a momentum of their own, continually attracting protesting elements of the working-class community around their banners.

In time, industrial worker organization would carry out actions on a scale of which artisans had only dreamed: in 1936 and again in 1968, within the space of a couple of weeks, millions of French workers went out on strike together; in the same period, across the entire country, in Lille, Toulouse, Nantes, and Marseilles, workers voted to support the national socialist and communist programs. But fresh opportunities brought fresh problems. The large national organizations which grew up were far more distant from their constituents than their artisanal predecessors. The direct democracy and informal organization characteristic of artisanal political life gave way to a far more indirect participation and bureaucratic organization; workers found it more difficult to make their voices heard and sometimes wondered whether anyone in their own organizations was even interested in their opinions. The opportunities and problems of industrial worker organizations were not uppermost in the minds of Stéphanois workers at the end of the nineteenth century, but their battles helped shape these organizations, then in process of formation.

Several conclusions emerge from this study of Stéphanois workers which might be of interest to social and economic historians. First, the presence of artisanal organization inside large and medium-sized factories and the stimulus this strategic position gave to mass strike actions should be noted. Too often, historians have concluded that the growing size of industry automatically means a decline in workers' control over production. But increased factory size did not mean the same thing as the introduction of industrial discipline or mechanization. The example of the Ripagè-rien glassworkers and the Chambonnaire fileworkers suggests that, at least for a time, a change in the scale of industry might leave workers' control of production relatively untouched. Artisans inside factory walls were put in contact with the machines which might one day replace them; as factory workers "inside the belly of the beast," artisans turned to militant unionism to assert their control over the new machines and to preserve their position.

The cases of Rive-de-Gier and Le Chambon-Feugerolles also show that the pursuit of craft and family interest did not always lead to politically conservative policies. Confronted with gradual technological change, artisanal workers in these two towns formed powerful alliances with industrial workers. The willingness, indeed the enthusiasm, with which artisanal fileworkers and glassworkers promoted industrial worker protest has implications for international comparisons of worker militancy in the late nineteenth century. Such extraordinary artisanal militancy suggests that, assuming the presence of large numbers of artisanal workers, slow technological change may have had more explosive potential for protest than rapid mechanization. The gradual development of industry in countries with a large artisanal base might be expected to produce more massive worker protests than the rapid development of industry in countries with a large industrial worker population. The rapid growth of the proletariat did not by itself produce mass strikes; the European industrial working class was too poor, geographically dispersed, and disunited to be able to carry out prolonged struggles on its own. Instead, the growth of a proletariat *alongside* a mass of threatened artisans, artisans who acted as catalytic agents of working-class revolt, produced mass strike protest.

The Selection of a Region

To see if different goals and methods of worker protest could be distinguished, I chose towns which all had a record of high strike activity but different industrial compositions. Of the three towns selected, one was predominantly artisanal, one predominantly industrial, and one mixed artisanal-industrial. In order to study closely relations between artisans and industrial workers, it is necessary to choose small towns. In large cities the variety of the labor movement and the very size of the city would make it difficult to separate the forces influencing workers' actions. Three criteria were used to select an area of study. I set out to find an area which had participated in strike waves, where participation was distributed across a geographic area, and which possessed industrial as well as artisanal workers.

The selection process was a sifting operation which comprised several stages. Participation in strike waves was the starting point of this process. According to Shorter and Tilly, a "strike wave" occurs when "both the number of strikes and the number of strikers in a given year exceed the mean of the previous five years by more than fifty percent." The strike wave of 1906 involved the largest number of strikers and strikes and the longest average duration of strikes of any period before World War I. Twenty departments with the greatest number of strikes per 100,000 workers in 1906 were selected from the figures in the *Statistique des grèves*. Three departments were omitted from this group: Seine, Bouches du Rhône, and Rhône. These three departments, which contain Paris, Marseilles, and Lyon, would all have been on such a list, but these cities were too large to form a part of a multi-city comparative study and strike activity in these towns dominated their departments. Next, the ten departments which had the highest absolute number of strikes were selected from these twenty. The larger the absolute number of strikes the easier it is to discover several cities which were the center of strike activity. The ten departments chosen were, in rank order: Pas-de-Calais, Loire, Jura, Isère, Morbihan, Meurthe, Ille-et-Villaine, Nord, Ardèche, and Puy-de-Dôme. If the ten departments with the highest percentage of strikers had been selected, there would have been only a few differences, and the first four departments on our first list were also the first four in the second list.

Departments were then chosen which had three cities under 40,000 which had strikes in 1906 and in either 1899 or 1900. I wanted to find cities which had participated in strike activity before 1906, and both 1899 and 1900 were strike years in which the number of strikes drastically increased. Departments with three cities having strike activity were chosen in order to find departments where the strike movement was dispersed. Four departments met this criteria: Nord, Loire, Jura, and Isère.

The 1906 industrial census made it possible to get some idea of the industry in each department. Using this census, I eliminated the Jura from the list because it had a very small number of industrial workers. The 1906 census is broken down into arrondissements and it seemed desirable to find three cities in the same arrondissement, since studying the arrondissement makes it easier to locate clusters of small towns which, though administratively separate, all belong to the same industrial environment and structure. Also, looking at the entire arrondissement means that different definitions of city limits can be reconciled: if a factory moves out of the city limits and into a nearby suburb, it still remains in the study. With this consideration in mind, the Nord was excluded. There was much artisanal industry in the Nord, but predominantly artisanal towns seemed to be in different arrondissements from mixed artisanal-industrial towns. Two departments remained: the Isère and the Loire. At this point, I decided to leave the decision up to the archives or, rather, the departmental catalogues. I chose the Loire because its records of catalogued material were far richer than those of the Isère.

I decided to leave the term "predominantly" rather loosely defined in order to retain some flexibility in choosing between a limited number of areas. In the appropriate chapters the types of artisanal worker in each of the three selected towns have been described at some length. There were four towns in the arrondissement of Saint-Etienne which might have been chosen. Le Chambon-Feugerolles had several strikes in 1899, 1900, and 1906, and Saint-Chamond had two strikes in 1906 and three strikes in 1899. The next two choices were Rive-de-Gier, which had five strikes in 1906 and participated in a regional miners' strike in 1899, and Firminy, which had three strikes in 1906 and had particpated in the same miners' strike. Rive-de-Gier was chosen mainly because of its mixed artisanal-industrial structure.

Perhaps the most debatable point in this entire system of industrial classification is that of coalmining. Shorter and Tilly classify miners as an artisanal occupation. While nineteenth-century coalmining was certainly not an industrial occupation, some might question its classification as an artisanal occupation (see Table 32). This proved to be a moot point, since more detailed investigation revealed that only a small minority of miners actually lived in any of our towns. Most Stéphanois miners lived in their own small coalmining communities. On occasion the population of these communities spilled over into nearby communes, but the miners in the communes of Rive-de-Gier and, particularly, Le Chambon-Feugerolles were actually a rural population who were part of a quite different urban network.

Table 32

Principal Occupations of Workers, 1891
(as percentage of total workforce in industry
and transport of each town)

Commune	Mining	Heavy Metalworking	Metal Trades	Glass	Textiles	Other
Rive-de-Gier (N = 3,302)	10.90%	54.99%	0.19%	28.04%	0	4.2%
Saint-Chamond (N = 4,518)	5.11	36.32	0.20	0	49.96	8.3
Le Chambon-Feugerolles (N = 3,802)	42.32	0	55.29	0.87	0	2.1

Manuscript census ADL 54/M/8. This estimate does not include 800 heavy metalworkers on the outskirts of Le Chambon.

The three towns selected were Le Chambon-Feugerolles (predominantly artisanal), Saint-Chamond (predominantly industrial), and Rive-de-Gier (mixed artisanal-industrial). These three towns were all in the arrondissement of Saint-Etienne.

Bibliography

I. PRIMARY SOURCES

ARCHIVES

Archives nationales (AN)
  Série BB/18: Procureurs généraux, 1450–2458.
  Série C: Classement provisoire, 3326–3373. Enquêtes sur la situation des ouvriers en France.
  Série F/7: Police générale.
  Série F/12: Industrie minière, situation économique, questions ouvrières.

Archives de la préfecture de police, Paris
  Série BA 171: L'Agent 47.

Musée sociale

Institut français d'histoire sociale

Archives départementales de la Loire (ADL)
  Série 3/M: Elections legislatives et senatoriales.
  Série 4/M: Elections cantonales.
  Série 5/M: Elections communales.
  Série 6/M: Conseils municipaux.
  Série 10/M: Evenements et affaires politiques.
  Série 19/M: Anarchistes.
  Série 40/M: Etablissements dangereuses et insalubres.
  Série 47/M: Instructions, statistiques, états récapitulatifs.
  Série 48/M: Mouvement de la population.
  Série 49/M: Dénombrements de la population.
  Série 56/M: Statistique industrielle.
  Série 88/M: Surveillance du travail des enfants et des femmes.
  Série 92/M: Grèves.
  Série 93/M: Syndicats et cooperatives.

Service vicinal: *Atlas des cartes cantonales du département de la Loire,* 1887.

Archives municipales de Saint-Etienne

Archives de la chambre de commerce de Saint-Etienne
Grèves et conditions d'industrie, cartons 59–106.

Bibliothèque municipale de Saint-Etienne

Archives municipales de Saint-Chamond
Délibérations du conseil municipal.

SELECTED NEWSPAPERS AND PERIODICALS

Abbreviations: Bibliothèque nationale (BN), Bibliothèque municipale de Saint-Etienne (BMSE), Musée sociale (MS).

L'Avenir de la Loire, Nov.-Dec., 1908 (BN)

L'Avenir des travailleurs de Rive-de-Gier, May-Dec., 1907 (BN)

La chanson plébienne, Jan.-Dec., 1900 (BMSE)

Le déshérité, Mar.-June 30, 1888 (BN)

Le drapeau rouge, July-Oct., 1901 (BN)

L'Echo socialiste, June, 1890 (BN)

L'Eclaireur de Rive-de-Gier, May, 1906–Dec., 1910 (BN)

L'Eclaireur de Saint-Chamond, Jan., 1899–Dec., 1911 (BN)

Germinal: Organe d'action et de combat syndicaliste de la Loire et de la région, Dec., 1905–May, 1906 (BN)

La Loire socialiste, July-Dec., 1888 (BN)

La lutte sociale, Feb., 1910–Aug., 1914 (BMSE)

Mémorial de la Loire et de la Haute-Loire, Dec., 1893–Jan., 1894 (BN)

Le peuple de la Loire, May-Dec., 1895 (BMSE)

Le républicain de la Loire et de la Haute-Loire, Aug., 1893 (BN)

Le réveil des verriers, Jan., 1891–Dec., 1894

Le socialiste-organe de la fédération socialiste autonome de la Loire, Dec., 1903–Aug., 1905 (BMSE)

Le stéphanois, Jan., 1899–May, 1911 (BN and BMSE)

Le temps, Jan.-Dec., 1893 (University of Chicago Library)

La tribune des travailleurs, Sept.-Nov., 1892 (BN)

La tribune républicaine, Oct., 1899–Dec., 1910 (BMSE)

L'Unité socialiste, Mar.-Apr., 1900 (BN)

L'Unité socialiste—organe officiel de la fédération de la Loire, Jan., 1905–Apr., 1906 (BN)

FRENCH GOVERNMENT PUBLICATIONS

Bureau de l'hygiène publique. *Statistique sanitaire des villes de France.* Melun: Imprimerie administrative, 1900.

Bureau de la statistique générale. *Annuaire Statistique, 1961—Rétrospectif.* Paris: Imprimerie nationale, 1961.

———. *Annuaire statistique—1911.* Paris: Imprimerie nationale, 1912.

———. *Bulletin de la statistique générale.* 4 vols. 1911–14.

———. *Indices généraux du mouvement économique en France de 1901–1931.* Paris: Imprimerie nationale, 1932.

———. *Résultats statistiques du recensement général de la population, 1901.* Paris: Imprimerie nationale, 1902.

———. *Résultats statistiques du recensement général de la population, 1906.* Paris: Imprimerie nationale, 1906.

———. *Statistique annuelle—1884.* Paris: Imprimerie nationale, 1887.

———. *Statistique de la France—1848.* Vol. 2. Paris: Imprimerie nationale, 1848.

———. *Statistique de la France—1872.* Paris: Imprimerie nationale, 1872.

———. *Statistique de la France—Prix et salaires à diverses époques.* Strasbourg: Berger-Levrault, 1863.

———. *Statistique de la France—Résultats généraux de l'enquête effectuée dans les années 1861–1865.* Nancy: Berger-Levrault, 1873.

———. *Statistiques des familles et des habitations en 1911.* Paris: Imprimerie nationale, 1918.

Office du travail. *Annuaire des syndicats.* Paris: Imprimerie nationale, 1890–1914.

———. *Annuaire des associations ouvrières de production.* Paris: Berger-Levrault, 1898.

———. *Les associations professionnelles ouvrières.* 4 vols. Paris: Imprimerie nationale, 1899–1904.

———. *Bordereaux des salaires pour diverses catégories d'ouvriers en 1900 et 1901.* Paris: Imprimerie nationale, 1902.

———. *Documents sur la question du chômage.* Paris: Imprimerie nationale, 1896.

———. *Résultats statistiques du recensement des industries et professions—Dénombrement général de la population du 29 mars 1896.* 4 vols. Paris: Imprimerie nationale, 1899–1901.

———. *Résultats statistiques du recensement des industries et professions—1906.* 4 vols. Paris: Imprimerie nationale, 1908.

———. *Salaires et coût de l'existence à diverses époques, jusqu'en 1910.* Paris: Imprimerie nationale, 1911.

———. *Salaires et durée du travail, coût de la vie pour certaines catégories en 1906.* Paris: Imprimerie nationale, 1907.

———. *Salaires et durée du travail dans l'industrie française.* 4 vols. Paris: Imprimerie nationale, 1893–97.

———. *Statistique des grèves.* Paris: Imprimerie nationale, 1890–1914.

———. *Statistiques du recensement de la population, 1901.* 4 vols. Paris: Imprimerie nationale, 1906.

CONGRESSES

Fédération des verriers de France
1891 (MS).
1892 (BN).
1893 (reprinted in the Mar., 1894, issues of *Le réveil des verriers*).

Fédération française des travailleurs du verre
1903–09 (MS).

Union fédérale des ouvriers métallurgistes de la France
1897–1909 (MS).

Chambre syndicale de la fabrique de quincaillerie et petite métallurgie de la Loire et de la Haute-Loire
1905–14 (BMSE).

Comité des forges de la Loire
1911–12 (BMSE).

BOOKS AND ARTICLES

Aftalion, Albert. "Le salaire réel et sa nouvelle orientation." *Revue d'économie politique* 26 (1912), 541–52.

Appert, L., and J. Henrivaux. *La verrerie depuis vingt ans.* Paris: E. Bernard, 1894.

Ardouin-Dumazet, M. *Voyage en France. No. 11.* Paris: Berger-Levrault, 1897.

Association française pour l'avancement des sciences. *Saint-Etienne.* 2 vols. Saint-Etienne: Théolier, 1897.

Aubert, G. *Fabrique de limes et de rapes-usines à Cosne, (Nièvre).* Paris: Publications industrielles, 1900.

Audiganne, Armand. *Les populations ouvrières et les industries de la France.* 2 vols. Paris: Capelle Libraire, 1854.

————. "La crise du travail dans Paris." *Revue des deux mondes* 93 (May 15, 1871), 301.

Balas Frères. *L'Industrie française des tresses et lacets.* Lyon: Association typographique, 1890.

Barbaret, Joseph. *Le travail en France: Monographies professionnelles.* Vols. 1–3. Paris: Berger-Levrault, 1886–87.

Baret, H. *Manuel de rubanerie, passementerie, et lacets.* Paris: Ballière, 1924.

Barron, Louis. *Les fleuves de France—La Loire.* Paris: Renouard, 1888.

Beauquis, A. *Histoire économique de la soie.* Paris: Donot and Pinot, 1900.

Benoist, Charles. "Le travail dans la grande industrie," pts. 1 and 2. *Revue des deux mondes* 12 (Dec., 1902) and 14 (June, 1903), 637–66.

————. "Vers la représentation proportionelle." *Revue des deux mondes* 2 (Mar., 1911).

Bonneff, Léon, and Maurice Bonneff. *La vie tragique des travailleurs.* Paris: Marcel Rivière, 1914.

Bontemps, Georges. *Guide du verrier, traité historique et pratique de la fabrication des verres, cristaux, vitraux.* Paris: Libraire du dictionnaire des arts et manufactures, 1868.

Chambeyron, J. B. *Recherches historiques sur la ville de Rive-de-Gier.* Lyon: Imprimerie de Léon Bartel, 1844.

Charneau, A. *Note sur les fours et appareils de verrerie.* Paris: E. Bernard, 1886.

Compagnie des aciéries de la marine. *Usines de Saint-Chamond.* 3 vols. (Photographs.) Paris: E. Mesière, n.d. (c. 1900–1914).

Condamin, James. *Histoire de Saint-Chamond et de la seigneurie de Jarez depuis les temps les plus reculés jusqu'à nos jours.* Paris: Alphonse Picard, 1890.

Corbon, Anthime. *Le secret du peuple de Paris.* Paris: Pagnenere, 1863.

"Cost of Living in French Towns." *House of Commons Sessional Papers*, vol. 91 (1909).

Courtot, Louis, and Eugene Rey. *Rapport des délégués ouvriers de la chambre syndicale des verriers réunis de Lyon à l'exposition universelle de Paris en 1889.* Lyon: Association typographique, 1890.

Curey, M. C. *L'Artillerie de Saint-Chamond à l'exposition universelle de 1900.* Paris: Berger-Levrault, 1901.

Deffernez, Dr. *Des souffleurs de verre, hygiène, maladies et accidents.* Vol. 5 of *Mémoires couronnés et autres mémoires publiées par l'académie royale de medicine de Belgique.* Brussels: Henri Manceaux, 1880.

Dégoute, M. *Rapport du délégué des boulonniers réunis et similaires de la ville de Lyon à l'exposition universelle de Paris en 1889.* Lyon: Association typographique, 1890.

Delesalle, Paul. "Les congrès des travailleurs du verre." *Le mouvement socialiste* 18 (Feb., 1906), 203–14.

Didron, Eduard, and M. Clémandot. *Rapport sur les cristaux, la verrerie et les vitraux à l'exposition universelle internationale de 1878 à Paris.* Paris: Imprimerie nationale, 1880.

Dubois, E., and A. Julian. "Industrie de la rubanerie à Saint-Etienne." In *Les moteurs électriques dans les industries à domicile*, vol. 3. Brussels: Office de publicité, 1902.

Ducarre, M. "Salaires et rapports entre ouvriers et patrons." *Assemblée nationale*, no. 3379 (1875).

Euverte, J. "De l'organisation de la main-d'oeuvre dans la grande industrie." *Journal des économistes* 19–20 (Sept., 1870), 340–89.

Faure, Petrus. *Un témoin raconte.* Saint-Etienne: Dumas, 1962.

Frachon, Benoît. "Souvenirs de Benoit Frachon—À l'appel d'octobre." *Institut Maurice Thorez—Cahiers* (Apr.-June, 1967), 63–72.

Garnier, Tony. *Une cité industrielle: Étude pour la construction des villes.* 2 vols. Paris: Massin, n.d. (c. 1911).

Godart, Justin. *L'Ouvrier en soie.* Lyon: Bernoux and Cumin, 1899.

Gonon, J. F. *Histoire de la chanson stéphanoise et forézienne depuis son origine jusqu'à notre epoque.* Saint-Etienne: Imprimerie cooperative, union typographique, 1906.

Griffuelhes, Victor. *L'Action syndicaliste.* Paris: Marcel Rivière, 1908.

———. "Les grèves et le syndicalisme français." *Le mouvement socialiste* 18 (Mar., 1906), 249–55.

———. "L'Inferiorité des capitalistes français." *Le mouvement socialiste* 28 (Dec., 1910), 329–32.

———. *Voyage révolutionnaire: Impressions d'un propagandiste.* Paris: Marcel Rivière, 1910.

Guesde, Jules, and Paul Lafargue. *Le programme du parti ouvrier.* Paris: Henri Oriol, 1833.

Halbwachs, Maurice. "Budgets de familles ouvrières et paysannes en France, en 1907." *Bulletin de la statistique générale de la France* 5 (Oct., 1914), 47–83.

———. *La classe ouvrière et les niveaux de vie.* Reims: Action populaire, 1908.

———. *Évolution des besoins dans les classes ouvrières.* Paris: Felix Alcan, 1933.

———. "Revenus et dépenses de ménages des travailleurs: Un enquête officielle d'avant guerre." *Revue d'économie politique* 35 (Jan.-Feb:, 1921), 50–59.

Hare, Augustus J. C. *South-Eastern France*. London: George Allen, 1890.

Huret, Jules. *Les grèves*. Paris: Editions de la revue blanche, 1902.

Kropotkin, Peter. *Fields, Factories, and Workshops*. New York: Greenwood Press, 1960 (1898).

Lagardelle, Hubert, ed. *La grève générale et le socialisme: Enquête internationale*. Paris: Marcel Rivière, 1905.

Le Play, F. "Description des procédés métallurgiques employés dans le pays de Gaulles." *Annales des mines* 13 (1848), 10–26.

Leroy, Maxime. *Les techniques nouvelles du syndicalisme*. Paris: Garnier Frères, 1921.

Leroy-Beaulieu, Paul. *De l'état moral et intellectuel des populations ouvrières et de son influence sur le taux des salaires*. Paris: Libraire Guillaumin, 1868.

———. "Le travail des femmes dans la petite industrie et l'instruction professionelle." *Revue des deux mondes* 99 (May 15, 1872), 332–60.

———. "Les ouvrières de fabrique autrefois et aujourd'hui." *Revue des deux mondes* 97 (Feb. 1, 1872). 630–57.

Levasseur, E. *The American Workman*. Baltimore, Md.: Johns Hopkins University Press, 1960.

Limousin, Charles. "L'Instruction professionnelle et l'industrie nouvelle." *Journal des économistes* 48 (Oct., 1901), 2–24.

Maitron, Jean, ed. *Ravachol et les anarchistes*. Paris: Julliard, 1964.

Marrel Frères. *Usines de Rive-de-Gier*. Paris: Le génie civil, 1893.

Meugy, A. *Histoire des mines de Rive-de-Gier*. Paris: Edouard Cornely, 1848.

Michaud, René. *J'avais vingt ans: Un jeune ouvrier au debut du siècle*. Paris: Editions syndicalistes, 1967.

Nansouty, Max. *Compagnie des hauts fourneaux, forges et aciéries de la marine*. Paris: Le génie civil, 1894.

Pataud, Emile, and Emile Pouget. *Comment nous ferons la révolution*. Paris: Editions de la guerre sociale, 1911.

Peligot, Eugène. *La verre, son histoire, sa fabrication*. Paris: G. Masson, 1877.

Pelletier, Pierre. *Les verriers dans le Lyonnais et le Forez*. Paris: by the author, 1887.

Pelloutier, Fernand. *Histoire des bourses du travail*. Paris: Alfred Costes, 1901.

Picquenard, Charles. "Le bilan financier des grèves." *Revue d'économie politique* 22 (May, 1908), 356–77.

Poulot, Denis. *Le sublime ou le travailleur comme il est en 1870 et ce qu'il peut faire*. Paris: Lacroix and Verboeckhaven, 1872.

Reclus, Onésime. *La France à vol d'oiseau*. Vol. 2. Paris: Flammarion, 1908.

Reybaud, Louis. *Études sur le régime des manufactures: Conditions des ouvrières en soie.* Paris: Michel Levy, 1859.

―――. *Le fer et la houille.* Paris: Michel Levy, 1874.

Rist, Charles. "La progression des grèves en France et sa valeur symptomatique." *Revue d'économie politique* 21 (1907), 161–93.

―――. "Relations entre les variations annuelles du chômage, des grèves, et des prix." *Revue d'économie politique* (1912), 748–58.

―――. "La situation financière des syndicats ouvriers français." *Revue économique internationale* 1 (Jan., 1911).

Robert, Charles. "Monteur d'outils en acier." *Les ouvriers des deux mondes* 2, no. 16 (1858), 285–311.

Roquille, Guillaume. *Poèmes français et patois: Oeuvres complètes de Guillaume Roquille de Rive-de-Gier.* Saint-Etienne: Imprimerie de la Loire républicaine, 1883.

Rousseau, J. J. *Confessions.* New York: E. P. Dutton, 1931 (1770).

Sabatier, Camille. "Le morcellisme dans l'industrie." *Revue d'économie politique* 21 (1907), 736–60.

Sauzay, A. *La verrerie depuis les temps les plus reculés jusqu' à nos jours.* Paris: Libraire Hachette, 1884.

Schloss, David F. *Methods of Industrial Remuneration.* London: Williams and Nargate, 1892.

Seilhac, Léon de. *Une enquête sociale: La grève de Carmaux et la verrerie d'Albi.* Paris: Perrin, 1897.

―――. *Une expérience socialiste: La verrerie ouvrière d'Albi.* Paris: Arthur Rousseau, 1913.

―――. *Les grèves du Chambon.* Paris: Arthur Rousseau, 1912.

Steele, Henry. *The Working Classes in France: A Social Study.* London: Twentieth Century Press, 1904.

Taine, Hippolyte. *Notes on England.* London: Thames and Hudson, 1957.

Vacher, Jacques. *Poésies et chansons de Jacques Vacher.* Saint-Etienne: Imprimerie de la Loire républicaine, 1898.

Valesh, Eva McDonald. "Conditions of Labor in Europe," *American Federationist* 3 (May, 1896), 42.

Vidal de la Blache, Paul. "Régions françaises." *La revue de Paris,* Dec. 15, 1910, pp. 821–49.

Villermé, M. *Les cités ouvrières.* Paris: J. B. Ballière, 1850.

Yvetot, Georges. "La section des bourses du travail." *Le mouvement socialiste* 15 (Jan., 1905), 116–27.

―――. "La deuxième conférence des bourses du travail." *Le mouvement socialiste* 21 (Apr., 1907), 373–83.

BIBLIOGRAPHICAL AIDS

Brécy, Robert. *Le mouvement syndical en France 1871–1921: Éssai bibliographique.* Paris: Mouton, 1963.

Dale, Leon A. *A Bibliography of French Labor.* New York: Augustus M. Kelley, 1969.

Ferguson, Eugene S. *Bibliography of the History of Technology.* Cambridge, Mass.: MIT Press, 1968.

Sheffield City Libraries. "Select Bibliography on Filecutting Machines." *Research Bibliographies,* n.s., no. 49 (Apr., 1948).

INTERVIEWS

On July 25, 1974, at his home in Le Chambon-Feugerolles, I tape-recorded an interview with Mr. Petrus Faure, the pre–World War I Chambonnaire syndicalist leader and student of the Stéphanois working-class movement.

II SECONDARY SOURCES

BOOKS

Agulhon, Maurice. *Une ville ouvrière au temps du socialisme utopique: Toulon 1815–1851.* Paris: Mouton, 1970.

Amman, Peter H. *Revolution and Mass Democracy: The Paris Club Movement in 1848.* Princeton, N.J.: Princeton University Press, 1975.

Anderson, Michael. *Family Structure in Nineteenth Century Lancashire.* Cambridge: Cambridge University Press, 1971.

Andréani, Edgard. *Grèves et fluctuations: La France de 1890 à 1914.* Paris: Editions Cujas, 1968.

Ashton, T. S. *An Eighteenth-Century Industrialist, Peter Stubbs of Warrington, 1756–1806.* Manchester: Manchester University Press, 1939.

Bairoch, Paul, *et al. The Working Population and Its Structure.* Vol. 1. Brussels: Editions de l'institut de sociologie de l'université libre de Bruxelles, 1968.

Banks, J. A. *Marxist Sociology in Action.* London: Faber and Faber, 1970.

Barnett, George E. *Chapters on Machinery and Wages.* New York: Arcturus Press, 1926.

Barral, Pierre. *Le département de l'Isère sous la Troisième République 1870–1940: Histoire sociale et politique.* Cahiers de la fondation nationale des sciences politiques, no. 115. Paris: Armand Colin, 1962.

Belleville, Pierre. *Une nouvelle classe ouvrière.* Paris: Julliard, 1963.

Bernot, Lucien, and René Blanchard. *Nouville, un village français.* Paris: Institut d'ethnologie, 1953.

Bernstein, Samuel. *Beginnings of Marxian Socialism in France.* New York: Russel and Russel, 1965.

Bezucha, Robert J. *The Lyon Uprising of 1834: Social and Political Conflict in the Early July Monarchy.* Cambridge, Mass.: Harvard University Press, 1974.

Bienefeld, M. A. *Working Hours in British Industry: An Economic History.* London: Weidenfeld and Nicolson, 1972.

Blauner, Robert. *Alienation and Freedom: The Factory Worker and His Industry.* Chicago: University of Chicago Press, 1964.

Bott, Elizabeth. *Family and Social Network: Roles, Norms, and External Relationships in Ordinary Urban Families.* New York: Free Press, 1971.

Bouvier, Jean, François Furet, and Marcel Gillet. *Le mouvement de profit en France au 19ᵉ siècle.* Paris: Mouton, 1965.

Boyer, Laurent. *Les élections politiques dans le département de la Loire à temps de l'assemblée nationale et du Maréchal MacMahon.* Paris: Sirez, 1963.

Braverman, Harry. *Labor and Monopoly Capital: The Degradation of Work in the Twentieth Century.* New York: Monthly Review Press, 1974.

Brecher, Jeremy. *Strike!* San Francisco: Straight Arrow Books, 1972.

Brody, David. *Steelworking in America: The Nonunion Era.* Cambridge, Mass.: Harvard University Press, 1960.

Brown, E. H. Phelps, with Margaret H. Browne. *A Century of Pay.* New York: St. Martins Press, 1968.

Cadbury, Edward, Cecile Matheson, and George Shann. *Women's Work and Wages: A Phase of Life in the Industrial City.* Chicago: University of Chicago Press, 1906.

Caplow, Theodore. *The Sociology of Work.* Minneapolis: University of Minnesota Press, 1954.

Charles, Jean. *Les débuts du mouvement syndicale à Besançon: La fédération ouvière 1891–1914.* Paris: Editions sociales, 1962.

Chevalier, Emile. *Les salaires au XIXᵉ siècle.* Paris: Arthur Rousseau, 1887.

Chomienne, C. *Histoire de la ville de Rive-de-Gier, du canton, et de ses principales industries.* Saint-Etienne: no publisher, 1912.

Clayre, Alasdair. *Work and Play: Ideas and Experiences of Aork and Leisure.* London: Weidenfeld and Nicolson, 1974.

Cole, Robert E. *Japanese Blue Collar, the Changing Tradition.* Berkeley: University of California Press, 1971.

Collier, Frances. *The Family Economy of the Working Classes in the Cotton Industry 1784–1833.* Manchester: Manchester University Press, 1964.

Collinet, Michel. *L'Ouvrier français: Essai sur la condition ouvrière 1900–1950*. Paris: Editions sociales, 1951.

D'Avenel, G. *Le mécanisme dans la vie moderne*. 5 vols. Paris: Armand Colin, 1896.

Dawley, Alan. *Class and Community: The Industrial Revolution in Lynn*. Cambridge, Mass.: Harvard University Press, 1976.

Donot, P. *Études historiques sur les origines de la fabrication des rubans, des lacets, du moulinage, de la teinture, du commerce des fers, et de la clouterie dans la ville de Saint-Chamond*. Lyon: H. George, 1889.

Dubreuil, H. *Robots or Men? A French Workman's Experience in American Industry*. New York: Harper, 1930.

Du Maroussem, Pierre. *La question ouvrière*. 3 vols. Paris: Arthur Rousseau, 1894.

Dunham, Arthur Louis. *Anglo-French Treaty of Commerce of 1860 and the Progress of the Industrial Revolution in France*. Ann Arbor: University of Michigan Press, 1930.

————. *The Industrial Revolution in France 1815–1848*. New York: Exposition Press, 1955.

Dupeux, Georges. *Aspects de l'histoire sociale et politique du Loir-et-Cher 1848–1914*. Paris: Mouton, 1962.

Duveau, Georges. *La vie ouvrière en France sous le Second Empire*. Paris: Gallimard, 1946.

Faure, Petrus. *Le Chambon rouge: Histoire des organisations ouvrières et des grèves au Chambon-Feugerolles*. Le Chambon-Feugerolles: Editions du syndicat unitaire des métaux, 1929.

————. *Histoire de la métallurgie au Chambon-Feugerolles*. Le Chambon-Feugerolles: Jué, 1931.

————. *Histoire du mouvement ouvrier dans le département de la Loire*. Saint-Etienne: Dumas, 1956.

Fournier, M. *Guillaume Roquille, poète ripagérien*. Saint-Etienne: Imprimerie de la Loire républicaine, n.d.

————. *Le roman d'un petit verrier*. Paris: Libraire Gedalge, 1925.

————. *Tableaux de la vie Saint-Chamonnais*. Saint-Chamond: Bordron, 1949.

————. *La vallée ardente: Scènes de la vie populaire*. Saint-Etienne: Libraire Dubouchet, 1938.

————. *La vie d'une cité: Impressions de Rive-de-Gier*. Saint-Etienne: Imprimerie de la Loire républicaine, 1936.

Fried, Marc. *The World of the Urban Working Class*. Cambridge, Mass.: Harvard University Press, 1973.

Friedenson, Patrick. *Histoire des usines Renault.* 2 vols. Paris: Editions du Seuil, 1972.

Galenson, Walter, and S. M. Lipset. *Labor and Trade Unionism: An Interdisciplinary Reader.* New York: John Wiley, 1960.

Gamson, William. *Power and Discontent.* Homewood, Ill.: Dorsey Press, 1968.

————. *The Strategy of Social Protest.* Homewood, Ill.: Dorsey Press, 1975.

Gaskell, P. *Artisans and Machinery.* London: John W. Parker, 1835.

Goault, Francois. *Comment la France est devenue républicaine.* Cahiers de la fondation nationale des sciences politiques, no. 62. Paris: Armand Colin, 1954.

Goetz-Girey, Robert. *La pensée syndicale français, militants et théoriciens.* Paris: Armand Colin, 1948.

Goldberg, Harvey. *The Life of Jean Jaures.* Madison: University of Wisconsin Press, 1962.

Goldthorpe, J. E., *et al. The Affluent Worker: Industrial Attitudes and Behaviour.* Cambridge: Cambridge University Press, 1968.

Gouldner, Alvin W. *Patterns of Industrial Bureaucracy.* New York: Free Press, 1954.

————. *Wildcat Strike: A Study in Worker-Management Relations.* New York: Harper, 1954.

Gras, L.-J. *Le conseil de commerce de Saint-Etienne et les industries locales au commencement du XIXe siècle.* Saint-Etienne: Théolier, 1899.

————. *Essai sur l'histoire de la quincaillerie et petite métallurgie . . . à Saint-Etienne et dans la région stéphanoise.* Saint-Etienne: Théolier, 1904.

————. *Histoire de la rubanerie et des industries de la soie à Saint-Etienne et dans la région stéphanoise suivie d'une histoire.* Saint-Etienne: Théolier, 1906.

————. *Histoire des eaux minérales du Forez, suivie de notes historiques sur l'industrie de la verrerie en Forez et en Jarez.* Saint-Etienne: Théolier, 1923.

————. *Histoire des premiers chemins de fer français et du premiers tramways de France.* Saint-Etienne: Théolier, 1924.

————. *Histoire du commerce locale et des industries qui s'y rattachent dans la région stéphanoise et forézienne.* Saint-Etienne: Théolier, 1910.

————. *Histoire économique de la métallurgie de la Loire, suivi d'une notice de la construction mécanique et l'industrie des cycles et des automobiles dans la région stéphanoise.* Saint-Etienne: Théolier, 1908.

————. *Histoire économique générale des mines de la Loire.* 2 vols. Saint-Etienne: Théolier, 1922.

————. *Notices historiques—les toiles de Panissaires—les origines de l'industrie des cotonnades en Roanne et en Beaujolais—la chapellerie du Chazelles.* Saint-Etienne: Théolier, 1924.

————. *Le prix de blé pendant trois siècles.* Saint-Etienne: Théolier, 1906.

Guilbert,Madeleine. *Les femmes et l'organisation syndicale avante 1914.* Paris: Centre nationale de la recherche scientifique, 1966.

Guillaume, Pierre. *La compagnie des mines de la Loire 1846–1854: Essai sur l'apparition de la grande industrie capitaliste en France.* Paris: Presses universitaires de France, 1966.

Gurr, T. *Why Men Rebel.* Princeton, N.J.: Princeton University Press, 1970.

Hamilton, Richard T. *Affluence and the French Worker in the Fourth Republic.* Princeton, N.J.: Princeton University Press, 1967.

Hamon, Léo, ed. *Les nouveaux comportements de la classe ouvrière.* Paris: Presses universitaires de France, 1960.

Hewitt, Margaret. *Wives and Mothers in Victorian Industry.* London: Rockliff, 1958.

Hobsbawm, Eric J. *The Age of Capital, 1848–1875.*New York: Charles Scribner's Sons, 1975.

Hufton, Olwen. *The Poor of Eighteenth Century France, 1750–1789.* Oxford: Clarendon Press, 1974.

Ingham, Geoffrey K. *Size of Industrial Organization and Worker Behavior.* Cambridge: Cambridge University Press, 1970.

Johnson, Christopher H. *Utopian Communism in France: Cabet and the Icarians.* Ithaca, Cornell University Press, 1970.

Julliard, Jacques. *Clémenceau, briseur de grèves.* Paris: Julliard, 1965.

————. *Fernand Pelloutier et les origines du syndicalisme d'action directe.* Paris: Editions du Seuil, 1971.

Kahn, Robert L., and Elise Boulding. *Power and Conflict in Organizations.* New York: Basic Books, 1964.

Kerr, Clark, John T. Dunlop, and C. A. Meyer. *Industrialism and Industrial Man.* Cambridge, Mass.: Harvard University Press, 1960.

Kindleberger, Charles P. *Economic Growth in France and Britain 1851–1950.* Cambridge, Mass.: Harvard University Press, 1964.

Knowles, K. S. C. J. *Strikes—A Study in Industrial Conflict.* New York: Philosophical Library, 1952.

Kornhauser, Arthur, Robert Dubin, and Arthur M. Ross, eds. *Industrial Conflict.* New York: McGraw-Hill, 1954.

Kriegel, Anne. *Aux origines du communisme français 1914–1920.* 2 vols. Paris: Mouton, 1964.

————. *Le pain et les roses: jalons pour une histoire des socialismes.* Paris: Presses universitaires de France, 1968.

Lefranc, Georges. *Grèves d'hier et d'aujourd'hui*. Paris: Aubier-Montaigne, 1969.

――――. *Le mouvement socialiste sous la troisième république*. Paris: Payot, 1963.

――――. *Le mouvement syndical sous la troisième république*. Paris: Payot, 1967.

LeMasters, E. E. *Blue Collar Aristocrats*. Madison: University of Wisconsin Press, 1975.

Leroy, Maxime. *La coutume ouvrière*. 2 vols. Paris: Girard and Brière, 1913.

Levasseur, E. *Questions ouvrières et industrielles en France sous la troisième république*. Paris: Rousseau, 1907.

Levine, David. *Family Formation in an Age of Nascent Capitalism*. New York: Academic Press, 1977.

L'Huillier, Fernand. *La lutte ouvrière à la fin du Second Empire*. Paris: Armand Colin, 1957.

Liepmann, Kate K. *The Journey to Work: Its Significance for Industrial and Community Life*. London: Kegan Paul, 1944.

Lloyd, G. I. H. *The Cutlery Trades: An Historical Essay in the Economics of Small-Scale Production*. London: Frank Cass, 1913.

Lorwin, Louis. *Syndicalism in France*. New York: Columbia University Press, 1914.

Lucas, Colin. *The Structure of the Terror: The Example of Javogues and the Loire*. Oxford: Oxford University Press, 1973.

Maitron, Jean. *Histoire du mouvement anarchiste en France, 1880–1914*. Paris: Société universitaire, 1951.

Mallet, Serge. *La nouvelle classe ouvrière*. Paris: Editions du Seuil, 1963.

Markovitch, T. J. *L'Industrie française de 1789 à 1964—Analyse des faits*. Cahiers de l'ISEA, May, 1966.

Merley, Jean. *L'Industrie en Haute-Loire à la fin de la monarchie de juillet aux débuts de la troisième république*. Lyon: Centre d'histoire économique et sociale de la région lyonnaise, 1972.

Moisoneer, Maurice. *Anarcho-syndicalisme ou Leninisme?* Paris: Université-Nouvelle, 1969.

Monatte, Pierre. *Trois scissions syndicales*. Paris: Les éditions ouvrières, 1958.

Moss, Bernard H. *The Origins of the French Labor Movement: The Socialism of the Skilled Worker 1830–1914*. Berkeley: University of California Press, 1976.

Mottez, Bernard. *Systemes de salaires et politiques patronales*. Paris: Centre nationale de la recherche scientifique, 1966.

Nef, John U. *Industry and Government in France and England, 1540–1640.* Ithaca, N.Y.: Cornell University Press, 1957 (1940).

Nelson, David. *Managers and Workers: Origins of the New Factory System in the United States, 1880–1920.* Madison: University of Wisconsin Press, 1975.

Neufeld, Maurice F. *Italy: School for Awakening Countries: The Italian Labor Movement in Its Political, Social and Economic Setting from 1800 to 1960.* Ithaca, N.Y.: Cornell University Press, 1961.

Nicholson, J. Shield. *The Effects of Machinery on Wages.* London: Swan and Sonnenschein, 1878.

Nolan, Aaron. *The Founding of the French Socialist Party 1893–1905.* Cambridge, Mass.: Harvard University Press, 1956.

Oberschall, Anthony. *Social Conflict and Social Movements.* Englewood Cliffs, N.J.: Prentice-Hall, 1973.

Pagé, Camille. *La coutellerie depuis l'origine à nos jours: La fabrication antique et moderne.* 4 vols. Chatellerault: H. Rivière, 1895–98.

Pawlowski, Christophe. *Tony Garnier et les débuts de l'urbanisme fonctionnel en France.* Paris: Centre de recherche d'urbanisme, 1967.

Perrin, Maxime. *Saint-Etienne et sa région économique: Un type de la vie industrielle en France.* Tours: Arrault, 1937.

Perrot, Michelle. *Les ouvriers en grève: France, 1871–1890.* 2 vols. Paris: Mouton, 1975.

Pierrard, Pierre. *La vie ouvrière à Lille sous le Second Empire.* Paris: Bloud and Gay, 1965.

Pollard, Sidney. *The Genesis of Modern Management.* London: Edward Arnold, 1959.

———. *A History of Labour in Sheffield.* Liverpool: Liverpool University Press, 1959.

Ridley, F. F. *Revolutionary Syndicalism in France: The Direct Action of Its Time.* Cambridge: Cambridge University Press, 1970.

Ross, Arthur M., and Paul T. Hartman. *Changing Patterns of Industrial Conflict.* New York: John Wiley, 1960.

Rowntree, B. Seebohm. *Poverty: A Study of Town Life.* London: Macmillan, 1902.

Rudé, George. *The Crowd in the French Revolution.* Oxford: Clarendon Press, 1959.

———. *The Crowd In History.* New York: John Wiley, 1964.

Schofer, Lawrence. *The Formation of a Modern Labor Force: Upper Silesia 1865–1914.* Berkeley: University of California Press, 1975.

Scott, Joan Wallach. *The Glassworkers of Carmaux: French Craftsmen and*

Political Action in a Nineteenth-Century City. Cambridge, Mass.: Harvard University Press, 1974.

Scoville, Warren C. *Capitalism and French Glassmaking, 1640–1789.* Berkeley: University of California Press, 1950.

———. *Revolution in Glassmaking: Entrepreneurship and Technological Change in the American Industry 1880–1920.* Cambridge, Mass.: Harvard University Press, 1948.

Shorter, Edward. *The Making of the Modern Family.* New York: Basic Books, 1975.

———, and Charles Tilly. *Strikes in France, 1830–1968.* London: Cambridge University Press, 1974.

Simiand, François. *Le salaire, l'évolution sociale et la monnaie.* 3 vols. Paris: Alcan, 1932.

———. *Salaire des ouvriers des mines de charbon en France.* Paris: Cornely, 1907.

Singer-Kérel, Jeanne. *Le coût de la vie à Paris de 1840 à 1954.* Paris: Armand Colin, 1961.

Sjoberg, Gideon. *The Preindustrial City.* New York: Free Press, 1960.

Slichter, Sumner. *Modern Economic Society.* New York: Henry Holt, 1928.

———. *Union Policies and Industrial Management.* Washington, D.C.: Brookings Institution, 1941.

Smelser, Neil J. *Social Change in the Industrial Revolution.* Chicago: University of Chicago Press, 1959.

Sorlin, Pierre. *Waldeck-Rousseau.* Paris: Armand Colin, 1966.

Stafford, David. *From Anarchism to Reformism: A Study of the Political Activities within the First International and the French Socialist Movement 1870–1890.* Toronto: University of Toronto Press, 1971.

Stearns, Peter. *The Lives of Labor: Work in a Maturing Industrial Society.* New York: Holmes and Meier, 1975.

———. *Revolutionary Syndicalism and French Labor: A Cause without Rebels.* New Brunswick, N.J.: Rutgers University Press, 1971.

———, and Harvey Mitchell. *Workers and Protest—The European Labor Movement, The Working Classes, and the Origins of Social Democracy 1890–1914.* Itasca, Ill.: F. E. Peacock, 1971.

Sturt, George. *The Wheelwright's Shop.* Cambridge: Cambridge University Press, 1923.

Suarez, George. *Briand: Sa vie—son oeuvre.* 6 vols. Paris: Plon, 1938–52.

Tannenbaum, Arnold S., and Robert L. Kahn. *Participation in Union Locals.* Evanston, Ill.: Row, Peterson, 1958.

Taylor, John. *From Self-Help to Glamour: The Workingman's Club 1860 to*

1972. Ruskin College History Workshop, Mar., 1972. Mimeographed pamphlet.

Thiollier, Lucien. *La chambre de commerce de Saint-Etienne et les industries de sa circonscription, 1833–1890*. Saint-Etienne: Théolier, 1891.

Thompson, E. P. *The Making of the English Working Class*. New York: Vintage Books, 1963.

Thompson, Wilbur R. *A Preface to Urban Economics*. Baltimore, Md.: Johns Hopkins University Press, 1965.

Tilly, Charles, and James Rule. *Measuring Political Upheaval*. Princeton, N.J.: Center for International Studies, 1965.

——, Louise Tilly, and Richard Tilly. *The Rebellious Century 1830–1930*. Cambridge, Mass.: Harvard University Press, 1975.

Touraine, Alain. *La conscience ouvrière*. Paris: Editions du Seuil, 1966.

——. *L'Évolution du travail ouvrier aux usines Renault*. Paris: Centre nationale de la recherche scientifique, 1955.

——, and Orietta Regazzo. *Ouvriers d'origine agricole*. Paris: Editions du Seuil, 1969.

Trempé, Rolande. *Les mineurs de Carmaux 1848–1914*. Paris: Les éditions ouvrières, 1971.

Ulman, Lloyd. *The Rise of the National Trade Union*. Cambridge, Mass.: Harvard University Press, 1955.

Vial, Jean. *L'Industrialisation de la sidérurgie française 1814–1864*. 2 vols. Paris: Mouton, 1967.

Walker, Charles R. *Steel: The Diary of a Furnace Worker*. Boston: Atlantic Monthly Press, 1923.

——. *Steeltown, an Industrial Case History*. New York: Harper Brothers, 1964.

——, and Robert H. Guest. *The Man on the Assembly Line*. Cambridge, Mass.: Harvard University Press, 1952.

Ware, Norman, *The Industrial Worker, 1840–1860*. Boston: Houghton Mifflin, 1924.

Warner, Lloyd, and J. O. Low. *The Social System of the Modern Factory*. New Haven, Conn.: Yale University Press, 1947.

Warner, Sam Bass, Jr. *The Private City*. Philadelphia: University of Pennsylvania Press, 1968.

Weber, Adna Ferrin. *The Growth of Cities in the Nineteenth Century: A Study in Statistics*. New York: Columbia University Press, 1899.

Weber, Eugen. *Peasants into Frenchmen: The Modernization of Rural France 1870–1914*. Stanford, Calif.: Stanford University Press, 1976.

Willard, Claude. *Le mouvement socialiste en France 1893–1905: Les guesdistes*. Paris: Editions sociales, 1965.

Zeldin, Theodore. *France 1848–1945*. Vol. 1. Oxford: Clarendon Press, 1973.

Zola, Emile. *L'Assommoir*. London: Penguin Books, 1970.

ARTICLES

Adam, Gerard. "Ou en est le débat sur la nouvelle classe ouvrière?" *Revue française de sciences politiques* 23 (June, 1972), 509–28.

Aminzade, Ron. "Mobilization and Collective Violence: The Working Class of Marseilles, 1830–1870." Unpublished paper, 1974.

Amman, Peter H. "Revolution: A Redefinition." *Political Science Quarterly* 77 (1962), 36–53.

Amsden, John, and Stephen Brier. "Coal Miners on Strike: The Transformation of Strike Demands and the Formation of a National Union." *Journal of Interdisciplinary History* 7 (Spring, 1977), 583–616.

Armengaud, André. "Population in Europe 1700–1914." In *The Fontana Economic History of Europe*, ed. Carlo M. Cipolla. Vol. 3. London: Fontana, 1973.

Arnonowitz, Stanley. "Lordstown: Disruption on the Assembly Line." In *False Promises: The Shaping of American Working Class Consciousness*. New York: McGraw-Hill, 1973. Pp. 21–50.

Baker, Donald N. "Seven Perspectives on the Socialist Movement of the Third Republic." *Historical Reflections/Reflexions historiques* 1 (Winter, 1974), 169–212.

Bensman, Joseph, and Israel Gerner. "Crime and Punishment in the Factory: The Function of Deviancy in Maintaining the Social System." In *Organizational Issues in Industrial Society*, ed. Jon M. Shepard. Englewood Cliffs, N.J.: Prentice-Hall, 1972. Pp. 181–97.

Bernard, Pierre. "Attitudes au travail et action ouvrière." *Sociologie du travail* 4 (Oct.-Dec., 1962), 349–366.

Bestor, A. E. "Evolution of the Socialist Vocabulary." *Journal of the History of Ideas* 9 (June, 1948), 259–302.

Betham-Edwards, Mrs. "Household Budgets Abroad: France." *Cornhill Magazine* 90 (Sept., 1904), 336–48.

Blumer, Herbert. "Early Industrialization and the Labouring Classes." In *Organizational Issues in Industrial Society*, ed. Jon M. Shepard. Englewood Cliffs, N.J.: Prentice-Hall, 1972. Pp. 10–16.

Boissier, Albert. "Essai sur l'histoire et sur les origines de l'industrie du clou forgé dans la région de Firminy." *Revue de folklore français* 12 (Apr.-June, 1941), 65–101.

Bonnet, Jean-Charles. "Les travailleurs étrangers dans la Loire sous la troisième république." *Cahiers d'histoire* 16, no. 1 (1971), 67–80.

Bonnet, S. "Political Alignments and Religious Attitudes within the Italian Immigration to the Metallurgical Districts of Lorraine." *Journal of Social History* 2 (1968), 123–55.

Bouvier, Jean. "Aux origines de la troisième république: Les réflexes sociaux des milieux d'affaires." *Revue historique* 210 (Oct.-Dec., 1953), 271–306.

———. "Mouvement ouvrier et conjonctures économiques." *Le Mouvement social* 48 (July-Sept., 1964), 3–30.

Bowditch, John. "The Concept of Elan Vital: A Rationalization of Weakness." In *Modern France*, ed. E. M. Earle. Princeton, N. J.: Princeton University Press, 1951.

Braque, René. "Aux origines du syndicalisme dans les milieux ruraux du centre de la France." *Le mouvement social* 42 (Jan.-Mar., 1963), 79–116.

Brizard, Germaine. "Chansons populaires du Velay et du Forez—Traditions populaires chantées." *Revue de folklore français* 1 (May-June, 1930), 125–26.

Brocard, Lucien. "La grosse métallurgie française et le mouvement des prix de 1890 à 1913." *Revue d'histoire économique et sociale* 10 (1922), 303–506.

Burgess, Keith. "Technological Change and the 1852 Lock-Out in the British Engineering Industry." *International Review of Social History* 14 (1969), 215–36.

———. "Trade Union Policy and the 1852 Lock-Out in the British Engineering Industry." *International Review of Social History*, 17 (1972), 645.

Cahen, Mme. "Évolution de la population active en France depuis cent ans d'après les dénombrements quinquennaux." *Études et conjonctures* 12 (May-June, 1953), 230–88.

———. "Évolution des conditions de logement en France depuis cent ans." *Études et conjonctures* nos. 10–11 (Oct.-Nov., 1957), 985–1376.

———. "La concentration des établissements en France de 1896 à 1936." *Études et conjonctures* 9 (Sept., 1954), 846–47.

Cahnman, Werner J. "The Historical Sociology of Cities: A Critical Review." *Social Forces* 45 (Dec., 1966), 155–60.

Calvignac, J. B. "Mémoires d'un militant mineur: J. B. Calvignac, maire de Carmaux." *Le mouvement social* 43 (Apr.-June, 1963), 121–38.

Caron, François. "Essai d'analyse historique d'un psychologie du travail." *Le mouvement social* n. 50 (Jan.-Mar., 1965), 3–40.

Cass, Millard. "The Relationship of Size of Firm and Strike Activity." *Monthly Labor Review* 80 (1957), 1330–34.

Caulier-Mathy, Mlle. "La composition d'un proletariat industriel: Le cas de l'entreprise Cockerill." *Revue d'histoire de la sidérurgie* 4 (Oct.-Dec., 1963–64), 207–22.

Chatelain, Abel. "Les usines-internats et les migrations féminines dans la région lyonnaise." *Revue d'histoire économique et sociale* 48 (1970), 373–94.

Chatelard, Claude. "La misère à Saint-Etienne de 1870 à 1914." *Études foréziennes* 4 (1971), 139–56.

Clarke, J. A. "French Socialist Congresses 1876–1914." *Journal of Modern Hisors* 31 (1959), 124–29.

Clough, Shepard B. "Retardative Factors in French Economic Development in the 19th and 20th Centuries." In *Journal of Economic History* supplement, "Tasks of Economic History," 1946–47. Pp. 91–102.

Commons, John R. "American Shoemakers 1648–1895: A Sketch of Industrial Evolution." In *Labor and Administration*. New York: A. M. Kelly, 1913.

Courtheaux, Jean-Paul. "Naissance d'une conscience de classe dans le proletariat textile du Nord? 1830–1870." *Revue économique* 8 (1957), 114–39.

———. "Privilèges et misères d'un métier sidérurgique au XIXe siècle: Le puddleur." *Revue d'histoire économique et sociale* 37 (1959), 161–84.

Crew, David. "Social Mobility in a German Town." *Journal of Social History* 6 (Fall, 1973), 447–63.

Crouzet, François. "Essai de construction d'un indice annuel de la production industrielle française au XIXe siècle." *Annales: Économies, sociétés, civilisations* 25 (May-June, 1970), 56–91.

Crozier, Michel. "Sociologie du syndicalisme." In *Traite de sociologie du travail*, ed. Georges Friedman and Pierre Naville. Vol. 2. Paris: Armand Colin, 1954.

Daumard, Adeline. "L'Évolution des structures sociales en France à l'époque de l'industrialisation (1815–1914)." *Revue historique* 502 (Apr.-June, 1971), 325–46.

Dauphin, C., and P. Pezerat. "Les consommations populaires dans la seconde moitié du XIXe siècle à travers les monographies de l'école de Le Play." *Annales: Économies, sociétés, civilisations* 30 (Mar.-June, 1975), 537–52.

Davies, J. "Toward a Theory of Revolution." *American Sociological Review* 27 (1962), 5–19.

Delabre, Bernard. "La grève de 1869 dans le bassin minier stéphanois." *Études foréziennes* 4 (1971), 109–38.

Derfler, Leslie. "Reformism and Jules Guesde: 1891–1904." *International Review of Social History* 12 (1967), 66–80.

Dingle, A. E. "Drink and Working-Class Living Standards in Great

Britain 1870–1914." *Economic History Review*, ser. 2, 25, no. 4 (Nov., 1972), 608–22.

Dreyfus, F. G. "L'Industrie de la verrerie en Bas-Languedoc de Colbert à la révolution industrielle du XIXe siècle." *Annales du Midi* 63 (Apr., 1951), 43–70.

Droulers, Paul. "Le cardinal de Bonald et la grève des mineurs de Rive-de-Gier en 1844." *Cahier historique* 6 (1961), 265–85.

Dubin, Robert. "Industrial Workers' Worlds: A Study of the Central Life Interests of Industrial Workers." *Social Problems* 3 (Jan., 1956), 131–42.

Dunlop, John T. "The Development of Labor Organization: A Theoretical Framework." In *Insights into Labor Issues*, ed. Richard A. Lester and Joseph Shister. New York: Macmillan, 1948.

Duveau, Georges. "Comment étudier la vie ouvrière: Les méthodes d'investigation." *Revue d'histoire économique et sociale* 26 (1941–47), 11–21.

Elwitt, Sanford H. "Politics and Social Classes in the Loire: The Triumph of Republican Order 1869–1873." *French Historical Studies* 6 (1969), 93–112.

Flonneau, Jean-Marie. "Crise de vie chère et mouvement syndical, 1910–1914." *Le mouvement social* 72 (July-Sept., 1970), 49–81.

Fohlen, Claude. "Esquisse d'une évolution industrielle: Roubaix au XIXeme siècle." *Revue du Nord* 32–33 (Apr.-Sept., 1951), 92–102.

Form, William H. "The Accommodation of Rural and Urban Workers to Industrial Discipline and Urban Living: A Four Nation Study." In *Organizational Issues in Industrial Society*, ed. Jon M. Shepard. Englewood Cliffs, N.J.: Prentice-Hall, 1972.

Furet, François. "Pour une définiion des classes inférieures à l'époque moderne." *Annales: Économies, sociétés, civilisations* 18 (May-June, 1963), 463–80.

Gaillard, Jeanne. "Les usines Cail et les ouvriers métallurgistes de Grenelle." *Le mouvement social* 33–34 (Oct., 1960–Mar., 1961), 35–53.

Galloway, D. T. "Machine Tools." In *A History of Technology*, ed. Charles Singer *et al.* Vol. 5. Oxford: Clarendon Press, 1958.

Garden, Maurice. "Ouvriers et artisans au XVIII siècle." *Revue d'histoire économique et sociale* 48 (1970), 28–45.

Gilbert, K. R. "Machine Tools." In *A History of Technology*, ed. Singer *et al.* Vol. 4. Oxford: Clarendon Press, 1958.

Gille, Bertrand. "Analyse de l'industrie sidérurgique française à la veille de 1830." *Revue d'histoire de la sidérurgie* 3 (Apr.-June, 1962), 83–111.

———. "La formation du proletariat ouvrier dans l'industrie sidérurgique française." *Revue d'histoire de la sidérurgie* 4 (Oct.-Dec., 1963–64), 244–51.

Gittelman, H. M. "Perspectives on American Industrial Violence." *Business History Review* 47, no. 1 (Spring, 1973), 1–23.

Gossez, Remy. "Une grève des mineurs à l'avènement de Napoleon III." *Actes du 78ᵉ congres des sociétés savantes* (1954).

Gras, Christian. "L'Ouvrier mouleur à travers le journal de sa fédération: La fonderie (1900–1909)." *Le mouvement social* 53 (Oct.-Dec., 1965), 51–68.

Gray, R. Q. "Styles of Life, the 'Labor Aristocracy' and Class Relations in Late Nineteenth Century Edinburgh." *International Review of Social History* 18 (1973), pt. 3, 428–52.

Guillaume, Pierre. "Les débuts de la grande industrie houillère dans la Loire: Les mines de Roche-la-Moliere et de Firminy sous la restauration." *Cahiers d'histoire* 4 (1959), 147–66.

————. "Grèves et organisation ouvrière chez les mineurs de la Loire au milieu du XIXᵉ siècle." *Le mouvement social* 43 (1963), 5–18.

————. "La situation économique et sociale du département de la Loire d'après l'enquête sur le travail agricole et industriel du 25 mai 1848." *Revue d'histoire moderne et contemporaine* 10 (Jan.-Mar., 1963), 5–34.

Habbakuk, H. J. "Family Structure and Economic Change in Nineteenth Century Europe." *Journal of Economic History* 15 (1955), 1–12.

Hanagan, Michael P. "Artisan and Skilled Worker: The Problem of Definition." *International Labor and Working Class History* 12 (Nov., 1977), 28–31.

————. "The Logic of Solidarity: Social Structure in Le Chambon-Feugerolles." *Journal of Urban History* 3 (Aug., 1977), 409–26.

Hardach, Gerd H. "Les problèmes de main-d'oeuvre à Decazeville." *Revue d'histoire de la sidérurgie* 8 (1967), 51–68.

Harley, C. K. "Skilled Labor and the Choice of Technique in Edwardian Industry." *Explorations in Economic History*, Ser. 2, 11 (Summer, 1974), 391–414.

Harrison, Brian. "Drink and Sobriety in England (1815–1872): A Critical Bibliography." *International Review of Social History* 12 (1967), 204–76.

————. "Pubs." In *The Victorian City: Images and Realities*, ed. H. J. Dyos and Michael Wolff. Vol. 1. London: Routledge and Kegan Paul, 1973.

Heron, Andre. "Le taylorisme, hier et demain." *Le temps modernes* (Aug.-Sept., 1975), pp. 220–78.

Hobsbawm, Eric J. "Economic Fluctuations and Some Social Movements since 1800." *Economic History Review*, ser. 2, 5 (1952), 1–25.

————. "The Labor Aristocracy of Nineteenth Century Britain." In *Workers in the Industrial Revolution*, ed. Peter N. Stearns and Daniel J. Walkowitz. New Brunswick, N.J.: Transaction Books, 1974. Pp. 138–76.

———. "The Machine Breakers." In *Labouring Men: Studies in the History of Labour*. New York: Basic Books, 1964. Pp. 7–26.

———. "The Formation of the Industrial Working Class: Some Problems." *Third International Conference of Economic History—Munich 1965 —Papers*. Paris: Mouton, 1968.

Holt, James. "Trade Unionism in the British and U.S. Steel Industries 1888–1912: A Comparative Study." *Labor History* 18 (Winter, 1977), 5–36.

Howard, M. P. "The Strikes and Lockouts in the Iron Industry and the Formation of the Ironworkers Union 1862–1869." *International Review of Social History* 18 (1973), pt. 3, 396–427.

Hufton, Olwen. "Women and the Family Economy in Eighteenth-Century France." *French Historical Studies* 9 (Spring, 1975), 1–22.

Isard, Walter. "Some Locational Factors in the Iron and Steel Industry since the Early Nineteenth Century." *Journal of Political Economy* 56 (June 3, 1948), 318–28.

Jackson, R. T. "Mining Settlements in Western Europe: The Landscape and the Community." In *Urbanization and Its Problems: Essays in Honor of E. W. Gilbert*, ed. R. P. Beckinsale and J. M. Houston. New York: Barnes and Noble, 1968. Pp. 146–70.

Jones, Gareth Stedman. " Working Class Culture and Working Class Politics in London, 1870–1900." *Journal of Social History* 7 (Summer, 1974), 460–508.

Julliard, Jacques. "Théorie syndicaliste révolutionnaire et politique gréviste." *Le mouvement social* 65 (Oct.-Dec., 1968), 55–70.

Katz, Michael B. "Occupational Classification in History." *Journal of Interdisciplinary History*, 3 (1972), 63–88.

Kelso, Maxwell. "The French Lador Movement during the Last Years of the Second Empire." In *Essays in the History of Modern Europe*, ed. Donald C. ˋMcKay. New York: Harper, 1936. Pp. 98–113.

———."The Inception of the Modern French Labor Movement 1871–1879: A Reappraisal." *Journal of Modern History* 8 (June, 1'36), 173–93.

Kerr, Clark, and Abraham Siegel. "The Interindustry Propensity to Strike: An International Comparison." In *Industrial Conflict*, ed. Arthur Kornhauser, Robert Dubin, and Arthur M. Ross. New York: McGraw-Hill, 1954. Pp. 189–212.

Kriegel, Anne. "Histoire ouvrière au XIX et XX siècles." *Revue historique* 90 (Apr.-June, 1966), 455–90.

Lacombe, Robert. "Notes de sociologie historique: Le choc de la révolution industrielle sur une petite ville du Lyonnais—Rive-de-Gier." *L'Ethnographie*, n.s., 64 (1970), 1–25.

Lampard, Eric E. "The Urbanizing World." In *The Victorian City: Images and Realities*, ed. H. J. Dyos and Michael Wolff. Vol. 1. London: Routledge and Kegan Paul, 1973. Pp. 3–58.

———. "The History of Cities in the Economically Advanced Areas." *Economic Development and Cultural Change* 3 (Jan., 1955), 81–136.

Landauer, Carl. "The Origin of Socialist Reformism in France." *International Review of Social History* 12 (1967), 81–107.

Landes, D. S. "French Business and the Business Man." In *Modern France*, ed. M. H. Earle. Princeton, N.J.: Princeton University Press, 1951. Pp. 334–53.

Laubier, Patrick de. "Esquisse d'une théorie du syndicalisme." *Sociologie du travail* 10 (1968), 362–93.

Laurie, Bruce, Theodore Hershberg, and George Alter. "Immigrants and Industry: The Philadelphia Experience 1850–1880." *Journal of Social History* 9 (Winter, 1975), 219–67.

Léon, Pierre. "Industrialisation en France, en tant que facteur de croissance économique, du début du XVIIIeme siècle à nos jours." *Première conférence d'histoire économique: Stockholm—1960.* Paris: Mouton, 1960.

———. "Points de vue sur le monde ouvrier dans la France du XVIIIe siècle." *Third International Congress of Economic History—Munich 1965 —Papers.* Paris: Mouton, 1968.

———. "La région lyonnaise dans l'histoire économique et sociale de la France." *Revue historique* 237 (Jan.-Mar., 1967), 31–62.

Lequin, Yves. "Les archives de la bourse du travail d'Annecy." *Le mouvement social* 73 (Oct.-Dec., 1970), 114–16.

———. "Classe ouvrière et idéologie dans la région lyonnaise à la fin du XIXe siècle." *Le mouvement social* 6 (Oct.-Dec., 1969), 3–20.

———"La formation du prolétariat industriel dans la région lyonnaise au XIXe siècle: Approches méthodologiques et premiers résultats." *Le mouvement social* 97 (Oct.-Dec., 1976), 121–37.

———. "Sources et méthodes des grèves dans la second moitié du 19eme siècle: L'Exemple d'Isère." *Cahiers d'histoire* 12, nos. 1–2 (1967).

Leroy, C. "Le culte du Saint-Eloi en Artois et dans le Nord de la France." *Revue de folklore français* 5 (1934), 217–52.

Lévy-Leboyer, Maurice. "La croissance économique en France au XIXeme siècle: Résultats préliminaires." *Annales: Économies, sociétés, civilisations* 23 (July-Aug., 1968), 788–807.

———. "L'Héritage de Simiand: Prix, profit et termes d'échange au XIXe siècle." *Revue historique* 243 (Jan.-Mar., 1970), 77–120.

Lhomme, Jean. "Les enseignements théoriques à retirer d'une étude sur les salaires dans la longue periode." *Revue économique* 16 (Jan., 1965), 18–61.

————. "Le pouvoir d'achat de l'ouvrier français au cours d'un siècle." *Le mouvement social* 63 (Apr.-June, 1968), 41–70.

Lipset, Seymour Martin, and Stein Rokkan. "Cleavage Structures, Party Systems, and Voter Alignments: An Introduction." In *Party Systems and Voter Alignments: Cross-National Perspectives*, ed. Seymour Martin Lipset and Stein Rokkan. New York: Free Press, 1967. Pp. 1–64.

Lorçin, Jean. "Un essai de stratigraphie sociale; Chefs d'atelier et compagnons dans la grève des passementiers de Saint-Étienne en 1900." *Cahiers d'histoire* 13, no. 2 (1968) 181–82.

————. "Une source privée: Les archives de la chambre de commerce." *Études foréziennes* 1 (1968), 205–11.

Lorwin, Val R. "France." In *Comparative Labor Movements*, ed. Walter Galenson. New York: Prentice-Hall, 1955. Pp. 319–409.

————. "Reflections on the History of the French and American Labor Movement." *Journal of Economic History* 17 (1957), 15–44.

Loubère, Leo. "Coal Miners, Strikes and Politics in the Lower Languedoc 1880–1914." *Journal of Social History* 2 (Fall, 1968), 25–50.

————. "The French Left-Wing Radicals, Their Views on Trade Unionism, 1870–1898." *International Review of Social History* 7 (July, 1962), 203–30.

————. "Left-Wing Radicals, Strikes and the Military 1880–1907." *French Historical Studies* 3 (Mar., 1963), 93–105.

————. "Les radicaux d'extrême-gauche en France et les rapports entre patrons et ouvriers 1871–1900." *Revue d'histoire économique et sociale* 42 (1964), 89–103.

Maitron, Jean. "La personalité du militant ouvrier français dans la seconde moitié du XIXe siècle." *Le mouvement social* 33–34 (Oct., 1960–Mar., 1961), 68–86.

————. "Archives conservées par les bourses du travail." *Le mouvement social* 36 (July-Sept., 1961), 28–37.

Manuel, Frank E. "The Luddite Movement in France." *Journal of Modern History* 10 (June, 1938), 180–211.

Marchal, André. "Réflexions sur une théorie économique de développement du syndicalisme ouvrier." *Revue économique* 2 (Feb., 1951), 45–61.

Marczewski, Jean. "Le produit physique de l'économie française de 1789 à 1913: Comparison avec la Grande-Bretagne." *Cahiers de l'ISEA* (July, 1965).

Markovitch, Tihomir J. "Le revenu industriel et artisanal sous la monarchie de juillet et le Second Empire." *Économies et sociétés*, ser. AF, vol. 4 (Apr., 1967).

————. "Les cycles industriels en France: Essai d'élaboration préalable d'indices annuels de la production industrielle pour le XIXeme siècle."

Le mouvement social n. 63 (Apr.-June, 1968), 11–40.

———. "The Dominant Sectors of French Industry." In *Essays in French Economic History*, ed. Rondo Cameron. Homewood, Ill.: Richard Irwin, 1970. Pp. 226–40.

Marrus, Michael. "Social Drinking in the Belle Epoque." *Journal of Social History* 7, no. 2 (Winter, 1974), 115–41.

Masse, Jean. "Les grèves des mineurs et carriers du Var de 1871 à 1921." *Annales du Midi* (Apr., 1967), 196–218.

Maurice, Marc. "Déterminants du militantisme et projet syndical des ouvriers et des techniciens." *Sociologie du travail* 7 (1965), 254–72.

Mendels, Franklin F. "Protoindustrialization: The First Phase of the Process of Industrialization." *Journal of Economic History* 32 (Mar., 1972), 241–61.

Merley, Jean. "Les élections de 1869 dans le département de la Loire." *Cahier historique* 6 (1961), 59–93.

Mills, C. Wright. A review of *Social Life of a Modern Community*. *American Sociological Review* 7 (1942), 263–71

Monds, Jean. "Workers' Control and the Historians: A New Economism." *New Left Review* 97 (May-June, 1976), 81–100.

Money, John. "Taverns, Coffeehouses and Clubs: Local Politics and Popular Articulacy in the Birmingham Area in the Age of the American Revolution." *Historical Journal* 14 (1971), 15–47.

Montgomery, David. "The New Unionism and the Transformation of Workers' Consciousness in America 1909–1922." *Journal of Social History* 7, no. 4 (Summer, 1974), 509–21.

———. "Spontaneity and Organization: Some Comments." *Radical America* 7 (Nov.-Dec., 1973), 70–80.

———. "Workers' Control of Machine Production in the Nineteenth Century." *Labor History* 17 (Fall, 1976), 485–509.

———. "The Working Classes of the Pre-Industrial American City 1780–1830." *Labor History* 19 (Winter, 1968), 3–22.

Moodie, Thomas. "The Guesdists and the Third Republic: The Lesson of the Boulanger Crisis." Paper presented to the Society for French istorical Studies. Ann Arbor, Mich. 1966.

Moutet, Aimée. "Les origiňes du systèm de Taylor en France." *Le mouvement·social* 58 (1967), 3–39.

Néré, Jacques. "Aspects du déroulement des grèves en France durant la période 1883–1889." *Revue d'histoire économique et sociale* 3 (1956), 286–302.

———. "Une statistique de salaire et de l'emploi en France dans le dernier tiers de XIXeme siècle." *Revue d'histoire économique et sociale* 2 (1955), 224–30.

Nettl, Peter. "The German Social Democratic Party 1890–1914 as a Political Model." *Past and Present* 30 (Apr., 1965), 65–96.

Neufeld, Maurice F. "The Inevitability of Political Unionism in Underdeveloped Countries: Italy, the Exemplar." *Industrial and Labor Relations Review* 13 (Apr., 1960), 363–86.

Olson, Mancur. "Rapid Growth as a Destabilizing Force." *Journal of Economic History* 23 (1963), 529–88.

Perrot, Michelle. "État des travaux universitaires inédits fait depuis 1945 et concernant le mouvement ouvrier en France (1815–1939)." *Le mouvement social* 33–34 (Oct., 1960–Mar., 1961), 7–20.

————. "Grèves, grèvistes et conjoncture: Vieux problèmes, travaux neufs." *Le mouvement social* n. 63 (Apr.-June, 1968), 109–24.

————. "La presse syndicale des ouvriers mineurs 1890–1914." *Le mouvement social* n. 43 (Apr.-June, 1963), 93–115.

Perroux, François. "Prises de vue sur la croissance de l'économie française 1780–1950." In *Income and Wealth*, ser. 5, ed. Simon Kuznetz. London: Bowes and Boaes, 1955. Pp. 41–78.

Pollard, Sidney. "Wages and Earnings in the Sheffield Trades 1851–1914." *Yorkshire Bulletin of Economic and Social Research* 6, no. 1 (Feb., 1954), 49–64.

Poperen, Maurice. "Création des bourses du travail en Anjou, 1892–1894." *Le mouvement social* 40 (July-Sept., 1962), 39–55.

Poussou, J. P. "Les mouvements migratoires en France." In *Annales de démographie historique—1970—Migrations*. Paris: Mouton, 1971.

Reberioux, M. "Socialistes et syndicalistes français." *Annales: Économies, sociétés, civilsations* 19 (1964), 979–95.

Reddy, William. "Family and Factory: French Linen Weavers in the Belle Epoque." *Journal of Social History* 8 (Winter, 1975), 102–12.

Rees, Albert. "Industrial Conflict and Business Fluctuations." *Journal of Political Economy* 10 (Oct., 1952), 224–30.

Revans, R. W. "Industrial Morale and Size of Unit." *Political Quarterly* 27 (1956), 303–11.

Reynaud, Jean-David. "La nouvelle classe ouvrière, la technologie et l'histoire." *Revue française de science politique* 22 (June, 1972), 529–42.

Rimlinger, Gaston V. "International Differences in the Strike Propensity of Coal Miners: Experiences in Four Countries." *Industrial and Labor Relations Review* 12 (Apr., 1959), 389–403.

Rist, Charles. "La durée du travail dans l'industrie française." *Revue d'économie politique* 61 (1897), 371–95.

Rosenberg, Nathan. "Technological Change in the Machine Tool Industry 1840–1910." *Journal of Economic History* 23 (1963), 414–43.

Rougerie, Jacques. "Composition d'une population insurgée, l'exemple de la commune." *Le mouvement social* 48 (July-Sept., 1964), 31–48.

———. "Remarques sur l'histoire des salaires à Paris au XIXe siècle." *Le mouvement social* 63 (Apr.-June, 1968), 71–108.

Roy, Donald. "Efficiency and 'the Fix': Informal Intergroup Relations in a Piecework Machine Shop." In *Organizational Issues in Industrial Society*, ed. Jon M. Shepard. Englewood Cliffs, N.J.: Prentice-Hall, 1972. Pp. 152–72.

Schnetzler, Jacques. "Un demi-siècle d'évolution démographique dans la région de Saint-Etienne, 1820–1876." *Études foréziennes* 1 (1968), 157–90.

———. "L'Évolution démographique de la région de Saint-Etienne de 1876 à 1946." *Études foréziennes* 4 (1971), 157–96.

Scott, Joan, and Louise Tilly. "Women's Work and the Family in Nineteenth-Century Europe." *Comparative Studies in Society and History* 17 (1975), 36–64.

Sewell, William H., Jr. "The Working Class of Marseilles under the Second Republic: Social Structure and Political Behavior." In *Workers in the Industrial Revolution*, ed. Peter N. Stearns and Daniel J. Walkowitz. New Brunswick, N.J.: Transaction Books, 1974. Pp. 75–116.

Silly, J. B. "La concentration dans l'industrie sidérurgique en France sous le Second Empire." *Revue d'histoire de la sidérurgie* 3 (Jan.-Mar., 1963), 19–48.

Smith, Victor. "Chants de quêtes—Noëls du premier de l'an—Chants du mai." *Romania* 2 (1873), 59–71.

———. "Chants du Velay et du Forez—Chants de saints et de damnés." *Romania* 4 (1875), 437–52.

Soboul, Albert. "Aux origines de la classe ouvrière industrielle parisienne (fin XVIIIe–début XIXe siècle)." *Third International Conference of Economic History—Munich 1965—Papers*. Paris: Mouton, 1968.

Spitzer, Alan B. "Anarchy and Culture: Fernand Pelloutier and the Dilemma of Revolutionary Syndicalism." *International Review of Social History* 8 (1963), 379–88.

Stearns, Peter N. "Against the Strike Threat: Employers' Policy towards Labor Agitation in France 1900–1914." *Journal of Modern History* 40 (Dec., 1968), 474–500.

———. "Measuring the Evolution of Strike Movements." *International Review of Social History* 19 (1974), 1, 1–27.

———. "National Character and European Labor History." In *Workers in the Industrial Revolution*, ed. Peter N. Stearns and Daniel J. Walkowitz. New Brunswick, N.J.: Transaction Books, 1974. Pp. 1–12.

————. "National Character and European Labor Movements." *Journal of Social History* 4 (1970), 95–124.

Stinchcombe, Arthur L. "Bureaucratic and Craft Administration: A Comparative Study." *Administrative Science Quarterly* 4 (Sept., 1959), 168–87.

————. "Social Structure and Organization." In *Handbook of Organizations*, ed. James S. March. Chicago: Rand-McNally, 1965. Pp. 142–93.

————. "Social Structure and Politics." In *Handbook of Political Science*, ed. Fred I. Greenstein and Nelson W. Polsby. Vol. 3. Reading, Pa.: Addison-Wesley, 1975. Pp. 577–622.

Stone, Katherine. "The Origins of Job Structure in the Steel Industry." *Review of Radical Political Economics* 6, no. 2 (Summer, 1974), 61–97.

Tarlé, Eugene. "La grande coalition des mineurs de Rive-de-Gier." *Revue historique* 137 (1936), 249–78.

Thomas, Keith. "Work and Leisure in Pre-Industrial Society." *Past and Present* 29 (1964), 50–62.

Thompson, E. P. "Time, Work-Discipline and Industrial Capitalism." *Past and Present* 38 (1967), 56–97.

Tiano, André. "L'Action des syndicats ouvriers: État des travaux." *Revue française de science politique* 10, no. 4 (Dec., 1960), 912–30.

Tilly, Charles. "From Mobilization to Political Conflict." Unpublished paper, Mar. 1970.

————. "Migrations in Modern European History." Working Paper no. 145, Center for Research on Social Organization.

————. "Revolutions and Collective Violence." In *Handbook of Political Science*, ed. Fred I. Greenstein and Nelson W. Polsby. Vol. 3. Reading, Pa.: Addison-Wesley, 1975, Pp. 483–556.

————. "Sociology, History, and the Origins of the European Proletariat." Address to American Historical Association annual meeting, 1976.

————. and Lynn Lees. "Le peuple de juin, 1848." *Annales: Économies, sociétés, civilisations* 29 (Sept.-Oct., 1974), 1061–91.

————, Joan Scott, and Miriam Cohen. "Women's Work and European Fertility Patterns." *Journal of Interdisciplinary History* 6 (Winter, 1976), 447–76.

Toutain, Jean-Claude. "La consommation alimentaire en France de 1789 à 1964." *Cahiers de l'ISEA* 5, no. 11 (Nov., 1971).

Vance, James E., Jr. "Housing the Worker: Determinative and Contingent Ties in Nineteenth Century Birmingham." *Economic Geography* 43 (Apr., 1967), 125–6.

————. "Housing the Worker: The Employment Linkage as a Force in Urban Structure." *Economic Geography* 42 (Oct., 1966), 294–325.

Verdes, Jennine. "Le syndicalisme révolutionnaire et le mouvement ouvrier français avant 1914." *Cahiers internationaux de sociologie* 36 (Jan.-June, 1964), 117–31.

Vincent, M. L. A. "Population active, production et productivité dans 21 branches de l'économie française (1896–1962)." *Études et conjonctures* 20 (Feb., 1965), 73–108.

Vuillemin, Jules. "Les syndicats ouvriers et les salaires." *Économie appliquée* 5 (Apr.-Sept., 1952), 261–336.

Weber, Eugen. "Gymnastics and Sports in Fin-de-Siècle France: Opium of the Classes." *American Historical Review* 6, no. 1 (1971), 70–98.

Weill, Gerard. "Le rôle des facteurs structurels dans l'évolution des rémunérations salariales au XIXe siècle." *Revue économique* 10, no. 2 (Mar., 1959), 237–67.

Welton, Thomas A. "On Forty Years' Industrial Change in England and Wales." *Transactions of the Manchester Statistical Society, 1897–1898,* pp. 153–266.

Wilson, Charles. "Economy and Society in Late Victorian Britain." *Economic History Review,* ser. 2, 18 (Aug., 1965), 183–98.

Winock, M. "La scission de Chatellerault et la naissance du parti 'allemaniste' (1890–1891)." *Le mouvement social* 75 (Apr.-June, 1971), 33–62.

THESES, DIPLOMES D'ÉTUDES SUPÉRIEURES, AND MÉMOIRES

Baker, Robert Parsons. *"A Regional Study of Working Class Organization in France: Socialism in the Nord 1870–1924."* Dissertation, Stanford University, 1972.

Bloomberg, Susan Eleanor. "Industrialization and Skilled Workers: Newark, 1826–1860." Dissertation, University of Michigan, 1974.

Bowditch, John. "A History of the General Confederation of Labor in France." Dissertation, Harvard University, 1948.

Butler, James C. "Fernand Pelloutier and the Emergence of the French Syndicalist Movement 1880–1906." Dissertation, Ohio State University, 1960.

Caldwell, T. "Workers' Self-Education in France." Dissertation, University of Leeds, n.d.

Calhoun, A. Fryar. "The Politics of Internal Order: French Government and Revolutionary Labor 1898–1914." 2 vols. Ph.D. dissertation, Princeton University, 1973.

Cellier, Jean. "Le logement à Saint-Etienne." DES, Université de Grenoble, 1949.

Chatelard, Claude. "La misère à Saint-Etienne entre 1870 et 1914." DES, Université de Lyon, 1966.

Cumbler, John Taylor. "Continuity and Disruption: Working Class Community in Lynn and Fall River, Massachusetts, 1880–1850." Dissertation, University of Michigan, 1974.

Durousset, Maurice. "La vie ouvrière dans la région stéphanoise sous la monarchie de juillet et la second république." DES, Université de Lyon, 1960.

Foster, John Odel. "Capitalism and Class Consciousness in Early Nineteenth Century England." Dissertation, Cambridge University, 1967.

Jacobs, Janet. "A Community of French Workers, Social Life and Labour Conflicts in the Stéphanois Region, 1890–1914," Dissertation, St. Anthony's College, Oxford, 1973.

Laubier, Patrick de. "Essai d'interprétation du syndicalisme révolutionnaire en France de 1894 à 1914." Mémoire, Université de Paris, 1962.

Lehning, James. "Peasant Families and Rural Industrialization: The Village of Marlhes, 1840–1914." Ph.D. dissertation, Northwestern University, 1977.

Martin, Jean-Paul. "Le syndicalisme révolutionnaire chez les métallurgistes de l'Ondaine 1906–1914." Mémoire, Université de Saint-Etienne, 1972.

Merriman, John. "Radicalization and Repression: The Experience of the Limousin 1848–1851." Dissertation, University of Michigan, 1972.

Snyder, David Richard. "Determinants of Industrial Conflict: Historical Models of Strikes in France, Italy and the United States." Dissertation, University of Michigan, 1974.

Tilly, Louise A. "The Working Class of Milan 1881–1911." Ph.D. dissertation, University of Toronto, 1973.

Vidal, Jean-François. "Le commune de 1871 à Saint-Etienne." DES, Université de Saint-Etienne, 1970.

Index

Agriculture and manufacturing,
    preindustrial, 38
Alcohol consumption, Stéphanois, 76–77,
    137
Anarchist clubs, Saint-Chamond, 138–40
Andréani, 78
Apprenticeship
    in artisanal industries, 14–15
    construction workers, Saint-Chamond,
        149
    fileworkers, Le Chambon, 180
    glassworkers, Rive-de-Gier, 98
    metalworkers, Saint-Chamond, 134–35
Ardouin-Dumazet, 98
    on fileworkers, Le Chambon, 181
Artisanal economy, France, late 1800s,
    4–13
Artisanal industry, disappearance,
    Saint-Chamond, 44
Artisanal workers
    and industrial unions, 21–23
    lifestyle, vs. industrial workers, 15–16
    in May Day strikes, Stéphanois, 51
    Paris, mid-1800s, 6–7
    politicized, and trade union movement,
        24–25
    ribbonmakers, Saint-Chamond, 42, 142
    and Stéphanois economic development,
        42
    strike activity, Le Chambon, 165–66
    and technological change, 13–20
    textile industry, Saint-Chamond, 142–43
    unionization, Stéphanois, 50
    see also Glassworkers; Skill hierarchy
Assembly plant, metalworking,
    Saint-Chamond, 132
Association des forges et aciéries de la
    marine, 114
L'Assommoir (Zola), 194

Audiganne, Armand
    on drunkenness in cafés, 137
    on Parsian industry, 6–7
Autonomy, skilled workers, and industrial
    work system, 64–65

Barral, Pierre, 80
La bataille syndicaliste, 192
Beauquis, 143
Benoist, Charles, 64
    on forging shop, 197–98
    on unskilled metalworkers, 133
Berrill, K., 5
Besson, M., 167
Birthplace, glassworkers, Rive-de-Gier,
    107–8
Blanc, Pierre, 105
Boltworkers
    and general strike, Le Chambon,
        167–68, 170–71
    strike supported by fileworkers, 190–91
    work structure and strike militancy,
        194–96
Bonneff, 195, 196
Bottleworkers, 93-94
    Roquille on, 104
    see also Glassworkers
Bourse du travail, 21, 24, 100, 102–3, 110
Boycott, Trablaine file factory, Le
    Chambon, 188–89
Braidmakers, Saint-Chamond, 143–44
    strike on shift system, 66
    unionization, 50
Bread prices, 73–76
Briand, Aristide, 157–58, 167
Brunon, M., 90, 110, 112

Café
    and alcohol consumption, 77, 137

boltworkers, Le Chambon, 183, 195
glassworkers, Rive-de-Gier, 102, 104, 105
and political life, Saint-Chamond metalworkers, 137–42
Career migration, Stéphanois, 40–41
Carmaux, glassworkers, 106, 107
Carnot, 140
Carriagemaking
France vs. England and U.S., 7
technological change in, 18
Cercle d'études sociales, 140–41
Chambre syndicale des fabricants de boulonnerie de la Loire, 196
Chambre syndicale de la petite métallurgie et quincaillerie, 191
Chambre syndicale des fabricants de limes, 183
Chambre syndicale des fabricants de limes du département de la Loire et de la Haute Loire, 184
Chambre syndicale des ouvriers métallurgistes du Chambon-Feugerolles et ses extensions, 171
Chambre syndicale des ouvriers verriers de Rive-de-Gier, 94
Charpentier, Edmund, 112
Château Claudinon, 200
Chatelain, Abel, 148
Chevalier, Emile, 69
Children
boltworkers, Le Chambon, 194, 195
and family economy, Saint-Chamond, 144-45
glassworkers, Rive-de-Gier, 95
Piedmontese, as glassworkers, 111
in textile industry, 66
Cité Claudinon, 200
Cities, Stéphanois, and artisanal workers, 42
Clark, G. N., 5
Claudinon, Georges, 199, 200
Claudinon, Jacques, 199, 200
Claudinon et cie, 196, 197, 199–200
Clemenceau, Georges, 166
Coalminers
preindustrial organization, Stéphanois, 42
unionization, 50
Coalmining
late 1800s, 46
in Rive-de-Gier, 42
and industrialization, Stéphanois, 44
Comité des forges, 170, 191
Compagnie des aciéries de la marine, 127, 130–31, 152, 154–55, 157
Compagnonnage organizations, Stéphanois artisanal workers, 42
Condamin, James, on industrial pollution, 45–46
Confédération générale du travail (CGT), 16
Construction workers
in May Day strikes, Stéphanois, 51
Saint-Chamond, pre-WWI, 127
unionization, Stéphanois, 50
wage structure, 72
work structure and strike militancy, Saint-Chamond, 149–50
Corbon, Anthime, on mechanization, 17
Cost of living, Stéphanois, 73–79
Craft unions
in 1800s, 21–22
Sheffield file trades, 174, 175, 177
see also Union(s)
Crouzet, François, 5
Crystal-glassworkers, 94, 97–98
Cutlers, preindustrial organization, Stéphanois, 42

Depression, late 1800s, 46–47
De Seilhac, Léon, 48, 175
on fileworkers, 184
on general strike, Le Chambon, 171
Dingle, A. F., 77
Discipline
French vs. U.S. factory, 11–12
militant, Rive-de-Gier unions, 92
Ducarre committee, 10
Dunières, May Day procession, 39
Dupeux, Georges, 80
Dyers
in May Day strikes, Stéphanois, 51
Saint-Chamond, 127, 143, 144

L'Eclaireur de Saint-Chamond, 150–51, 187

Economic development, Stéphanois, 41–48
Electrification, and artisanal industry, 10
Employers
    antagonism to Rive-de-Gier unions, 109
    boltmaking, Le Chambon, 196
    filemaking, Le Chambon, 184
    and industrial work system, 64–66
    organization, Le Chambon, 191–92
    power, and unemployment, 153–55
    workday regulation, 65–66
Engels, Friedrich, 45
Engineer, and mechanization,
    metalworking, 131, 132
England
    economy, vs. France, 4–6
    file trades craft unions, 174, 175, 177
Environment, Stéphanois, and
    industrialization, 45–46
Euverte, J., on task system, 64
Exodus of the infants, and general strike,
    Le Chambon, 173

Factory
    discipline, U.S. vs. French, 11–12
    union shop floor committees,
        Rive-de-Gier glassworkers, 108–9
    see also Industrial work system; Work
        structure and strike militancy
Family patterns
    fileworkers, Le Chambon, 189–90
    glassworkers, Rive-de-Gier, 95–96
    metalworkers, Rive-de-Gier, 115
    textileworkers, Saint-Chamond, 144–45
Faure, Petrus, 40, 195
    on fileworkers, Le Chambon, 171–72
    on strikes, Saint-Chamond, 61
    on work conditions, 67
Filecutting, Le Chambon, 179–81
Filemaking, and Stéphanois
    industrialization, 44
Fileworkers
    and general strike, Le Chambon,
        167–68, 171
    mechanization, and strikes, Le
        Chambon, 61
    support of boltworkers' strike, Le
        Chambon, 190–91
    unionization, 50
    work structure and strike militancy, Le

Chambon, 178–84
Food prices, 73–76
Foreign workers
    Piedmontese children as glassworkers,
        111
    as strikebreakers, Rive-de-Gier
        glassworkers' strike, 112–13
Foreman
    authority, and time system, 65
    and work discipline, 68
Forgers, wages, Saint-Chamond, 133
Forging
    mechanical vs. hand, 113–15
    and on-the-job contacts, 117–18
Foundrymen, wages, Saint-Chamond, 133
Fournier, M.
    on glassworkers' café, 105
    on glassworkers' housing, 99–100
Frachon, Benôit, 195–96
Franchise, electoral, and trade unionism,
    23

Gambetta, Leon, 21
Gamin, 94, 96, 98
Garnier, Tony, 43
Garod, café, 105
Gaudin, 89
General strike
    Le Chambon, 167–72
    Sheffield file trades, 174, 175
Glassmaking
    and industrialization, 43–44
    mechanization, and strike activity,
        Rive-de-Gier, 61–62
    in Rive-de-Gier, 42
    technological change in, 18
    workday, 66
Glassworkers
    career migration, 40
    in May Day strikes, Stéphanois, 51
    and metalworkers' strike, Rive-de-Gier,
        89–92
    skill hierarchy, 93–94, 96–97
    strike experience, Rive-de-Gier, 92–93
    unionization, Stéphanois, 50
    work structure and strike militancy,
        Rive-de-Gier, 93–105
The Glassworkers of Carmaux (Scott), 106
Grand garçon, 94, 96, 98

Grand National Consolidated Craft Unions
(British), 22
Gras, L.-J., 145
Griffuelhes, Victor, on mechanized
weavers, 16–17

Harley, C. K., 10
Henri, IV, 42, 142
Hobsbawm, Eric, 7
Housing
glassworkers, Rive-de-Gier, 94, 99–100
textile company dormitories,
Saint-Chamond, 147–48
see also Residential patterns

Index of dissimilarity
construction workers, Saint-Chamond,
149–50
glassworkers, Rive-de-Gier, 100
metalworkers, Rive-de-Gier, 118–19;
Saint-Chamond, 136–37
textileworkers, Saint-Chamond, 145–46
Industrial economy, England, vs. artisanal
economy, France, 4–6
Industrial Fatigue Research Board, 97
Industrialization
and environment, 45–46
rural, Stéphanois, 37–39
Industrial Revolution, and Stéphanois
economic development, 42
Industrial unions, artisanal, 21–23
See also Industrial workers; Industrial
work system; Strike(s); Union(s)
Industrial workers
emergence of, 12–13
lifestyle, vs. artisanal workers, 15–16
in May Day strikes, Stéphanois, 51
metalworkers strike, Rive-de-Gier,
87–89
Saint-Chamond, pre-WWI, 127
strike activity, Le Chambon, 165–66
see also Strike(s); Union(s)
Industrial work system
and market for Saint-chamond products,
151
metalworking, Saint-Chamond, 128,
130–31
rise of, 62–68
Industry

change, and working class coalition,
20–25
Stéphanois region, 34
Industry-wide unionism, Le Chambon,
173–76
Inflation
and cost of living, pre-WWI, 75–76
and strike activity, Saint-Chamond
construction workers, 149–50
and worker protest, Saint-Chamond,
150–55

Jackson, James, 43
Jaures, Jean, 88
Jury, Victor, 148
on employer paternalism, 155

Kinship ties, and glassworker solidarity, 98
Knights of Labor (American), 22
Kropotkin, Peter, 13
on mechanization, 9–10

Labor exchange, *see Bourse du travail*
Lafont, Ernest, 192
Lagardelle, Hubert, 192
on workers' democracy, 193
La Fayette, nailmaking in, 37–38
Le Chambon-Feugerolles
cutlery trade in, 42
general strike, 167–72
revolutionary syndicalism, 192–94
strike, May Day, 1906, 3, 51
strike activity, 58–61
strike militancy, 165–67
union organization, 172–78
working-class coalition, 184–92
work structure and strike militancy:
boltworkers, 194–96; fileworkers,
178–84; metalworkers, 196–201
Leonardo da Vinci, 185
Le Play, on metalworkers, 129–30
Le réveil chambonnaire, 184–92
Leroy-Beaulieu, Paul, on working-class
cafés, 137
Levine, David, 37
Lhomme, Jean, 75
Lifestyles, artisanal vs. industrial workers,
15–16
"The Limitation of Production" (Vinay),
108

Limousin, Charles
  on employer decision to mechanize, 16
  on mechanization and discipline, 12
Living standard, Stéphanois, 72–80
Lockout and general strike, Le Chambon, 170–71
London Board of Trade, 72, 73, 74, 75
Lorçin, Jean, 48

Manufacture and agriculture, preindustrial, 38
Markovitch, Tihomir, 6, 7
Marrel Frères metal plant, 93, 115–17
Marrus, Michael, 77
Martin, Jean-Paul, on Le Chambon fileworkers, 172
Masons, in May Day strikes, Stéphanois, 51
May Day strikes
  Rive-de-Gier glassworkers, 92–93
  Stéphanois, 3, 50–51, 67
Meat prices, 73–76
Mechanization
  artisanal workers' resistance to, 13–20
  file industry, Le Chambon, 185–89
  Kropotkin on, 9–10,
  of Saint-Chamond metalworking, 128–29, 131–32
Mermier, M., 170
Metal trades, general union, Le Chambon, 171–72
Metalworkers
  career migration, 40
  in May Day strikes, Stéphanois, 51
  and general strike, Le Chambon, 167–68, 170–71
  and metal fabrication industry, Stéphanois, 46–47
  patron saint of, 38
  strike, Rive-de-Gier, 87–89
  unionization, Stéphanois, 50
  wages and strike activity, 79–80
  workday, 66
  work structure and strike militancy: Le Chambon, 196–201; Rive-de-Gier, 113–20; Saint-Chamond, 129–42
Metalworking
  early 1900s, 10–11
  and industrialization, Stéphanois, 44–45

  paternalism, 156
  semiskilled workers in, 18
  task system, 63
  wage structure, 70, 71
Michel, Louise, 140
Migration pattern
  Stéphanois, 35–41
  textileworkers, Saint-Chamond, 147
Millerand, 167
Miners
  in May Day strikes, Stéphanois, 51
  wage structure, 70, 71
  workday, 66
Montgolfier, Adrien de, 110, 156
Mont Pilat, rural industry, 37
Monts du Forez, rural industry, 37
Monts du Lyonnaise, rural industry, 37
Moulin, Laurent, career migration, 41

Nailmaking, in La Fayette, 37–38
Napoleon III, 20
Nef, John U., 5
Negrel, M., 105

Ouvrièrisme, 138

Padrone, and Italian children as glassworkers, 111
Paris, artisanal workers, mid-1800s, 6–7
Paternalism
  Claudinon et cie, 199–200
  foundations, Saint-Chamond, 155–59
Payre, 140
Pensions, and paternalism, Saint-Chamond, 155–56
Philloux, 90
Piece-rate system, 65
Plate-glassworkers, strike on work teams, 68
Politics
  Saint Chamond metalworkers, 138–42
  and union activity, Rive-de-Gier, 110–12
  and working-class coalition, 20–25
Pollution, industrial, Condamin on, 45–46
Population, Stéphanois, 35
Porteur, 94, 96
Potterymaking, technological change in, 18
Poulot, Denis, 62–63, 65

Protest, and worker organization,
Stéphanois, 48–52
Puddlers, Saint-Chamond, 129, 131–32
Putting-out system, filecutting, Le
Chambon, 180

Ravachol, 138
career migration, 41
Rent, and cost of living, 77
Residential pattern
boltworkers, Le Chambon, 195
construction workers, Saint-Chamond,
149, 150
fileworkers, Le Chambon, 181
glassworkers, Rive-de-Gier, 98–106
metalworkers: Le Chambon, 198–99;
Rive-de-Gier, 118–19;
Saint-Chamond, 136–37
textileworkers, Saint-Chamond, 145–46
Revue d'économie politique, 10
Reybaud, Luis, 63, 113, 131
on family economy, Saint-Chamond,
144–45
on Stéphanois cost of living, 73
Ribbonmakers
preindustrial organization, Stéphanois,
42
strike, 1900, 48
unionization, 50
workday, 66
Ribbonmaking
artisanal, Saint-Chamond, 42, 142
and industrialization, Stéphanois, 44
in La Fayette, 38
Richarme, Petrus, 107, 110
Richarme works, 96, 98
Siemens oven in, 107
workers by birthplace, 108⁻
Rist, Charles, 177
Rive-de-Gier
coal and glass industries in, 42
coal mine shutdown, 46
metalworkers' strike, 87–89
plate-glassworkers' strike on work teams,
68
strikes, 58–61, 87–89
unionization, 50
unions in, 92–93
worker solidarity and strike action,
89–92

working-class coalition, 105–13
work structure and strike militancy:
glassworkers, 93–105; metalworkers,
113–20
Roquille, Guillaume, 95, 114
on glassworkers, 104
Roucharge, café, 141
Rural industry, textiles, Saint-Chamond,
142–43

Sabatier, Camille, 10, 13
Saint-Chamond
disappearance of artisanal industry, 44
inflation, unemployment, and worker
protest, 150–55
paternalism foundations, 155–59
ribbon industry, 42
strike activity, 58–61
working-class quiescence, 126–29
work structure and strike militancy:
construction workers, 149–50;
metalworkers, 129–42; textileworkers,
142–49
Saint-Eloi, metalworkers' patron saint, 38
Saint-Etienne
labor force and union membership, 49
wage structure, 70–71
Scott, Joan, 106
Section française de l'internationale ouvrière
(SFIO), 158
Semiskilled workers
emergence of, 12–13
and industrial unions, 21–22
and May Day strikes, Stéphanois, 51
in metalworking, 18, 115, 133
unionization, Stéphanois, 49–50
and wage structure, 69
see also Industrial workers; Metalworkers
Sheffield, England
file trades, 177
general strike, 174, 175
Shoemaking, technological change in, 18
Shoeworkers, political resolutions, 24
Shorter, Edward, 17, 89
Siemens continuous-fusion oven, 107
and glassworker strikes, Rive-de-Gier,
61–62
Siemens-Martin open hearth ovens, and
steel production, 131–32
Silk millers, preindustrial organization,

Stéphanois, 42
Silk production and manufacture, Saint-Chamond, 142–43
Silkthrowers, Saint-Chamond, 142, 143
Simons, Eric N., on filecutter, 186
Singer-Kérel, Jeanne, 74, 75
Skill, variety, in artisanal industries, 14–15
Skilled workers
autonomy, and industrial work system, 64–65
and May Day strikes, Stéphanois, 51
unionization, 49–50
and wage structure, 69
see also Strike(s); Union(s)
Skill hierarchy
glassworkers, Rive-de-Gier, 93–94, 96–97
metalworkers: Le Chambon, 197; Saint-Chamond, 129–30, 133–34
Smith, Victor, on Stéphanois rural life, 39
Socialists
Le Chambon, 193–94
Rive-de-Gier, 112
Saint-Chamond, 140–42, 158
Société anonyme des verriers, 96
Société industrielle, 152
Solidarity
and cafés, 137
construction workers, Saint-Chamond, 149
fileworkers, Le Chambon, 183
and strike action, Rive-de-Gier, 89–92
see also Working-class coalition
Souffleur, 94, 95, 96, 98
Standard of living, Stéphanois, 72–80
Stearns, Peter, 75
Steel industry
and great depression, late 1800s, 46–47
mechanization, Saint-Chamond, 128–29, 131–32
see also Metalworkers
Stéphanois
cantons, 36
economic development, 41–48
migration pattern, 35–41
preindustrial task system, 63–64
setting, 33–35
standard of living, 72–80
strikes, 3, 50–51, 57–62, 67
wage structure, 68–72

worker organization and growth of protest, 48–52
Strike(s)
braidmakers, Saint-Chamond, 66
and cost of living, 77–78, 80
general, Le Chambon, 167–72
glassworkers, Rive-de-Gier, 68, 92–93, 109, 112–13
and inflation, Saint-Chamond construction workers, 149–50
patterns, 1870–1914, 57–61
ribbonworkers, Stéphanois, 48
Saint-Chamond, 127–28
Stéphanois, 3, 50–51, 57–62, 67
textileworkers, 1890–1914, 17
window-glassworkers, 119
on workday, 66–67
on work discipline, 67–68
and worker solidarity, Rive-de-Gier, 87–92
and working-class coalition, 20–25
see also Union(s); Work structure and strike militancy
Strike kitchens (*soupes communistes*), Le Chambon metalworkers, 168, 178, 179, 190, 191
Strike militancy, Le Chambon-Feugerolles, 165–67
see also Work structure and strike militancy
Stubbs, Peter, 185
Subcontracting, and task system, 63–64
Supervisor, and mechanization, metalworking, 131, 132
Syndicalism, in Le Chambon, 61, 192–94

Task system
metalworking, 113–14
preindustrial, 63–64
and wages, 65
Technological change
artisanal workers' resistance to, 13–20
England vs. France, 1800s, 6
and fileworkers, Le Chambon, 184–85
and strike activity, 57
Technology, glassworking, Rive-de-Gier, 107
Le temps, 108
Terrenoire, steel company shutdown, late 1800s, 46–47

Textile industry
  Stéphanois, 38–39
  strikes, Saint-Chamond, 127
  wage structure, 70, 71
  workday, 66
Textileworkers
  France vs. England and U.S., 8–9
  and industrial workday, 66
  strikes, 1890–1914, 17
  unionization, Stéphanois, 50
  work structure and strike militancy,
    Saint-Chamond, 142–49
Tilly, Charles, 17, 89
Tilly, Louise, 96
Time system, and foreman's authority, 65
Trablaine file factory, 187–89
Trade Unions, *see* Union(s)
Training, in artisanal industry, 15
  See also Apprenticeship
Tramway workers, in May Day strikes,
    Stéphanois, 51
Tuiebault-Sisson
  on glassworker union committees, 108
  on mechanical vs. hand forging, 114–15
  on metal production, 131–32
Typographers, in May Day strikes,
    Stéphanois, 51
Tyr, Jean-Marie, 168–69

Unemployment
  and career migration, 40–41
  glassworkers, 95
  and worker protest, Saint-Chamond,
    150–55
Union(s)
  Anglo-American vs. French, 20–25
  and economic crisis, Saint-Chamond,
    152–53
  factory shop floor committees,
    Rive-de-Gier glassworkers, 108–9
  formative period, 23–24
  glassworker meetings in cafés, 105
  Le Chambon, 172–78
  organization, and growth of worker
    protest, Stéphanois, 48–52
  in Rive-de-Gier, 92–93
  and working-class coalition, 20–25
  and working-class quiescence,
    Saint-Chamond, 126–29
  see also Strike(s); Work structure and
    strike militancy
Union des fabricants de limes de France,
    189
*L'Unité socialiste-organe hebdomadaire de la
    fédération de la Loire,* 141
Unskilled workers
  glassworkers, 94
  metalworkers: Rive-de-Gier, 115;
    Saint-Chamond, 133
  unionization, Stéphanois, 49–50
  women in textile industry, 17
  see also Industrial workers

Verrerie Sainte-Clotilde, 107
Vinay, Pierre, 90
  on production, 108

Wage rollout, Stéphanois, 72
Wages
  boltworkers, Le Chambon, 194
  construction workers, Saint-Chamond,
    149
  and cost of living, 78–80
  fileworkers, 181, 183; and Trablaine
    boycott, 188–89
  glassworkers, Rive-de-Gier, 94–95
  metalworkers: Le Chambon, 196–97;
    Rive-de-Gier, 115; Saint-Chamond,
    132–33
  in Stéphanois industry, 68–72
  and task system, 65
  textileworkers, Saint-Chamond, 144
Waldeck-Rousseau, Pierre, 21
Weavers, in May Day strikes, Stéphanois,
    51
Weill, Gerard, 69
Whyte, W. F., on crystal-glassworkers,
    97–98
Window-glassworkers, 94
  Roquille on, 104
  strikes, 119
Women
  boltworkers, Le Chambon, 194–95
  fileworkers, Le Chambon, 183
  and glassmaking, 95–96
  participation in textile strikes, 17
  ribbon weaving, La Fayette, 38
  textileworkers, 66; Saint-Chamond, 142,
    143–44
Work conditions, factories, 67

Workday
   regulation by employer, 65–66
   strikes on, 66–67
Work discipline, conflict over, 67–68
Worker protest, Saint-Chamond, and
   inflation and unemployment, 150–55
Worker control, France, 1800s, 3–4
Work groups
   construction workers, Saint-Chamond,
   149
   glassworkers, Rive-de-Gier, 96–98
   metalworkers: Rive-de-Gier, 115, 118;
   Saint-Chamond, 132
Working class
   migration patterns, Stéphanois, 35–41
   quiescence, Saint-Chamond, 126–29
Working-class coalition
   formation of, 20–25
   Le Chambon, 184–92

   Rive-de-Gier, 105–13
   see also Solidarity; Strike(s); Union(s)
Work patterns, glassworkers, 95, 97–98
Work structure and strike militancy
   Le Chambon: boltworkers, 194–96;
   fileworkers, 178–84; metalworkers,
   196–201
   and political role of café, 138
   Rive-de-Gier: glassworkers, 93–105;
   ·metalworkers, 113–20
   Saint-Chamond: construction workers,
   149–50; metalworkers, 129–42;
   textileworkers, 142–49
Work system. *See* Industrial work system
Work teams, glassworkers, 94, 96–99

"Yellow" union, Le Chambon, 168, 170

Zola, Emile, 194